THE

CALIF

JEANNETTE

AMER

LOUISE

COOK

INNOVATIONS
REGIONAL

ILLUSTRATIONS BY

A FIRESIDE BOOK   PUBLISHED BY SIMON & SCHUSTER INC.

ORNIA-

FERRARY

ICAN

FISZER

BOOK

ON AMERICAN DISHES

RODICA PRATO

NEW YORK LONDON TORONTO SYDNEY TOKYO

FIRESIDE
SIMON & SCHUSTER BUILDING
ROCKEFELLER CENTER
1230 AVENUE OF THE AMERICAS
NEW YORK, NEW YORK 10020

DESIGNED BY KAROLINA HARRIS
MANUFACTURED IN THE UNITED STATES OF AMERICA

1 3 5 7 9 10 8 6 4 2

1 3 5 7 9 10 8 6 4 2 PBK.

LIBRARY OF CONGRESS CATALOGING IN PUBLICATION DATA
FERRARY, JEANNETTE, DATE.
THE CALIFORNIA-AMERICAN COOKBOOK.

BIBLIOGRAPHY: P.
INCLUDES INDEX.
1. COOKERY. AMERICAN—CALIFORNIA STYLE. I. FISZER,
LOUISE. II. TITLE.
TX715.F425   1985   641.59794   85-14224

ISBN 0-671-50503-3
ISBN 0-671-67310-6 PBK.

ACKNOWLEDGMENTS

First we would like to thank the three most patient people we know: Peter Carroll, Frances Mayes, and Leslie Hsu read and reread every paragraph, recipe, revision, addendum, and helpful hint we could come up with. Frances also lent us books, tested recipes, and even donated a couple of recipes. The completed manuscript benefited from a thorough reading by Janis Popp and from some stringent recipe testing by Kirsten Lucid, Don Lowe, Tani Barlow, and Leslie Hsu. We thank M.F.K. Fisher for her support and her unreserved confidence before, during, and after. We thank her also for making the resources of her library available to us, as did Toni Illick and Elaine Cahn. Our editor, Carole Lalli, we thank not only for her meticulous editing but also for her indomitable good spirit and coast-to-coast availability. Fred Hill, our agent and friend, was wonderful, just plain wonderful.

In a general sense we realize a significant debt to the chefs, bakers, home cooks, food professionals, and students who shared their knowledge and added to ours. We are grateful to Elizabeth Wise for her loyalty and sensitivity beyond the call of duty. We would like to officially thank all our parents—the Ferrarys, Bessie Carroll, the Kemplers—for their encouragement, enthusiasm, and odd favors—like not flying out to visit us at inauspicious moments. We thank Matthew Carroll for putting in alphabetical order a lot of things that were in no particular order to begin with; and Natasha Carroll-Ferrary, now suddenly four years old, for adding a note of reality to this project by demanding, amidst all the creation and refinement of recipes, something to eat.

5

CONTENTS

CONTENTS

CALIFORNIA-AMERICAN COOKING:
State of the Art

California has always been more than slightly fanatic about food. Maybe that's because the people who moved to California have always been more than a little bit homesick. Whether they came for the gold in the hills or, more recently, for the electronics in the Valley, people have found comfort and community in the pleasures of the table. Meals were more than nourishment; cafés and restaurants were extensions of breakfast nooks and dining rooms.

So it goes. People are still coming to California, from everywhere, leaving behind more, as it turns out, than they realized. The ties of family and tradition become more attractive from a distance. The greatest benefit and the most disturbing frustration of life in California are one: this very remoteness. Everyone's real past becomes myth. During holiday seasons, people in California are always creating a "family" for the occasion, inviting close and kindred friends who, in five years, will have moved back or moved up, or, too often, moved on. That really may be better than being bored with a bunch of snoring uncles, but always the suspicion remains that really it isn't. So we live here, cursed and blessed with distance, with the yearning for the proximity we came here to escape, the continuity that would be automatic, and resented, if we lived a few blocks away from parents and cousins.

It is only natural, then, that California should become so interested and involved in the cooking of all the country's regions, accepting and welcoming all foods and food customs. These traditions are, after all, our own styles, the Thanksgivings, Sunday dinners, and cookouts we left behind: the scrapple and the hominy, the baked beans and clam chowder, barbecue and chimichangas. These influences have tremendous impact on the food and eating styles in California. In addition, California itself is a land of plenty, where a glorious variety of foods grows nearby and in profusion. We seem to have everything at our disposal. Some would argue that California cuisine is the sum total of all this—a brilliant collaboration between the dishes gathered from everywhere else, and the best of the state's bounty—the melting pot's melting pot. Others contend that its final effect means California has no cuisine of its own. If we have succeeded in our task, the truth of the matter lies somewhere in this book.

California cooking reflects these influences; it does not simply absorb them. It is inspired by, not determined by these resources. Recently, California chefs have begun to transform this national wealth, to draw upon its excellence, modify where desirable, and create an appealing cuisine that serves people today. This is really what people have always done, by natural selection—taken what they could use, what worked. It is especially true in this country which has, in terms of food, inherited the whole world as its province.

The various nationalities which settled everywhere in this country inadvertently and cumulatively created true American cookery. This "perilously simple cuisine," as Raymond Sokolov calls it in *Fading Feast*, "arose in farmhouses as adaptations to rural conditions. . . . [M]ainline American cookery at its best, the food of the farmhouse, [was] splendid there, close to the soil." The current enchantment with American food can certainly be traced to the charm of this farmhouse fare; but much of the appeal lies not so much in specific dishes themselves as in their manner of execution—not what was cooked, but how. In spirit, we are closer to the grill and the rolling pin and the cast-iron skillet than we are to the pastry tube, bain marie, and soufflé dish. We prefer the straightforward and the tangible to the elusive and fragile. When it comes to food, we don't like to take chances. We favor success. We are trying to recapture that perilous simplicity.

The recipes in this book reflect this heritage: American food in the California style. And yet "California-style" restaurants open every day, in every state—including California!—and to the amazement of many, these restaurants are vastly different from each other. Some seem Mediterranean, their menus full of fish soups, cheese and olives, a thousand pastas; others boast nouveau grits, blueberry muffins, Cajun sausages. Rich, thick chiles prevail equally with mesquite-grilled monkfish. But the California style does have its common denominators: its sense of history, an excitement over the culinary traditions of Americans, replete with all their ethnic and regional diversity. For you, the cook, or the bedtime cookbook reader, that's where the fun begins!

This book is for the home cook. It spills over with the excitement generated by many of California's innovative chefs, whose celebrated names have been by now overly borrowed. But because this volume is meant for the nonprofessional, it was developed with a realistic appreciation of the kinds of produce and products available to the home consumer. Our recipes do not demand ingredients that are almost impossible to find or that can be located only in the most exclusive specialty shops in major cities. On the other hand, every recipe has its novelties, its elements of the unexpected, its tempting blends and contrasts. These recipes have pleased our students, our families, and our friends, not only once but the many times we made, revised, and recast them. We hope you will find each recipe the kind that begs to be assembled, cooked up, served forth, eaten with gusto, and prepared again, by popular demand.

You will find more than recipes in this book. With each recipe we offer accompanying information about its ethnic, cultural, or environmental background, its ingredients, technique of preparation, and/or evolution. Wherever possible, we show how and where recipes or cooking styles originate, what changes them, how they came to California, why they are popular now. In providing this information, we wanted to highlight the importance of food and its preparation as part of our heritage, to show that food has roots and also has branches. As M. F. K. Fisher says in *How to Cook a Wolf:* "No recipe in the world is independent of the tides, the moon, the physical and emotional temperatures surrounding its performance."

HOW TO USE THIS BOOK:
Stalking the Wild Asterisk

There is nothing so exasperating as finding an asterisk that seems to lead nowhere. In this book, a single asterisk (*) signifies "Gathered Crumbs," located at the end of the book. "Gathered Crumbs" explains frequently used terms and techniques and some basic recipes for stocks, pâte brisée, crème fraiche, and other ingredients used in several places throughout the book.

A double asterisk (**) indicates the "Pantry Fancies" section, which contains informal recipes and useful information about some of the currently popular foods and ingredients that have recently been working their way from gourmet food shops to national supermarket chains. Many of these "new" foods are as old as maple syrup and balsamic vinegar; they are easy to use, convenient to store, and add an extra dimension to many dishes. They are frequently overlooked, however, and even very American specialties common in one area of the country are quite foreign to another. Whenever we use any of these enticing items, we double-asterisk them so you can, if you wish, find out more about them in the "Pantry Fancies" section.

Some recipes are followed by short Notes. These helpful hints discuss an ingredient or technique that pertains specifically to that recipe. For example, the Chile Corn Chowder contains a Chile Note after the recipe about how to gauge the heat of chile peppers. The White Chocolate–Hazelnut Mousse w/Raspberry Sauce is followed by a Cream Note, which will assure lighter yet creamier results, and a Hazelnut Note, which instructs about grinding the nuts.

We have tried to make this book fit the way people live. For example, we have no big central chapter called "Main Courses." Instead we have several chapters from which the cook can choose what, if anything, should be "main" and where it should come in the meal. "Littlemeals" is a collection of informal, one-dish meals, pastas, pizzas, calzones, and substantial salads. Many of the "Specials of the Day" are also simple to prepare, but they are meant for special occasions, dinner parties, gatherings with friends. Among the "Soups for All Seasons" recipes, several might be served as meals in themselves, while others are appropriate as first courses. The "Appetizer Salads" are intended as light first courses, while the more elaborate and heartier salads are grouped as Event Salads in the "Littlemeals" chapter. Many of the "Fresh Starts" might be appetizers, finger foods, or first courses as the occasion demands. The "Vegetables" are in alphabetical order and often include suggested alternatives. This allows the cook to adapt the recipe to what is fresh and available. "The Bread Basket" contains yeast breads, muffins, biscuits, scones, and even foccacie—in other words, a variety, to go with any menu of the moment. "Fresh Finales" are desserts: fruit pies, pound cakes, ice creams, sherbets, cookies, soufflés.

While this method of organization is conducive to conventional meal planning (selecting appetizers, breads, main courses, desserts), it also accommodates today's needs for less structured meals, and will appeal to the increasing numbers of people who enjoy building a meal around a series of appetizers or salads or, yes, even desserts! In fact, to many who enjoy cooking, the art of the meal lies not so much in the success of each individual dish, but in the creative combining of courses for the total dinner. We wanted in no way to interfere with the fun of that adventure.

On the other hand, we have put together a section of suggested menus in which we combine courses and dishes in ways that take advantage of contrasting tastes, textures, and ingredients. The wine recommendations accompanying these menus also take into account the various flavors of the meal. For this reason, we sometimes include different wines for the different parts of the meal.

Finally, for further details about the culinary information in the background of our recipes, we have provided a brief bibliography following the recipes.

FRESH
STARTS

Whether called hors d'oeuvres, starters, or premeal snacks, this category of food has historically been associated with drink. The earliest bars in America were located in corner grocery stores where a drinking area was set off from the more domestic transactions. Naturally there was plenty of food in these grocery stores, but no real facilities for cooking or for actual dining. People ate, literally, what they could get their hands on.

Eventually bars became established in separate quarters, some in unpretentious basements, others in fancy hotels. The fare became more elaborate. Many places instituted the "free lunch," an array of foods, from oysters on the half shell to joints of beef, offered for the price of a drink.

Prohibition curtailed some of this activity, but creative alternatives were constantly in the offing. People resorted to private— actually clandestine—cocktail parties where a new style of eating emerged, based on finger foods, tidbits that could be easily manipulated with the "free" hand. These bite-size dainties soon became institutionalized as a social custom and as a separate section in American cookbooks, usually called "Appetizers" or "Canapés."

World War I also contributed to the new food style. The practicalities of the workday forced people to transfer their day's big meal from the afternoon to the evening. Predinner snacks helped stave off hunger and stimulate, or decimate, the appetite, depending on the particular assortment.

Some say that because of the deemphasis on sit-down meals and family dinners, we have now become a land of snack eaters. Delis, street carts, and gourmet groceries cater to this preference, offering an ever more various sampling of delicacies. The trend has even been identified and reported by the Wall Street Journal as "grazing," a habit apparently quite suitable to young professionals who prefer eating conveniently when hunger strikes. This may not necessarily be conducive to the development of refined palates or fine cuisine, but it may help explain why appetizers have once again come into vogue. At their best, they are like a big box of assorted chocolates; a beautifully arranged panoply of hors d'oeuvres allows people to enjoy tasting a variety of foods and to choose only what appeals to them. A selection of the following dishes would make delicious fare for an early evening appetizer party. But each of these little morsels is really intended as a light, not-too-fussy prelude to a meal, a way to awaken the palate and get everything off to a nice "fresh start."

Mushroom-Hazelnut Pâté
Chicken Pâté Layered with Brandied Chicken Livers
Pâté of Fresh and Smoked Salmon
Triangle Crepes Filled with Boursin and Smoked Salmon
Smoked Trout Mousse with Horseradish and Golden Caviar
Shrimp in Sherry-Vinegar Mayonnaise
Seviche of Scallops and Snapper
with Green Peppercorns
Mussels in Mustard
California Caponata
Carrot and Zucchini Sticks in Raspberry Vinegar
Tomato-Coriander Tartlets
Cucumber Rounds Stuffed with Gorgonzola
Ricotta Pesto with Belgian Endive
Goat Cheese Tarts with Sun-dried Tomatoes
Roquefort Crisps
California Grape Leaves Filled with
Dried Apricots and Pine Nuts
Savory Nutlets
Pesto Pecans
Spiced Walnuts

Mushroom-Hazelnut Pâté

Eating mushrooms always showed a certain death-defying bravado because many edible varieties have lethal look-alikes. Nevertheless, mushroom "catsup" was a popular sauce among eighteenth-century Americans, who also liked their mushrooms stewed. Modern cultivating and preserving techniques widened the mushroom audience considerably. People trusted store-bought mushrooms, grown and selected by experts. But the safest and most available, and consequently most popular, mushrooms in this country were, until recently, the ones to be found in cans. These days, however, it is not unusual to find several different types of wild and cultivated mushrooms in many neighborhood supermarkets.

Some mushrooms taste surprisingly like meat: the "beefsteak," for example, and the shaggymane. The puffball can be breaded and fried as puffball "cutlets" or puffball "steak"; and the poly-pore, or "chicken mushroom," which tastes like chicken breast, can be made into fricassee and polypore croquettes. Mushroom "burgers" are a current favorite in Michigan, one of the few areas in the known universe blessed with forests of morels, per-haps the most coveted of wild mushrooms. The nutritional value of mushrooms ranges from dubious to high in protein, though not all the protein can be assimilated.

Our pâté, which sounds more meaty than it tastes, mingles the musty flavor of sautéed, cultivated mushrooms and toasted hazelnuts with an underlying suspicion of Pernod. It makes a richly delicious yet light hors d'oeuvre.

3 tablespoons vegetable oil
1 bunch green onions,.
   chopped
1 pound mushrooms, washed
   and chopped
1 teaspoon tarragon
2 cloves garlic, minced

¼ cup chopped fresh parsley
1 cup finely chopped toasted
   hazelnuts*
¼ pound butter
   salt and pepper
   dash Tabasco
1 tablespoon Pernod

Heat oil in a skillet and sauté onions until wilted. Add the mushrooms and cook about 15 minutes or until most of the moisture has evapo-rated. Add tarragon, garlic, parsley, hazelnuts, and butter. Cook an-other 8 minutes. Add remaining ingredients and mix well.

Put into crock or serving dish and chill until firm. May be garnished with sliced mushrooms. Serve with bread or crackers.

Serves 8 to 10

Chicken Pâté Layered with Brandied Chicken Livers

According to <u>Mrs. Rorer's Cookbook</u> of one hundred years ago, any housekeeper who makes pâtés will receive such praise and appreciation that "she will enter them at once on her weekly bills of fare." Perhaps Mrs. R. was attempting to demystify pâtés, which were similar, though not identical, to the traditional American liver and meat loaves. Pâtés were also made from badger, porcupine, and dormouse, and fashioned to look like birds, fish, or any shape that would inspire their consumption. In a traditional recipe for lark pâté, each slice was supposed to contain a whole lark, boned or not, depending on the cook's sense of humor. Pâtés, rough and smooth, hot and cold, became more popular in this country with the arrival of Italians, Germans, and French, whose recipes incorporate everything from woodcock, duck, and wild rabbit to the famous goose livers from Alsace.

These days, lighter pâtés, such as those made with pureed fish or the multicolored vegetable loaves, are in favor. Even chocolate and fruit are being used, for interesting new dessert pâtés. Our creamy, loaf-type pâté is made from tender chicken breast, accented with brandied nuggets of chicken liver. It could easily become part of the weekly bill of fare since it is not only delicious but, with the help of the food processor, simple to prepare.

2 tablespoons butter	2 egg whites
½ pound fresh chicken livers, cleaned and quartered	2 tablespoons chopped fresh parsley
salt and pepper	1 teaspoon thyme
¼ cup brandy	1 teaspoon ground nutmeg
1 pound boned and skinned chicken breast, cold	¼ teaspoon cayenne
	1¾ cups cold heavy cream

Melt butter in a skillet and sauté chicken livers over medium-high heat until lightly browned, about 6 minutes. Salt and pepper livers and pour brandy over them. Cook over high heat about 2 minutes, or until some brandy has evaporated. Set livers aside.

For the chicken pâté, or forcemeat itself, make sure the chicken has been trimmed of all fat. Cut chicken into cubes and place in processor bowl along with egg whites, herbs, and seasonings. Process until pureed and then slowly pour in the cream. Puree until you have obtained the texture of heavy whipped cream.

Preheat oven to 325°F and oil a 6-cup heat-proof mold (we like to use a loaf pan). Pour one-quarter of the chicken mixture into it. Then place one-third of the brandied livers over the chicken mixture. Repeat layers until chicken and livers have been used up. You should end with a layer of the chicken mixture.

Cover mold with a piece of oiled aluminum foil or parchment paper* and place mold in a slightly larger pan. Add water to the larger pan until it comes one-third of the way up the mold.

Bake about 50 minutes. Let cool and refrigerate overnight before serving.

May be served as a first course surrounded by a fresh tomato sauce (see page 265) or as an hors d'oeuvre on slices of French bread.

Serves 8 to 10

Pâté of Fresh and Smoked Salmon

Early pioneers in the Pacific Northwest were intrigued by a mysterious Indian red flag hung ominously on top of long poles. Eventually they came close enough to discover that the flag was actually a giant salmon, split and strung up like an early billboard to advertise that salmon was available. In fact, the Chinook Indians and the Tlingits of the Northwest coast had so much salmon they developed many ingenious and delicious methods of preserving this highly perishable food. They pulverized the dried flesh into a powder and mixed it with berries to make a sort of pemmican (a concentrated food used by the North American Indians). They sun-dried it into salmon jerky and, most commonly, they smoked it in several different ways, one of which was called "Siwash cheese." Later, settlers often salted salmon and folded it into creamed dishes and fish cakes, using it like salt cod. In our easy pâté, delicious strips of smoked salmon are laced through a smooth puree of the fresh fish.

1 pound fresh salmon, cooked, skinned, and boned	2 tablespoons lemon juice
	1 tablespoon good-quality mustard
¼ pound butter, room temperature	salt and pepper
½ cup cold heavy cream	¼ pound smoked salmon,** cut into thin strips
1 tablespoon chopped fresh dill	smoked salmon and fresh dill for garnish

In the bowl of a food processor, process fresh salmon and butter until smooth. While machine is running pour in cream. Process until pureed. Add remaining ingredients except smoked salmon. Process and remove to a mixing bowl.

By hand mix in smoked salmon. Pour pâté into a crock or serving bowl, cover, and refrigerate overnight.

Before serving, garnish with additional strips of smoked salmon and a sprig of fresh dill. Serve from crock surrounded with squares of black bread or mound on cucumber slices.

Serves 8 to 10

Triangle Crepes Filled with Boursin and Smoked Salmon

Crepes in this country date to colonial days, when they were made as thin as possible, spread with a topping or sprinkled with powdered sugar. A colorful version, made with beets, was called the "pink pancake." The French and English preferences for thin crepes prevailed in the evening's dessert course, but other influences became equally important. For breakfast, the Germans and Dutch preferred hearty thick waffles; settlers in New Jersey and Pennsylvania favored buckwheat cakes; in Rhode Island, travelers took along johnnycakes (or "journey" cakes) made with cornmeal. South Carolinians resorted to the ovens to cook their substantial favorite, the plantation skillet cake. Slapjacks and flapjacks were crepes with some width, as were all the "cakes" preceded by words like rice, corn, griddle, flannel, hominy, sourmilk, batter, buttermilk, and hot. Flannel cakes were lumberjack cuisine, possibly named for the flannel shirts that were common attire in the camps. Another theory has it that flannel is what the cakes tasted most like. "Flatcars" were griddle cakes named after the railroad cars on which the lumber was transported. When stacked in a pile, the cakes were known as "strings of flats."

Even fritters, tortillas, won ton skins, and Indian fry breads share some basic, crepelike similarities. Our version sounds least like, but perhaps most resembles, cheese-stuffed blintzes. These neat, two-bite-size crepes make excellent finger food. The home-made Boursin is delicious, but you can, of course, use one from the cheese shop.

Boursin Cheese

¼ pound cream cheese
¼ pound ricotta cheese
2 tablespoons heavy cream
3 tablespoons finely chopped fresh parsley, dill, or oregano

2 cloves garlic, minced
1 teaspoon salt
1 tablespoon freshly ground pepper

In food processor or blender mix all ingredients together until smooth. If possible, make this mixture 12 hours in advance to allow cheese to ripen and flavors to blend.

Crepes

2 eggs
½ cup milk
¼ cup water
1 cup flour
3 tablespoons chopped fresh parsley

2 tablespoons vegetable oil
salt and pepper
butter
¼ pound smoked salmon,** cut into 1-inch strips

In a bowl blend first seven ingredients until smooth. Cover and let stand at least 1 hour before using (see Note).

Heat crepe pan or small skillet over moderately high heat and butter very lightly. Hold pan off heat with one hand and with the other hand pour in ¼ cup batter. Quickly swirl batter around until it covers the surface of the pan and return the pan to heat. When the top of the crepe looks dry, turn it over and cook very briefly on the other side. Remove crepe from pan and continue cooking rest of batter in the same manner. If not using immediately, stack crepes between squares of waxed paper and wrap the batch in plastic.

To assemble crepes: Cut 24 crepes in half. Place about 1 tablespoon cheese and 1 strip of salmon on one side of a crepe half. Fold over to the other side, then fold again in half. The filling should now be enclosed in a triangular-shaped crepe package. Repeat with remaining crepes and filling. Arrange in an overlapping pattern on serving platter and cover well with plastic wrap if not using immediately. Crepes have a tendency to dry out very quickly.

Makes about 24

CREPE NOTES: There is a reason for waiting at least an hour to use the crepe batter. (Mrs. Rorer's 1886 cookbook advises that the batter "stand away in a cold place.") This allows the flour to dissolve and expand and the gluten to develop, resulting in a smoother batter and a more tender crepe.

These crepes can be made up to 2 days ahead, wrapped in dampened towels (paper or cloth) and kept refrigerated or frozen in a plastic bag or tight plastic wrapping. To freeze, stack crepes, separating them with strips of waxed paper. Set the stack on a paper plate, put another paper plate upside down on top of the stack, staple the edges, and freeze. This not only preserves the crepes, it keeps them from getting mangled in the freezer.

Smoked Trout Mousse with Horseradish and Golden Caviar

Although the first colonists around Chesapeake Bay found the waters teeming with fish, they lacked the instruments and methods to work this treasure into their food supply. They tried beating the fish in the water with frying pans and scooping them to shore, a method that was splashy but generally ineffectual. Captain John Smith's solution—nailing the fish to the ground with his sword—worked well enough for a few meals. But from that point on, many colonists depended on Native Americans to teach them fishing techniques and, equally important, their age-old ways of preserving the catch through salting, drying, kippering, and smoking.

Smoked trout and salmon are now commonly found in many areas of the country, but the greatest variety of smoked fish in any area is likely to be located in the nearest Jewish delicatessen. That would also be a convenient place to pick up the horse-radish, which, in our recipe, is incorporated directly into the mousse. The crowning golden touch—the caviar—might come from the Hudson River, the West Coast, or anywhere in between. Always popular in this country, caviar was at one time slathered on bread and served free in New York barrooms. These caviar sandwiches had a practical purpose, of course: to increase the thirst and thus the sale of nickel beer. If American "golden" is unavailable, black or red caviar (any old caviar, if you will) will garner few complaints.

½ pound smoked trout,** skinned and filleted
½ cup heavy cream
¼ pound butter, room temperature
¼ pound cream cheese, room temperature

2 tablespoons white prepared horseradish
2 tablespoons chopped fresh dill or parsley
2 ounces golden caviar**

In a food processor puree trout with cream until smooth. Add remaining ingredients except caviar and process again until smooth.

Pour into a serving crock (mixture will be loose, but will firm up in refrigerator) and cover with plastic wrap. Store in the refrigerator for at least 4 hours.

Garnish with golden caviar and serve with small slices of black bread and cucumber rounds. Makes about 1½ cups mousse.

Serves 8 to 10

Shrimp in Sherry-Vinegar Mayonnaise

In a sense, mayonnaise was one of the first health foods in this country. When nutrition became a popular concern at the beginning of this century, salads came into vogue; mayonnaise went along as their natural companion. By now this cold sauce is so common, we hardly think of it as French-born. Nor do we associate it with the excitement surrounding its origins, about which there are many conflicting reports. Mayonnaise may simply be a corruption of moyeunaise, from the old French moyeu, meaning "egg yolk." Far more provocative is our preferred version, which traces mayonnaise to the French victory over the British at Minorca's Port Mahón (hence mahon-naise). There it was supposedly invented by the French bon vivant, le duc de Richelieu, whose dinner guests often sipped their champagne and supped in the nude. Whether or not the mayonnaise was in any way responsible for such behavior has so far not been determined; but anything might happen with our version, heady with sherry vinegar and sweet shrimp. It's a tempting and easy way to find out.

1 egg
1 egg yolk
1 tablespoon good-quality
    mustard
5 tablespoons sherry
    vinegar**
1 cup vegetable or olive oil
    (or a mixture of both
    according to taste)

1 clove garlic, minced
    salt and pepper
1 pound tiny bay shrimp,
    cleaned and cooked
    capers, rinsed and drained,
    for garnish

To make mayonnaise, combine egg, yolk, mustard, and 2 tablespoons vinegar in the bowl of a food processor. Process until well blended, about 30 seconds. While motor is running, pour oil in very slowly in a thin, steady stream. Add remaining vinegar and garlic. Taste for salt and pepper and season accordingly.

Transfer mixture to a bowl and stir in shrimp. Let sit about an hour, covered, in refrigerator.

Spread on thin slices of black bread or baguette, each piece garnished with a caper.

Alternate serving suggestion: Place cooked artichoke leaves in concentric circles on round platter. Pile a small amount of shrimp-mayonnaise mixture in center of each leaf and top with a caper.

Serves 6 to 8

Seviche of Scallops and Snapper with Green Peppercorns

This seviche is the perfect recipe for those who usually do not like raw fish. Long marinating in spiced lime juice transforms the texture and flavor of the scallops and snapper, which taste "cooked" though they still retain their freshness and vibrancy. This seviche is also the perfect recipe for those who do like raw fish! Since the fish is not subjected to heat, it is not truly cooked. Swedish gravlax, made from dill-infused, salt-cured salmon, is another widely known, raw-cooked dish. Found in many cultures, these "raw" methods of "cooking" food are ancient and derive from the scarcity of fuel and the need to preserve the food supply.

Based on any number of South American seviches, this peppercorned combination of plump scallops and firm red snapper is further enlivened by showers of fresh coriander.

1 pound fresh bay or sea
scallops (if using sea
scallops, cut into quarters)
1 pound very fresh snapper,
cut in bite-size pieces
1 onion, coarsely chopped
4 green onions, sliced into
rings
1 red bell pepper, coarsely
chopped
1 1½-ounce can green
peppercorns,** rinsed,
drained and slightly
mashed with back of spoon
1 cup fresh lime juice (5 or 6
limes)
¼ cup olive oil
salt and pepper
¼ cup chopped fresh
coriander leaves, plus more
as garnish

Put scallops, snapper, onions, red pepper, and peppercorns in a glass or stainless-steel bowl. Pour lime juice over and toss until well coated. Cover bowl and refrigerate for at least 4 hours, or until fish looks opaque.

Drain the juices that have accumulated in the bowl and discard; add the remaining ingredients. Toss well and sprinkle with additional coriander.

Serve as a first course on a bed of shredded red lettuce or as an hors d'oeuvre with assorted breads and/or crackers.

Serves 6 to 8

Mussels in Mustard

Four thousand years ago, the Indians of Catalina Island, west of Los Angeles, enjoyed quite a few mussels. In fact, judging from the evidence of shell remains, it seemed they preferred them, four to one, over abalone. Further excavation into a lower stratum of shells, however, revealed an overwhelming predominance of abalone shells. This discovery led to the conclusion that people began eating mussels only after they had exhausted the abalone supply.

Several thousand years later, mussels returned to short-lived popularity, this time with the early European settlers on the East Coast. After that, mussels again disappeared for a few centuries from American cookbooks and from our tables. Their occasional loss of favor may be due to the sometimes fatal effects of indulging in mussels during certain parts of the year; but a strict quarantine now keeps them from the marketplace during this "unfriendly period," as West Coast Cook Book author Helen Evans Brown calls it. Actually, mussels are considered the least dangerous of mollusks since they are not consumed raw.

Plump and apricot-colored with gleaming blue-black shells, mussels are gorgeous in appearance and taste. Their sheer richness belies their low calorie content, their low place in the food chain, their high position as one of the most succulent foods of choice in a more nutrition-conscious world.

3 pounds mussels (see Note)	4 sprigs parsley
1 cup dry white wine	salt and pepper
1 onion, sliced	pinch cayenne

Sauce

3 tablespoons imported whole-grain mustard	salt and pepper
2 teaspoons red wine vinegar	2 cloves garlic, finely minced
4 tablespoons olive oil	2 tablespoons chopped fresh parsley

Scrub mussels to remove sand and dirt. Pull out beards.

Place mussels in a stockpot with the wine, onion, parsley, salt and pepper, and cayenne. Cover and bring to a boil, then simmer for about 5 minutes or until all the mussels have opened.

Remove mussels from the pot, reserving liquid for another use if you wish. Let cool.

Meanwhile, combine all sauce ingredients in a bowl. Remove mussels from shells and toss with mustard sauce.

Serve on slices of French bread or, as a first course, on a bed of lettuce.

Serves 6

MUSSEL NOTE: Store live mussels in a covered bowl of water in the refrigerator up to 3 or 4 days *before* cleaning, as they don't live long after. If you are not sure if a mussel is fresh, just smell it; your nose will supply the answer.

California Caponata

There are about as many recipes for caponata as there are Sicilians who will swear that their own version is the only authentic one. Except for a single essential ingredient—eggplant—the basic components can include any or all of the best from a summer garden: celery, zucchini, tomatoes, green peppers, garlic (naturally), onions and herbs, plus olives, capers, and momentary whims. Caponata in Palermo also has crayfish tails and tuna roe; in Syracuse it includes a goodly amount of chocolate shavings.

Caponata's myriad interpretations have multiplied further in this country, where additional regional influences have become part of the recipes. In our version, wine-soaked raisins and chopped walnuts add a California note and an unexpected meatiness. This recipe makes a particularly nice hors d'oeuvre.

¼ cup olive oil
3 Japanese eggplants or 2 young small eggplants, diced (see Note)
1 large onion, chopped
6 very ripe plum tomatoes, peeled, seeded, and chopped, or 15-ounce can imported Italian tomatoes, drained and chopped
1 tablespoon imported tomato paste**

1 tablespoon good red wine vinegar
¼ cup pitted and halved black olives
1½ tablespoons capers
salt and pepper
4 tablespoons coarsely chopped toasted walnuts*
4 tablespoons golden raisins, soaked in 2 tablespoons red wine for 1 hour

Heat olive oil in a skillet and sauté eggplants and onion for about 5 minutes.

Combine with remaining ingredients and cook, uncovered, about 10 minutes, over very low heat. Stir every so often to prevent burning or sticking to bottom of skillet. This dish should not be overcooked. The vegetables should remain crunchy.

May be served hot or at room temperature, piled in a crock and surrounded by crackers or slices of fresh, sweet baguettes. Or it may be spooned generously on lettuce leaves as a very unordinary salad or first course.

Serves 8

EGGPLANT NOTE: Young, tender eggplants are always our first choice in any eggplant recipe. Try to find Japanese eggplants, which are small and elongated, with few seeds; they are less bitter.

Carrot and Zucchini Sticks in Raspberry Vinegar

As a method of preserving food, the making of pickles and relishes was always very popular with American cooks, possibly because of our native penchant for any extra touch of sweetness. Pickles were made from anything—from peaches to nasturtium seeds—and their variety lent color and pungency all through the winter. Year-round availability of fresh produce has made pickling less necessary, though no less appreciated. Our recipe faintly echoes the time-honored pickling tradition, suffusing crisp-cooked vegetable sticks with a fruity marinade.

6 cups water
½ teaspoon salt
1 pound carrots, cut into ¼-inch-thick sticks
½ pound zucchini, cut into ¼-inch-thick sticks

½ cup raspberry vinegar**
2 tablespoons chopped fresh parsley
¼ cup olive oil
salt and pepper

In a large pot bring salted water to a boil. Add the carrot sticks and cook for 1 minute. Add the zucchini and cook 1 more minute. Drain in a colander.

Mix vinegar, parsley, oil, salt and pepper together until blended.

Remove vegetables to a storage jar or bowl and pour the marinade over the still-warm vegetables. Refrigerate at least 24 hours before serving.

Serves 6

Tomato-Coriander Tartlets

Shortly after "discovering" America, the Spanish also "discovered" the tomato, which was found in the lower Andes and brought back to Europe. With the European explorations and settlements, the tomato made a speedy return trip to the Americas, and though considered novel, if not poisonous, in some areas, tomatoes became well entrenched in others. In the American South, for example, tomatoes appeared in early recipes with okra and eggs or as catsup and even marmalade. Later, immigrating Italians entered all aspects of the produce business wherever they settled in this country, thereby introducing many vegetables into general knowledge. At the same time, the growing popularity of Italian cooking brought tomatoes much fond attention. The fact that tomatoes were among the first vegetables to be canned significantly increased their year-round availability and acceptance. Oddly enough, tomatoes became important on the West Coast only after the development of canned tomato puree. This was largely the achievement of Camillo Pregno, a grower whose improved preserving techniques expanded the horizons of cook and capitalist alike.

The coriander in our recipe reflects other influences: Chinese, Middle Eastern, Portuguese, and that of the American Southwest, where the Zuni Indians have long used this pungent herb in their cookery. In fact, it is coriander that gives these refined-looking tarts their unexpected sensuality.

1 recipe pâte brisée*	1 teaspoon ground coriander
4 tablespoons imported	salt and pepper
tomato paste**	½ cup chopped fresh
2 egg yolks	coriander leaves
½ cup heavy cream	

Preheat oven to 375°F.

Press 2 teaspoons dough into each of 24 ungreased tartlet molds or mini-muffin tins. Refrigerate molds while preparing filling.

In a bowl mix tomato paste, yolks, cream, ground coriander, and salt and pepper until well blended. Stir in ¼ cup chopped coriander.

Pour filling into prepared tartlet shells and sprinkle remaining chopped coriander evenly over tartlets. Bake for about 15 minutes or until filling is set.

Let cool for about 15 minutes on rack before attempting to remove tartlets from molds.

Makes 24

Cucumber Rounds Stuffed with Gorgonzola

"Over fish but under meat." This American rule of cookery concerned the cucumber, a vegetable that appealed to New World cooks, who seemed to like the challenge of trying to transform the basically bland cucumber into delicious salads and hot vegetable dishes. In this recipe, the very neutrality of cucumbers is the perfect foil for the pungent Gorgonzola, "il Re de Formaggio" (the King of Cheese), as it is called. With its walnut and cheese stuffing, this little hors d'oeuvre could even lead to an amendment of the above cucumber rule: over fish, under meat, but around Gorgonzola.

2 cucumbers	3 tablespoons finely chopped
¼ pound imported	walnuts and 24 walnut
Gorgonzola cheese	halves
¼ pound butter	

To prepare cucumbers for stuffing, strip-peel with vegetable peeler, leaving some of the skin for color if you wish. Cut cucumbers into 1-inch slices. With teaspoon or small melon baller, carefully remove the center seeds, leaving just a thin shell to hold stuffing.

To make filling, in a bowl mix Gorgonzola, butter, and chopped walnuts together until creamy and well blended.

Fit a pastry bag with a star tip and fill bag with the cheese mixture.

Pipe filling into hollow of each cucumber slice and top with a walnut half. Set on platter and cover with plastic wrap. Refrigerate until ready to serve.

Makes about 24

Ricotta Pesto with Belgian Endive

Basil is one of the few glories of a summer garden of which no one ever seems to have too much. During its precious short season, it is put into salads, into soups, and, with a little olive oil, into the freezer for the long basil-bare winter. One of its most appreciated expressions, pesto, is so versatile that it can be used to sauce fresh hot vegetables, sliced potatoes, and, of course, pasta in many forms. Leftover pesto, admittedly a rarity, can be mixed with creamy ricotta for this recipe, with its inviting contrast of faintly bitter and creamy rich.

   3 small heads Belgian endive
   ½ cup pesto*
   1 cup ricotta cheese

Break leaves off endive and wipe well. (We find when we wash the leaves they take on a bitter, acrid taste.)

In a bowl mix pesto and ricotta until well blended.

Fit a pastry bag with a star tip and fill bag with ricotta mixture. Pipe about 1 tablespoon mixture down center of each leaf.

Arrange decoratively on a serving platter.

Serves 8 to 10

Goat Cheese Tarts with Sun-dried Tomatoes

Eating dried tomatoes is not so new to some people in this country. At one time tomatoes were boiled in sugar syrup and then dried, sprinkled with sugar, and served as a sweet.

Once thought to be the bona fide forbidden fruit direct from Eden itself, these "love apples" were considered powerful aphrodisiacs. In spite of, or because of, this reputation, they eventually became this nation's most widely consumed fruit/vegetable.

Sun-dried, tomatoes acquire an intensely concentrated taste and a garnet sheen. Baked in mini-tarts with a piquant goat cheese, they are a visual and gastronomic enchantment.

1 recipe pâte brisée*	1 egg
¼ pound goat cheese** (see Note)	2 tablespoons chopped fresh parsley
2 tablespoons butter	6 sun-dried tomatoes,** quartered
¼ cup heavy cream	

Preheat oven to 375°F.

Press 2 teaspoons dough into each of 24 ungreased tartlet molds or mini-muffin tins. Refrigerate while preparing filling.

In a bowl mix remaining ingredients except tomatoes until smooth.

Remove tins from the refrigerator and place a tomato upright in each lined mold. Fill three quarters full with filling. Tomato should be peeking out at top.

Bake for about 18 minutes; let cool on cake rack before removing tarts from tins.

Makes 24

GOAT CHEESE NOTE: We recommend a Montrachet or one of the mild domestic goat cheeses for this recipe.

Roquefort Crisps

In the French caves of Combalou, Roquefort cheese ages most gracefully into the stuff that dreams (and these crisps) are made of. Over the centuries, this regal blue-veined cheese has inspired its share of poets and cooks as well as cheesemakers who have attempted to develop a similar masterpiece. In 1918, the California Experiment Station used goats' milk to produce what it considered a successful facsimile. Today we have several fine domestic blues in this country, most of which, however, begin in the cow barn. Oregon Blue is generally considered most similar to Roquefort, but it has Gorgonzola overtones. Other respected American blues include the Nauvoo, which dwells and ripens in limestone caves in Illinois along the Mississippi River.

A Wisconsin Blue, a marbly Maytag, or the impeccable Tolibia would be perfect in this recipe. Or if you must let them eat Roquefort, try Bee Brand, one of the fourteen members of the Roquefort Society permitted by French law to use the name of the cheese's home village.

We might add that Amelia Simmons, in her 1796 American Cookery, warns against adding to any cheese such "deceits" as saffron or "cocumberries." Fortunately, she made no reference to poppy seed.

¼ pound butter, room temperature	1 cup flour
	¼ teaspoon cayenne
½ pound Roquefort, room temperature	½ cup poppy seed

Place butter and cheese in a medium bowl and mix until blended with electric beater or by hand. Add the flour and cayenne and beat again until smooth.

Divide the mixture in half and place one portion on wax paper. Form the mixture into a log-shaped roll about 1½ inches in diameter. Repeat procedure with the other portion. Refrigerate for at least 12 hours.

Preheat oven to 400°F and grease a cookie sheet.

Slice the chilled rolls into thin wafers, ¼ inch thick, then sprinkle with poppy seed. Place on cookie sheet and bake for about 8 minutes.

Cool and store in an airtight container.

Makes about 60

California Grape Leaves Filled with Dried Apricots and Pine Nuts

Egg of the Sun: There is no mystery about how the yolk-colored apricot earned that early nickname from the Persians, who all but worshiped the fruit. When the early-ripening apricot was brought to the New World, the Cherokees felt similar reverence. They planted apricots with such enthusiasm, they soon found themselves surrounded by hillsides full of wild "field apricots." In the California missions, the padres cultivated and preserved the sunny little fruits, incorporating them into their rabbit stews and marinades. At present, only about five percent of the entire crop is consumed fresh because many consider dried apricots even more succulent, especially in flavorful combinations with other dried fruits, lamb, and other meats.

Our recipe reflects the apricot's Armenian connections by wrapping the fruit in grape leaves with ground lamb and pine nuts. Thanks to the wine industry, grape leaves are a local commodity in California, but grape leaves from anywhere will work as well.

30 grape leaves	pinch cinnamon
27 dried apricot halves	2 green onions, chopped
3 tablespoons pine nuts	1 tablespoon chopped fresh
½ pound ground lamb	mint leaves
¼ cup raw rice	2 tablespoons lemon juice
salt and pepper	water

Remove grape leaves from jar and rinse under running water to remove brine. Drain well and reserve.

To make filling, chop 12 apricot halves and mix in a bowl with pine nuts, lamb, rice, salt and pepper, cinnamon, and onions.

Lay grape leaf, vein side up, stem toward you. Place 1 tablespoon filling at base of leaf and roll up, tucking in excess leaf at sides to make a small bundle. Place seam side down in a large pot. Repeat with rest of leaves.

Place remaining apricot halves in between stuffed grape leaves. Sprinkle with mint and lemon juice. Add enough water to cover. Cover with lid and bring to a boil. Reduce heat and simmer for about 1 hour.

Serve cold or at room temperature.

Makes 30

Savory Nutlets

There are three varieties of nuts in this recipe, each with its own distinct character. The peanut is the most common and is usually found in the laps of baseball fans or spilling from the hands of little children. Once thought to be native to West Africa, peanuts have now been traced to Peru and Brazil. They may be one of those rare examples of a food that originated in both hemispheres.

The pecan, also native American, has, through a venerable succession of pies and waffles, become firmly based in the American South. Georgia, in fact, is the world's leading producer. The almond, which gives added taste and substance to the pastry shell, is now considered native to California, which provides half the world's supply. Together, the three nuts will make a nice big batch of Savory Nutlets.

Pastry

1½ cups flour
½ cup finely ground almonds
½ cup butter
2 tablespoons margarine or vegetable shortening

1 egg
½ teaspoon salt
¼ teaspoon cayenne

Filling

1½ cups heavy cream
¾ cup grated Parmesan cheese
1½ cups coarsely chopped pecans
1½ cups peanuts

¼ teaspoon cayenne
1 teaspoon dried thyme, or 2 tablespoons fresh thyme leaves
3 tablespoons butter

To make the pastry, mix all ingredients in a bowl until they're well blended and refrigerate, wrapped in plastic, about 1 hour.

Grease a 9″-x-13″ baking pan. Roll out pastry to fit pan, then place pastry in pan, bringing sides up about ¾ inch by pressing with fingers. Refrigerate, covered with plastic wrap, about 1 hour. Meanwhile, make filling.

Preheat oven to 375°F. In a saucepan heat cream and cheese until bubbly. Stir in nuts and seasonings and cook until mixture becomes somewhat thickened, about 5 minutes. Set aside.

Partially bake pastry for about 12 minutes. Remove from oven and spread nut mixture on pastry. Return to oven and bake for about 25 minutes. Remove from oven and dot with 3 tablespoons butter and bake another 5 minutes.

Let cool and cut into small squares.

Makes about 48

Pesto Pecans

Although Thomas Jefferson had nothing to do with this recipe, it might not have happened without him. At Monticello, he successfully propagated the pecan, which had not previously thrived in that area. He presented several of these prize trees to George Washington to be planted at Mount Vernon; three of them are still bearing pecans.

The word pecan is found in all the American Indian languages spoken in pecan-producing territories. Pecans were roasted, cooked with vegetables, ground as a thickener. Even their oil was used as a seasoning. Their scientific name means "Illinois hickory," but in Texas they mean strictly business for endless numbers of roadside tourist shops, which sell pecan confections as regional souvenirs. They make an especially memorable appearance in this recipe, tossed in a basil-bountiful sauce.

2 cups shelled pecans
   boiling water (see Note)
1 cup fresh basil leaves
3 cloves garlic

¼ cup olive oil
3 tablespoons grated
   Parmesan cheese
salt and pepper

Place pecans in a heat-proof bowl and cover with boiling water. Let stand for about 10 minutes, then drain thoroughly.

Preheat oven to 350°F, then place pecans on paper towel–lined cookie sheet and toast about 30 minutes, shaking cookie sheet from time to time to turn nuts. Remove nuts from oven.

In a food processor mince basil and garlic together until finely chopped.

In a large skillet heat oil until hot. Add pecans and cook, turning frequently with spatula until nuts appear shiny and coated with oil. This should take about 5 minutes. Add basil-garlic mixture and cook for another 5 minutes, tossing nuts until they are well coated. Sprinkle cheese over the nuts and cook for another minute.

Remove from the skillet and let cool. Sprinkle with salt and pepper to taste. Store in an airtight container.

Makes 2 cups

soak note: The boiling water soak helps remove any bitterness and enables the nuts to absorb more flavor.

Spiced Walnuts

Preserving walnuts by some means or another seems to have been a preoccupation of walnut devotees since time immemorial. Some have drenched them for months on end in herbed honey; others grind them into a spicy paste. In English pubs, which serve them pickled, shells and all, their physical appearance has been described by one observer as resembling something recovered from the compost heap. There is also an interesting American frontier recipe for pickled walnuts, minus their shells but with a combination of horseradish, mustard, and ginger, and left in a crock for an entire year before serving. This racy little recipe, with its snap of chile against cumin, also works well to preserve walnuts—provided, of course, you don't serve them, because if you serve them they seldom last the evening.

2 cups walnut halves	2 teaspoons ground cumin
¼ cup butter, melted	2 teaspoons kosher salt
1 tablespoon chile powder	

Preheat oven to 350°F.

Spread walnuts on a jelly-roll pan and pour melted butter over them, stirring to coat each nut well. Bake for 15 minutes.

Remove pan from oven and sprinkle with chile and cumin. Stir well again to distribute spices evenly. Bake for another 10 minutes.

Remove nuts from pan and place on paper toweling to absorb extra grease. Sprinkle with salt. Store in airtight container.

Makes 2 cups

SOUPS
FOR ALL SEASONS

People love soup. They seem happier when you put a big bowl of it before them. Sometimes we suspect people are so fond of soup because it gives them a chance to eat bread.

Certainly among the most comforting of all human sensations must be the tug of fingertips at the warm crust of a rough peasant loaf and the heady smell of the still-steaming, torn-off chunks. Indeed, restaurants rely on these seductive powers when they serve not only a full tureen of their aromatic soup of the moment but a basket of warm French bread. The meal that follows this tantalizing prelude is often a true anticlimax.

Soup has not always been so beloved in this country. Strongly influenced by English attitudes, Americans at first distrusted soups as "French and not quite honest." A hundred years ago soup had not exactly achieved popular acceptance, but it was commonly served in prisons, in the army, as saloon free lunches, and, last but at least luxurious, at the fanciest restaurants. At New York's Delmonico's, two soups were served with meals, a consommé and a cream.

Today we find soup especially accommodating to the demands of our life-styles. One of the results of smaller households, sporadic food shopping, last-minute meal planning, and ever-changing schedules is a lot of uncoordinated groceries in the bin. (Because she refuses to use the term "leftovers," Julia Child calls these "extra vegetables"!) This is the perfect scenario, because so many things can be made into a soup and almost anything can be pureed into a soup. It takes a certain touch, of course, but you get that after a while. A little homework with chicken backs and miscellaneous scraps and bones can provide an always-ready supply of flavorful stock, which gives any soup a big head start. Adding a bouillon cube to the cooking water is always a good possibility, as is using canned bouillon, but both these choices fall under the category of realistic alternatives rather than preferred procedures. There's really no sense in getting uppity about these things, however, as anyone who has ever tried to live up to the demands of an old cookbook —extracting the bone marrow, storing the celery leaves—would agree.

At any rate, soup can be most understanding. Perhaps its most appreciated contemporary attribute is its ability to taste just as good and often better when it is reheated. You can usually make it ahead and you might as well. In addition, the novice cook can produce a beautiful, textbook-perfect creation by carefully following directions, but the same cook may achieve equally successful results by throwing things together that just happened to go. On the other hand, even the most exacting recipe promises nothing without the participation and interaction of the cook in sampling and adjusting the changeable meld of ingredients. There is something that will make it all come together this afternoon differently than it did last Thursday: the sweetness of the butter, the pungency of the herbs, the assertiveness of the stock or vegetables.

Our favorite soups are ones that have surprises in them: a few last-minute oysters, a spray of tarragon from a friend's garden, an afterthought of grated orange peel. There is always the possibility of surprise if you keep certain things around and "discover" them at the auspicious moment: some olives, dried wild mushrooms, chile peppers, slivers of cheese, a bit of smoked salmon. Any soup-in-progress responds to you in special unexpected ways, so you have to pay attention, give it what it needs. On those days when you'd like the excitement without the experiment, however, you might try one of the trustworthy combinations in this chapter.

SOUP NOTE: You can vary the richness of these or any soups by adjusting the proportion of chicken stock, milk, and/or cream. For a lighter version, use all stock; for a velvety bisque substitute cream for milk. Potatoes are a natural thickener. You might keep in mind James Beard's suggestion of using instant mashed potatoes for the same purpose.

Fresh Cherry Tomato Soup with Grated Jack and Sourdough
Croutons
Coriandered Carrot Soup with Crushed Peanuts
Spinach-Parsnip Soup
Curried Winter Root Soup
Red Pepper and Eggplant Soup
Mushroom, Olive, and Cream Cheese Soup
Very Democratic Double-Mushroom Soup with Pernod and
Tarragon
Broccoli-Walnut Cream Soup
Almond-Garlic Soup
Yellow Split Pea and Fresh Green Pea Soup
Black and White Swirled Bean Soup

Real Succotash Soup
Chicken Minestrone with Angel Hair Pasta and Mace
Chunky Potato-Sorrel Soup
Good Green Soup
Zucchini and Peppery Watercress Soup
Crookneck Squash and Tomato Soup
Corn and Oyster Bisque
Creamy Crab and Artichoke Soup
Summer Tomato–Corn Pone Soup
Chile Corn Chowder
Cabernet Borscht with Beef and Beets
Spicy Lamb and Lentil Soup with Cilantro Cream
Guacamole Soup
Strawberry-Melon Soup with White Zinfandel
Seafood Gazpacho
Cool Cucumber and Hot Mustard Soup

Fresh Cherry Tomato Soup with Grated Jack and Sourdough Croutons

"Americans want nothing to do with soup, and . . . almost die laughing when they see us prepare our soup every day." Such was the observation of a Swiss traveler immigrating to this country in the early 1800s. Indeed, only a few cookbooks at that time bothered to include any recipes for soups (Mary Randolph's The Virginia Housewife and Sally Rutledge's The Carolina Housewife, for example), and these were usually bean or tomato soups. A growing French influence on American eating habits, especially among the upper classes, helped popularize soup; but so did the Panics of 1873 and 1893, when soup's economical qualities loomed larger than its gastronomical virtues.

Combining soup and cheese can also be traced to the French, but the particular cheese in our recipe originated with the Spanish padres in California. Called Queso de Pais, it was made in the seventeenth-century missions and is considered an indigenous American product. Later, following the Gold Rush, this cheese was the pet project of one David Jacks, who stamped it with his own name and its shipping point, Monterey.

In addition to the now-traditional Monterey Jack, our recipe takes advantage of the more developed flavor of the aged grating cheese, dry Jack. Both are melted temptingly on the sourdough croutons topping the soup.

4 tablespoons butter
1 large onion, chopped
2 cloves garlic, minced
2 baskets (24 ounces) ripe
  cherry tomatoes (see Note)
6 cups chicken stock*
  salt and pepper
2 tablespoons chopped fresh
  dill

¼ cup crème fraiche* or
  heavy cream
2 tablespoons honey
12 slices sourdough bread, ¼
  inch thick
6 tablespoons butter, melted
1 cup grated Monterey Jack
  cheese
½ cup grated dry Jack cheese

In a 4-quart saucepan melt the 4 tablespoons butter. Add onion and garlic and cook until wilted, about 8 minutes.

Meanwhile, stem and halve cherry tomatoes. Add to saucepan and simmer, partially covered, until tomatoes are soft and start to break down, about 10 minutes. Add the stock and bring to a boil. Reduce heat and simmer about 15 minutes.

Puree soup through food mill or in food processor and put through a strainer. Return puree to saucepan and add seasonings, cream, and honey. Keep soup warm but do not boil.

Toast bread until golden. Spread each slice with melted butter and set aside.

Ladle soup into 6 oven-proof bowls. Place 2 croutons on soup and sprinkle with cheeses. Arrange on cookie sheet and put under broiler until cheeses melt, about 5 minutes. Serve immediately.

Alternate method: Butter toasted bread slices, sprinkle with cheeses, then toast in oven or broiler until cheese is melted. Top filled soup bowls with cheese-crusted croutons and serve.

Serves 6

TOMATO NOTE: The honey in this recipe not only counterbalances the natural acidity of tomatoes, but enhances the vegetable's natural sweetness. If good fresh tomatoes are not available, imported Italian canned are preferable to domestic brands.

Coriandered Carrot Soup with Crushed Peanuts

At the 1904 St. Louis World's Fair, peanut butter made an impressive public debut as a high-protein, eminently digestible, surprisingly delicious health food. Soon it was sold in grocery stores, where proprietors stored roasted and crushed peanuts in barrels or tubs. Selling peanut butter was strenuous work because the nuts had to be stirred vigorously to mix in the separated oil before the mixture could be ladled out for individual customers. Peanut butter was also made at home—we have found an 1898 Atlanta recipe for the Peanut Butter Sandwich. When "real" butter was scarce, during wartime rationing, some restaurants that set out peanut butter as a lowly substitute were surprised to discover that their customers preferred it. A few connoisseurs insist that the best way to enjoy the homey spread is sprinkled with fresh chervil and tarragon and spread, ever so thinly, on fresh-baked gingerbread.

Sauces made from, or thickened with, peanut butter are daily fare throughout the world; peanut butter soup is as popular in the countries of Africa as it is in Virginia, where Jefferson had peanuts growing at Monticello in the early 1790s. This soup combines the flavors of sweet fresh carrots and roasted peanuts heightened with a last-minute scattering of coriander and crushed peanuts. We like to garnish pureed soups with some of their ingredients; it adds texture and accents the character of the soup.

3 tablespoons butter
1 onion, chopped
½ cup coarsely chopped dry-
   roasted peanuts
1 teaspoon ground coriander
½ cup chopped fresh
   coriander leaves

1½ pounds carrots, cleaned and
   sliced
5 cups chicken stock*
½ cup heavy cream
salt and pepper

In a 4-quart saucepan melt butter, add onion, and sauté until slightly wilted. Add peanuts, coriander, and carrots and sauté for another 8 minutes. (Reserve some coriander leaves and peanuts for garnish.) Add chicken stock and bring to a boil. Reduce heat and simmer gently, partially covered, another 10 minutes or until carrots are tender.

With strainer or slotted spoon remove solids to bowl of food processor or blender. Puree, adding enough of the remaining liquid from saucepan to make a fairly smooth mixture. It should have some texture, so don't puree too much. Return puree and all liquid to saucepan. Mix until well blended with cream and heat. Salt and pepper to taste.

Pour into bowls and garnish with fresh coriander and chopped peanuts.

Serves 6

Spinach-Parsnip Soup

According to some popular legends, parsnips can cure the worst toothache, heighten sexual arousal, and alleviate stomach discomforts; on the other hand, they can make you delirious and even bring on madness. A few centuries back, parsnips reportedly did all these things, though their reputation has settled down a bit lately. In fact, many people today have never heard of parsnips nor tasted their nutty sweetness.

Yet colonial New Englanders loved them sliced thin and served with salt cod. Because of their high sugar content, pars-

nips were often preserved as a sweet, fried as dessert fritters, and even made into wine. Their taste has been compared to seafood; and some famous old recipes, such as Poor Man's Lobster Salad, are made entirely of parsnips camouflaged in mayonnaise. Prosciutto often begins life as a parsnip-munching pig, whose flesh eventually becomes suffused with the delicate honey taste of the vegetable. A few scraps of parsnip are almost always present in any respectable pot-au-feu; a couple of whole parsnips can do wonders for a soup, such as this one, steamy and aromatic with nutmeg, dill, and Parmesan.

2 tablespoons butter	2 medium parsnips, peeled
2 cloves garlic, minced	and sliced
1 large bunch fresh spinach,	½ cup heavy cream
washed	4 tablespoons Parmesan
1 teaspoon grated nutmeg	cheese
1 teaspoon chopped fresh dill	salt and pepper
5 cups chicken stock*	

In a 4-quart saucepan melt butter and sauté garlic until limp. Reserve several leaves of spinach for garnish and sauté remaining spinach with stems until limp. Add nutmeg, dill, and chicken stock and bring to a boil. Stir in parsnips, reduce heat to a simmer, and cook, partially covered, for 15 minutes.

Puree mixture in blender or food processor. Return to saucepan and add remaining ingredients. Reheat gently.

Make a chiffonade* of reserved spinach leaves and sprinkle on top of each serving.

Serves 6

Curried Winter Root Soup

Everybody knows about Johnny Appleseed but too few of us have given "Turnip" Townshend his equally deserved place of honor. In his private English gardens, Lord Townshend (as he was known prior to his close association with the turnip) grew many varieties of this faintly sweet root vegetable. His enthusiasm gradually led to wider acceptance of the turnip and won for his lordship his presumably flattering nickname.

"Turnip's" labors were much needed on behalf of the unappreciated vegetable. At one time, turnips were used mainly to throw at people as a token of disapproval, a role eventually taken over by the tomato. Turnips were always inexpensive, long-lasting, fast-growing; they flourished in poor soil under adverse conditions. Consequently, they were associated with the poor, and their culinary potential was largely ignored. They were recognized for other attributes, however. New Englanders ate turnips to prevent scurvy. Turnips contain trace amounts of arsenic, which the human body needs and seldom gets from friendly sources (cabbages also provide it). Some species have been associated with "frensie and giddiness of the brain," which may not be all bad.

Turnips can range in size from the small, delicately sweet, white spring turnips with delicious, edible greens (usually thrown away by overly fastidious produce departments) to blood-red Alaskan turnips twelve inches thick. Some California specimens have weighed in at just under one hundred pounds.

Perhaps the finest characteristic of turnips is their extraordinary ability to absorb surrounding flavors. In a soup such as ours, not only do they yield their own fragrance, they increase in richness and succulence as they cook with the other root vegetables in the highly flavored curry. As Andre Simon says so fondly of turnips, "... they take to themselves the savour of their pot companions."

4 tablespoons butter	1 small white turnip, sliced
2 leeks, white part only, chopped	1 small apple, peeled, cored, and chopped
1–2 tablespoons curry powder (see Note)	4 cups chicken stock*
2 carrots, grated	1 cup crème fraiche* or yogurt
1 small celery root, peeled and cut into small pieces	salt and pepper

In a 4-quart saucepan melt butter and sauté leeks until soft. Add curry powder and cook until curry becomes fragrant.

Set aside ½ cup grated carrots and add the rest along with celery root, turnip, and apple to the pot. Cook until all ingredients are coated with curry mixture. Add the stock and bring to a boil. Reduce heat to simmer and cook, covered, for about 15 minutes, or until all vegetables are soft.

Remove vegetables to bowl of food processor and puree. Return puree to the pot and add the crème fraiche, salt and pepper. Heat through. Do not boil if using yogurt.

Sprinkle each serving with reserved grated carrots.

Serves 6

CURRY NOTE: The reason we are not more specific about the amount of curry powder is that each brand is a distinctive combination of spices in varying proportions. Try the almost fruity, highly flavored S&B curry powder. Some stores carry curry paste, such as the M. M. Poonjiaji brand, which we also recommend.

Red Pepper and Eggplant Soup

Bell peppers, stuffed with anything, were once the darlings of the one-dish-meal generation. Available in three main colors, all sweet peppers are similar in taste and, in fact, are merely advancing stages of ripeness: from green through yellow to red. Their structural benefits as containers are complemented by their glossy, smooth beauty, the reds being our particular favorite. Sleek red peppers make any dish glow, and their distinctive taste is further enhanced by roasting. Matched to the flavors of olive oil, garlic, and tomatoes, roasted red peppers are in their element, an alliance we've tried to capture here.

4 tablespoons olive oil
3 cloves garlic, minced
1 large onion, chopped
1 small eggplant, peeled and
   cut into small cubes
3 red bell peppers, roasted*
3 tablespoons imported
   tomato paste**

1 teaspoon fennel seed
1 teaspoon oregano
5 cups chicken stock*
½ cup chopped fresh parsley
   salt and pepper

In a 4-quart saucepan heat oil and add garlic, onion, and eggplant. Sauté over medium heat for about 8 minutes.

Remove skin, seeds, and veins from roasted red peppers and cut into strips. Add peppers, tomato paste, fennel, and oregano to saucepan, stir well, and cook for another 25 minutes. Add chicken stock and bring to a boil. Simmer for about 10 minutes.

Puree mixture in a food processor, return to pan, and reheat gently, stirring in parsley at the last minute. Taste for salt and pepper.

Serves 6

Mushroom, Olive, and Cream Cheese Soup

According to legend, you can tell by the colors of the rainbow just how good the olive crop is going to be. If there is truth in that, they must have some very nice rainbows over Lindsay, California, which has been the center of the industry in this country for over a half-century. A sign over the highway into town announces: "A nice town, a great olive."

That sign would have been hanging over Monticello if Thomas Jefferson had been successful with the olives he brought from Aix-en-Provence. Though they did not thrive in the South, neither did they diminish his esteem for the olive, which he felt was "of all the gifts of heaven to man . . . next to the most precious, if it be not the most precious." Another precious olive-related gift was given to the world by Herbert Kagley who, in 1933, developed the first olive pitter.

With some fresh mushrooms and creamy white cheese, this haunting olive soup recalls Lawrence Durrell's praise for the olive: "A taste older than meat, older than wine. A taste as old as cold water."

4 tablespoons butter	salt and pepper
1 bunch green onions, chopped	1 8-ounce can black olives,** drained and chopped
½ pound mushrooms, cleaned and chopped	4 cups chicken stock*
2 tablespoons lemon juice	¼ pound cream cheese
1 teaspoon chopped fresh dill	½ cup sour cream or plain yogurt for garnish

In a 4-quart saucepan melt butter and sauté onions and mushrooms until tender. Sprinkle with lemon juice and cook another minute. Add dill, salt and pepper, olives, and stock and bring to a boil. Reduce heat and add cream cheese. Simmer gently for 15 minutes.

At this point you may puree mixture in a food processor or blender if you want a smooth soup. We prefer to serve it as is for its interesting textures, with a dollop of sour cream or yogurt topped with additional chopped olives, if desired.

Serves 4 to 6

Very Democratic Double-Mushroom Soup with Pernod and Tarragon

Until the recent past mushrooms played hard to get. When they were difficult to cultivate, mushrooms made their rare appearances only on the tables of the wealthy. Then in the 1890s, at the Pasteur Institute of Paris, French scientists succeeded in unraveling the secrets of producing mushroom spawn. But they offered to share with the world only the spawn itself and not the technique of producing it. Finally, in the 1920s, American scientists made similar discoveries and freely published their findings. This resulted in widespread cultivation, brought mushrooms to the masses, and had flavorful implications for omelettes, sauces, and every conceivable soup. Democratization has led to yet another dilemma: With so many mushrooms at one's disposal, which soup is the one to make? This one is exceptional, with its foresty flavors of dried and fresh mushrooms and an undertone of Pernod.

4 tablespoons butter	2 teaspoons chopped fresh
1 large shallot, chopped	tarragon leaves
¾ pound mushrooms, cleaned	2 cups chicken stock*
and sliced	¼ cup Pernod
2 ounces dried porcini	1 cup half and half
mushrooms** (see Note),	salt and pepper
soaked in hot water for 30	
minutes	

In a 2-quart saucepan melt butter and sauté shallots and mushrooms until tender. Meanwhile, drain porcini mushrooms and reserve liquid. (If liquid looks sandy, pour through strainer lined with cheesecloth or paper towel.) Add porcini and tarragon to saucepan and continue to simmer for another 8 minutes, stirring frequently. Add the stock and porcini liquid and simmer, covered, for 15 minutes. Remove from heat.

With a slotted spoon, remove approximately half the mushroom-shallot mixture from saucepan and reserve. Puree contents of saucepan in a food processor or blender with Pernod and half and half.

Return to saucepan, add reserved mushroom-shallot mixture, and taste for salt and pepper. Reheat gently if necessary.

Serves 4

PORCINI NOTE: Although porcini are delicious in this soup, you can substitute other dried mushrooms, such as shitakes or morels, with equally tasty results.

Broccoli-Walnut Cream Soup

The Pennsylvania Dutch often planted their crops close to giant walnut trees, which they considered evidence of great fertility. They also incorporated the native nuts into their cooking, especially for their famously extravagant black walnut cakes. Many Native Americans had been using both sap and nuts in their cooking since 2000 B.C.

Our recipe has been influenced by many other walnut customs as well: Bulgarian "tarator," a walnut-cucumber soup; a walnut-cream sauce from Turkey; an Arab and Persian walnut paste used as a thickener for soups and sauces; and an Italian sauce in which walnuts are ground with olive oil, butter, and parsley. The broccoli deepens this soup's Italian accent and tempers the walnuts with a fresh vegetable taste.

2 tablespoons butter
2 cloves garlic, minced
1 shallot, minced
1 cup white wine
4 cups chicken stock*
1 large bunch broccoli,
    peeled and chopped, saving
    6 to 8 flowerets for garnish

½ cup finely chopped walnuts
    salt and pepper
½ teaspoon cayenne
1 teaspoon marjoram
1 cup heavy cream

In a 4-quart saucepan melt butter and sauté garlic and shallots until tender. Pour in wine and stock and bring to a boil. Add the broccoli, bring to a boil again, reduce heat to a simmer, and cook for about 10 minutes. Stir in walnuts and seasonings and cook for another 5 minutes.

Puree entire mixture in a food processor or blender, return to saucepan, and add the cream. Reheat gently but do not boil.

Serve garnished with broccoli flowerets.

Serves 6 to 8

Almond-Garlic Soup

Garlic Chip Cookies and Garlic Meringue Pie are not as unusual as they sound—at least not in Gilroy, California. During the last weekend in July, that city hosts the annual Garlic Festival where 130,000 participants and spectators have been known to devour over a ton and a half of garlic. The festival's cooking contest stirs up considerable interest among California "garliphiles," who submit hundreds of recipes, some of them actually edible. Not to be outdone, Berkeley, California, also hosts similar rituals, all of which amounts to an ever-spiraling number of garlic dishes throughout the state.

Garlic has always had loyal devotees, including the pre-Columbian Indians, who ate it in quantity as a vegetable. In the south of France, home of the classic Languedoc garlic soup, the little cloves are called the truffles of Provence. By contrast, California produces huge elephant garlic in which each clove equals a whole head of regular garlic.

This soup is a beautiful blending of garlic and almonds underscored by the sweet presence of leeks.

4 tablespoons butter
2 leeks, white part only,
   sliced

15 cloves garlic, peeled
1 cup finely ground almonds
   salt and pepper

5 cups chicken stock*
1 cup heavy cream

In a 4-quart saucepan melt butter and sauté leeks and garlic until soft. (Do not let garlic color or it will make soup bitter.) Add the almonds, salt and pepper, and stock. Bring to a boil and cover, then simmer for 20 minutes.

Puree in a blender or food processor. Return soup to saucepan, add cream, and reheat gently.

Serves 6 to 8

Yellow Split Pea and Fresh Green Pea Soup

Furs and dried peas were once constant companions; in fact, one wasn't possible without the other. Fur traders destined for the Hudson Bay Company's post at Fort Vancouver even toted their own salt pork with them to flavor the split pea soup that sustained them. Peas were a major crop in the fort's gardens, planted by Hudson Bay's Dr. McLoughlin. They grew so well in that region that today the state of Washington is the world's leading producer of dried peas.

As tasty as they may be, dried peas seem a totally different species from fresh. Thomas Jefferson was so in awe of his favorite vegetable that he cultivated several different varieties of peas at Monticello. According to his Garden Book, he also entered in an annual pea competition with his gardening friends; he lost these contests with little remorse since all participants were invited to enjoy the winner's entries.

Reportedly the Dutch are responsible for bringing split pea soup, one of their national dishes, to this country. In this two-part soup, old-time split pea soup still reigns supreme, but the tiny sparkling green peas turn it, at the last, into a new, fresh-tasting dish as well.

4 tablespoons vegetable oil

2 leeks, white part only, chopped

3 cloves garlic, minced

2 carrots, chopped

3 tablespoons chopped fresh parsley

½ teaspoon nutmeg

6 cups chicken stock*

1 bay leaf

½ pound yellow split peas

1½ cups shelled fresh or frozen young green peas

salt and pepper

fresh mint leaves, chopped, for garnish

In a 4-quart saucepan heat oil and add leeks, garlic, carrots, parsley, and nutmeg. Cook, stirring occasionally, until vegetables are tender, about 8 minutes. Add stock, bay leaf, and split peas. Bring to a boil, reduce to a simmer, and cook, covered, for about 1 hour.

Remove bay leaf and puree soup in a food processor or blender. Return soup to pot, add green peas, and cook for 5 minutes. Add salt and pepper to taste.

Serve with a sprinkling of chopped mint leaves.

Serves 8 to 10

Black and White Swirled Bean Soup

U.S. Senate Bean Soup may not exactly be food for the gods, but it has certainly been, for over a half-century, soup of the senators. Made from dried white beans, it is a specialty of the U.S.

Senate Restaurant in Washington, D.C. Credit for inventing this political potage is often laid at the feet of a certain Minnesota senator; however, there is sufficient dispute about this authorship to incite rage among those who embroil themselves in culinary controversies of this sort. For example, George and Berthe Herter, in their book Bull Cook and Authentic Historical Recipes and Practices, insist that bean soup is a national soup of Belgium and was originally created by a Belgian, Jean Debruyn.

This seems no less than unpatriotic, considering the bean soup tradition in this country. Boston was known as Beantown, and Navy Bean Soup was a virtual Sunday necessity all over New England, where it became a natural repository for the remnants of Saturday night's baked beans. In Massachusetts, the success or failure of "Forefathers Day" dinner depended entirely on the taste of the beans. New Hampshire's "Bean Porridge" was a hearty old bean-laden dish. The famous Black Bean Soup from New York's Coach House Restaurant is a hearty and relatively new one, the restaurant having opened in 1949. In this two-soups soup, each has spicy and distinctive flavors of its own. Swirled together, they make each spoonful of soup a surprise.

1 pound dried black beans	12 cloves garlic, finely minced
1 pound small dried white beans	1 onion, chopped
water	6 tablespoons good red wine vinegar
4 tablespoons olive oil	4 jalapeño peppers,* seeded and deveined
½ cup chopped fresh coriander leaves	salt and pepper
2 teaspoons ground cumin	

Rinse beans and soak in separate bowls overnight. Drain and rinse. Cook each batch of beans separately in enough water to cover, simmering gently for several hours, or until beans are soft.

Puree each batch of beans with their cooking liquid in a food processor or blender and place in separate bowls.

To the black beans add a puree of olive oil, coriander, cumin, and half the garlic and onion. To the white beans add a puree of vinegar, jalapeños, and the other half of the garlic and onion.

Heat each batch in different saucepans and taste for salt and pepper.

To serve, ladle ¾ cup black bean soup into a shallow bowl, and then ladle ¾ cup white bean soup over it, swirling gently with spoon. May be garnished with additional chopped coriander.

Serves 6 to 8

Real Succotash Soup

The entire question of succotash requires a certain suspension of disbelief. Most people think they know everything they ever wanted to know about succotash. At first, we agreed. Succotash is canned. They serve it in cafeterias and grammar school hot lunch programs (or tepid lunch programs, as the case may be). Marathon runners wouldn't touch the stuff. We decided it was time, in this culinary age of discovery, to take a fresh look at succotash.

The oldest recipe we found combines dried white beans and cooked dried corn with a couple of fowls, a hunk of beef brisket, salt pork, and seasonings. The final servings included only the beans, corn, and meat from one of the fowls. New England cooks used scarlet-flecked cranberry beans and fresh corn, when available. Equally legitimate succotashes mixed corn with lima beans or kidney beans. The Pennsylvania Dutch added green peppers, tomatoes, and onions and made their succotash into a kind of vegetable stew. The Indians who originally taught everyone else the art of "msickquatash" froze it in blocks and chopped off whatever they needed throughout the winter.

The point is that, until the canning industry divested the dish of its intrinsic and varied character, people loved succotash. Whether they used fresh vegetables or the earthy goodness of dried, they enjoyed this basic combination with and without additional ingredients. Author Evan Jones reports finding the diary of a Vermont pioneer farmer whose entries included nothing at all about food except for one day in the middle of August, 1898: "This day," he wrote, "I din'd upon Succotash."

We have chosen to do our interpretation in the form of a soup, smoldering with the smoky flavor of country ham and the sweetness of peas.

½ pound Smithfield or
country ham,** diced
1 onion, chopped
1 cup fresh or frozen green
peas
1 cup cooked lima beans

1 cup fresh or frozen corn
kernels
4 cups chicken stock*
1 cup milk
3 tablespoons fresh parsley
salt and pepper

In a 4-quart saucepan sauté ham until fat is rendered. Add onion and cook until soft. Add peas, beans, corn, and stock, and bring to a boil. With a slotted spoon remove approximately 1 cup of the vegetables and half the ham and set aside. Reduce heat to a simmer, and cook, covered, for 10 minutes.

In a food processor or blender puree soup until smooth, return to pot, and add milk, parsley, salt and pepper, and reserved ham and vegetables. Reheat gently.

Serves 6

Chicken Minestrone with Angel Hair Pasta and Mace

At one time, the world's most beautiful women drank up great quantities of a coveted beauty potion: chicken soup. Their goal was a plump silhouette, as curvaceous as a fat little chicken. They believed that the only way to look like the rounded, waddling birds was to consume them—literally to take their shapes. Recently, people have been less interested in identifying with chickens for cosmetic purposes. The little birds are pursued for higher goals, such as preparing this voluptuous chicken minestrone.

Minestrone, minestra, and minestrina are all Italian words for soup. Based on the same root as "minister," they convey the meaning of something "served" or "given," the essence of any soup. In this one, shreds of tender poached breast of chicken and fine strands of angel hair pasta impart a certain delicacy to a vegetable-laden, chunky assemblage.

4 tablespoons vegetable oil	1 teaspoon thyme
1 onion, chopped	6 cups chicken stock*
1 leek, white part only, chopped	3 cups water
2 stalks celery, sliced	3 carrots, peeled and sliced
1 red bell pepper, seeded, deveined, and cut into strips	1 cup dried garbanzo beans soaked overnight, or 2 16-ounce cans, drained
1 small fennel bulb, chopped	¼ cup chopped fresh parsley
½ head savoy cabbage, shredded	2 chicken breasts, skinned
4 plum tomatoes, seeded and coarsely chopped	8 ounces angel hair pasta (very thin pasta)
2 teaspoons mace	3 cloves garlic
	salt and pepper

In an 8-quart soup pot heat oil and sauté onion and leek until soft. Add celery, red pepper, fennel, and cabbage. Cook over medium heat for about 8 minutes, until all vegetables are tender. Add the tomatoes, mace, and thyme, stir well, and cook for another 3 minutes. Pour in the stock and water and bring to a boil slowly. (If a foam forms on surface skim it off.)

Stir in the carrots, beans, and parsley. Reduce heat to a simmer and cook, partially covered, for 1 hour.

Add the chicken breasts and cook for 20 minutes. (Make sure that the soup does not reach the boiling point or the chicken will be tough and stringy.) Remove chicken and allow to cool.

Meanwhile, add the pasta and cook for another 10 minutes.

Remove chicken from bones and cut into thin strips; add to soup. Press garlic through a garlic press directly into soup. Stir well and season with salt and pepper to taste.

Serves 12

Chunky Potato-Sorrel Soup

Potatoes have not always had an easy life. At one time, they were rejected by just about every nation and across all social strata. People who were starving wouldn't eat them, even as a last resort. In some cases, potato promoters resorted to tactics not unlike today's advertising campaigns, enlisting endorsements from the famous and the powerful to convince people of the potato's true potential. Louis XVI, for example, agreed to accept a bouquet of potato flowers as a sign of his approbation of the "Indian artichoke," as the native American tuber was disdainfully known to the French. But Louis didn't stop there. He plucked out one of the little potato posies and slipped it through his buttonhole, wearing it for all the world to see. Marie Antoinette, who apparently wanted to participate equally in these early days of potato p.r., planted a few potato flowers in her hair. Frederick the Great was even more effective, especially since his campaign employed armed troops to convince the people, who were suffering from famine, that they should consider the potato. In Wattenburg, Germany, appreciative citizens put up a statue of Sir Francis Drake holding a potato, probably a replica of the one he brought from across the seas. Meanwhile, back in America, Eliza Leslie was, by 1837, calling potatoes "part of every dinner."

By now we are familiar with several varieties of reds, waxies, and Idahos, with exotic blues, among others, beginning to come on the market. James Beard reports that any Peruvian potato market displays rainbows of colors and endless varieties. This should come as no surprise since the Incas calculated units of time by how long it took to cook a potato.

In this soup, chunks of potato are deliciously set off by the lemony-spinach taste of sorrel. It's good company at the formal feast as well as for cozy, hearty wintertime meals.

3 tablespoons butter

6 ounces sorrel leaves, cut in
chiffonade*

salt and pepper

1 teaspoon chopped fresh dill

5 cups chicken stock*

3 medium potatoes, cut into
1½-inch chunks

2 egg yolks

¾ cup heavy cream

In a 4-quart saucepan melt butter and sauté sorrel, stirring until sorrel seems to liquefy, for about 5 minutes. Add salt and pepper, dill, and stock. Bring to a boil and add potatoes. Reduce heat to a simmer, and cook for about 10 minutes or until potatoes are tender.

In a bowl mix yolks with cream and add a cup of soup to the mixture. Add soup-cream-yolk mixture back to soup and stir well on low heat. Cook for about 3 minutes, or just until soup thickens slightly. Do not boil or egg yolks will curdle.

Serves 6

Good Green Soup

In spite of being served to a group of discriminating gourmets several years ago, "Garbage Soup" never really caught on in the San Francisco Bay area. Its ingredients consisted of leftover salad greens with residual dressing, and whatever other inspirational scraps were about. Most surprising (and most surprised) were the diners to whom it was offered: distinguished members of the very exclusive, all-male Confrerie de la Marmite (Brotherhood of the Cooking Pot), a Swiss society with their only U.S. chapter located in San Francisco. That Garbage Soup was a true exclusive because its particular combination of leafy stems, stray bits, and wondrous revisited tastes was something that no one could duplicate—nor did anyone express any interest in doing so.

At any rate the "garbage" concept was the inspiration behind our Good Green Soup. We like to rummage through our vegetable bins and covered bowls in the fridge to see what we might put into it: yesterday's vegetables, a leftover lunch salad, Saturday night's elegant puree of broccoli. Anything that still has some hint of freshness left to it can qualify. Most of the time it will be a fine Good Green Soup; and occasionally it will be a Great Green Soup. However, on those days when you have no leftovers to start you off, you might try this one.

4 tablespoons butter
2 cups shredded lettuce
1 bunch spinach leaves,
   washed
2 leeks, white part only,
   chopped
3 celery stalks with leaves,
   chopped
1 10-ounce package frozen
   peas, or 1 pound fresh,
   shelled peas

½ cup chopped fresh parsley
1 teaspoon marjoram
1 teaspoon thyme
4 cups chicken stock*
1 cup half and half
   salt and pepper

In a 4-quart saucepan melt butter and add vegetables. Cook over low to medium heat until tender, about 8 minutes. Add herbs and stock and bring to a boil. Reduce heat, cover, and cook for 10 minutes more.

With a slotted spoon remove vegetables to a food processor or blender and puree with half and half. Return soup to pot, reheat gently, and season with salt and pepper to taste.

Serves 6

Zucchini and Peppery Watercress Soup

"Cuckow-floure" and "lady-smock" are two of the picturesque nicknames for watercress. Less romantically, it has been called an important weed. This insulting designation had no effect on the famous French palace chef, Taillevent, who prepared it for royal diners as a special course "to refresh the mouth." Since then watercress has been famous for its tingling, peppery qualities.

Although watercress is a weed found at the edges of rivers and streams, the grocery-store crop is more likely to come from shallow commercial tanks. The word "cress" refers to other plants, including Indian cress, also known as nasturtium, and winter cress, or rocket. These greens have entirely different tastes from the regally refreshing watercress, which is used in this lively zucchini soup.

4 tablespoons butter	pinch salt
1 bunch green onions, chopped	1 tablespoon freshly ground black or white pepper
1 pound zucchini, sliced	4 cups chicken stock*
3 tablespoons balsamic vinegar**	1 bunch watercress leaves
	½ cup heavy cream

In a 4-quart saucepan melt butter and sauté onions and zucchini. Add vinegar, salt, and pepper, and cook for 5 minutes. Add the stock, bring to a boil, and reduce heat to a simmer. Cook, covered, for 10 minutes.

Place mixture in a food processor or blender along with watercress leaves (save some for garnish). Puree, return to pot, and reheat gently with cream.

Serve topped with watercress leaves. As good cold as it is hot.

Serves 4 to 6

Crookneck Squash and Tomato Soup

"Squash" comes from a Narragansett Indian word: <u>askoot-as-quash</u>. According to some reliable evidence, squash was proba-

bly the first food cultivated by American Indians. For centuries, it continued to be part of the great Indian triad, along with maize and beans, that made up the basic diet of all North and South American Indians. Iroquois-speaking Indians made it into a soup, along with its flowers, plus some meal for thickening. By the time the first Europeans came along, the Pueblos in the Southwest had been eating squash for over 2000 years. Yet the first explorers ignored squash completely, thinking it was a type of bland, uninteresting melon.

Crooknecks don't look like other squashes and they don't pass for very good melons either. But they have been used, by at least one eminent American food authority, for other unsquashlike purposes. As Jonathan Norton Leonard recounts, in his American Cooking: New England, when he was a mere child he used to stretch a few rubber bands on a crookneck squash from top to bottom and make himself a sort of miniature guitar. For the less musically inclined, crooknecks can be simmered along with some oregano and peppery summer savory into a fine and aromatic soup.

4 tablespoons butter
1 leek, white part only,
  thinly sliced
1 pound crookneck squash,
  thinly sliced
½ teaspoon oregano
1 teaspoon fresh summer
  savory, or ½ teaspoon
  dried savory

5 cups chicken stock*
2 large ripe tomatoes, seeded
  and coarsely chopped
4 sun-dried tomatoes,** cut
  into strips
2 medium potatoes, diced
  salt and pepper

In a 4-quart saucepan melt butter and sauté leeks until tender. Add squash, oregano, and savory and cook for another 3 minutes. Add stock, bring to a boil, and add tomatoes and potatoes. Reduce to a simmer, cover, and cook for 10 minutes. Add salt and pepper to taste.

Serves 6

Corn and Oyster Bisque

"Oys! Oys! Oys!" the big burly men called, some with wet sloshing pails hanging from their shoulders, some pushing wheelbarrows. "Here's your fine fresh oysters! Come, buy!" And everybody did, especially in the Boston of 1830 when oystermen walked through the streets shouting their convincing chants. By then the American oyster fad that began in the 1700s was in full swing, and not only in the coastal towns where oysters were plentiful. People in interior settlements eagerly awaited the arrival of stagecoach wagons, called the "Oyster Line," which brought the oysters from Baltimore. In Buffalo and other lake towns, oyster lovers welcomed oyster-laden boats along the Erie Canal. The well-traveled oyster arrived on horseback, by spring wagon, and even, for one Chicago restaurant willing to pay the fare, by sleigh.

In those days the abundant oysters were not very expensive anywhere. Writing in the 1850s, an English traveler noted one obvious social distinction: "The rich consume oysters and Champaigne; the poorer classes consume oysters and lager bier." As in so many things, California excels in extremes, with its tiny Olympias (numbering 1400 to a gallon) and the large Pacific Kings (4 or 5 to a pint) equally popular. Today, an Oyster Investigation Laboratory at Bivalve, New Jersey, is testimony to our continuing interest in oysters.

This satiny bisque, chockful of luscious oysters and sweet kernels of corn, has its own reasons for popularity. Another might be deduced from the words on a poster from the Oyster Institute of North America: "Eat Oysters. Love Longer."

2 tablespoons butter	salt and pepper
1 onion, finely chopped	2 10-ounce jars large oysters
2 cloves garlic, minced	with liquid
1½ cups milk	chopped fresh parsley for
1 cup heavy cream	garnish
2 cups fresh or frozen corn kernels	

In a 4-quart saucepan melt butter and add the onion and garlic. Cook over low heat until onion becomes wilted, then add milk, cream, and corn. Bring to a boil and add the salt and pepper and oysters with liquid. (If oysters are extra large you might want to cut them in half.) Bring to a simmer but do not boil.

Remove from heat and let stand for 5 minutes. Sprinkle each serving with chopped parsley.

Serves 6

Creamy Crab and Artichoke Soup

Having at one time been called aphrodisiacs, artichokes are perhaps a little more interesting than they would otherwise be.

Certainly they look unusual, which is often a qualification for aphrodisiacs. They still seem exotic to many Americans, especially outside New York, San Francisco, and other cities with large Italian neighborhoods.

As aphrodisiacs no one seems to know just how artichokes work because no one knows if they work. For their pure physical involvement, however, artichokes rank as high as Dungeness crab (uncracked) or fresh corn on the cob. Like these other foods, an artichoke gets pretty much all your attention while you're eating it. Our soup combines both sweet crab meat and tender artichokes in ways that are comparatively easy to handle but are compellingly tasty enough to still claim quite a bit of attention.

3½ cups chicken stock*	1 tablespoon lemon juice
1 10-ounce package frozen	3 tablespoons brandy
artichoke hearts or	1 teaspoon thyme
bottoms, thawed	¼ teaspoon cayenne
salt and pepper	¼ pound crab meat, cooked
1½ cups heavy cream	

In a 4-quart saucepan bring stock to a boil and add artichokes; simmer for 10 minutes. In a food processor or blender puree soup and return to the pot. Add remaining ingredients. Reheat gently.

Serves 6

Summer Tomato–Corn Pone Soup

"Appone" is a simple Algonquin Indian bread made of cornmeal and water. For the early settlers, who had no wheat, "corn pone" was their only bread, and often their only food. Cooked in various ways, the cornmeal-water mix developed many different forms: hoecakes were lowered into an open fire on the end of a hoe; ashcakes were wrapped in vine leaves and thrown in the flames or placed directly on the ashes and washed off when cooked and piping hot.

These early associations with the primitive and the basic eventually gave corn pone the advantage of reverse snobbism. A century later, rich Virginia planters, who had plenty of wheat, were often known to prefer "the Pone." And Benjamin Franklin probably insulted everybody in 1766 by saying that any "hoe-cake hot from the fire is better than a Yorkshire muffin." For some reason, corn pone has often made for strange politics. Huey Long and Franklin Roosevelt engaged in public debate over whether corn pone should be dunked in one's soup (the Long approach) or broken into pieces and crumbled into it (FDR's preference).

Our California down-home soup, which takes advantage of both methods, might be called the "Great Compromiser." The taste of sweet onions and tomatoes intermingles with the squares of basil-suffused corn pone, which flavors the soup from the bottom up.

Pone

½ cup cornmeal	2 eggs, beaten
½ cup flour	½ cup butter or lard, melted
½ teaspoon baking soda	½ cup buttermilk
3 tablespoons sugar	½ cup finely chopped fresh
½ teaspoon salt	basil leaves

3 tablespoons butter	2 tablespoons honey
1 large sweet onion, finely	½ cup chopped fresh basil
chopped	leaves
2 pounds fresh tomatoes,	salt and pepper
coarsely chopped	4 cups chicken stock*

Preheat oven to 350°F and grease an 8-inch-square baking pan.

To make pone, mix first 5 ingredients in a bowl until blended. In a separate bowl combine eggs, butter, and buttermilk, then mix well with dry ingredients. Stir in basil.

Turn mixture into baking pan and bake for about 30 minutes. Allow to cool and cut into 6 squares.

Meanwhile, to make soup, melt butter in a 4-quart saucepan and sauté onion until soft. Add tomatoes and cook over medium heat for 5 minutes. Add remaining ingredients and simmer, covered, for 15 minutes.

Pass soup through a food mill and return to pot to heat through.

Place a square of corn pone in each of 6 bowls and pour soup over it.

Serves 6

Chile Corn Chowder

The chile pepper, the chowder, and most of the ingredients in this satisfying soup are native American, though all have gone on to international indispensability. Traced back to the Incan and Aztec cultures of 5000 B.C. Peru, chile peppers are now ubiquitous, providing the base for Hungarian paprika, cayenne, Tabasco sauce, and Indian curry. From California and New Mexico to Texas, the number of varieties of chile peppers is exceeded only by the number of dishes that utilize them. There is an international standard used to measure the heat of peppers on a scale from 1 to 120, and some of the fiery jalapeños rate only a 15.

This soup recalls several American regional specialties, beginning with the early corn chowders of Massachusetts, which reportedly traveled west on covered wagons into chile country. In Oregon, Salmon and Corn Chowder has long been a local favorite. In the Southwest, the Pueblo Indians made a Green Chile Stew, and Santa Fe's Posole includes both hominy, or hulled corn, and red chile pulp.

Strictly speaking, a stew may be prepared any number of ways, but a chowder must be built. The old New England expression "Building a chowder" accurately describes the process of constructing layers of alternating ingredients and covering it all with the liquid in which it cooks. As John Thorne explains in his wonderful pamphlet on the subject of chowder: "...a chowder represents the special preparation of some very ordinary ingredients, while a stew represents an ordinary preparation of some very special ingredient."

3 tablespoons butter	2 cups milk
3–4 jalapeño peppers,* seeded, deveined, and cut into strips (see Note)	1½ cups chicken stock*
	4 medium red potatoes, diced
1 tablespoon ground cumin	4 tablespoons grated dry Jack
1 tablespoon coriander	cheese
2 large tomatoes, peeled* and seeded	2 carrots, peeled and shredded
½ large onion	salt and pepper
4 cups fresh corn kernels (or frozen, thawed)	½ cup chopped fresh coriander leaves for garnish

In a 4-quart saucepan melt butter and sauté jalapeños over a low heat just until they turn slightly limp, about 3 minutes. Add ground cumin and coriander and stir. In a food processor or blender puree 1 tomato with the onion and add to jalapeños. Cook for about 5 minutes.

Meanwhile puree 3 cups corn kernels with the milk, then pass the mixture through a food mill. Add, along with the stock, to tomato-jalapeño mixture and bring to a boil. Add the potatoes and let simmer, covered, for about 8 minutes. Add the cheese, carrots, remaining tomato and corn, and cook for another 3 minutes, uncovered. Add salt and pepper to taste.

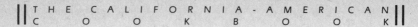
Sprinkle with chopped coriander just before serving.

Serves 6

CHILE NOTE: In this soup or any chile-flavored dish, you can get even more heat from chiles by chopping them, rather than slicing. This will release more of the potent oil concentrated in the veins.

It is difficult to determine accurately the hotness of a chile pepper before cooking it. Generally speaking, the smaller the chile the hotter it is. The most reliable test is your tongue: Cut the chile in half and put your tongue to one of the cut edges; don't chew or swallow, just feel for the intensity of heat on your tongue.

Cabernet Borscht with Beef and Beets

In a pinch I can make from a chicken soup a borscht, but to make from a borscht a chicken soup, this is beyond any cook.
Isaac Bashevis Singer quoting his Aunt Yentl,
New York Times, January 19, 1984

When preparing beets, even the most fastidious cook is bound to be caught red-handed. But the Pennsylvania Dutch have a felicitous attitude toward the beet and its intrusive habit of turning everything in its vicinity a deep unwashable crimson. If you can't beat them, these cooks decided long ago, you might as well dye some eggs with them. The result is Pickled Beets and Red Eggs, a dish which tastes as bright as it looks.

Borscht is the beet's other starring role, though its recipes and its spelling vary with its ethnic identity as well as with available ingredients. Some cooks advise adding red wine vinegar to keep the beets red, but that seldom seems necessary. We have included a dash of Cabernet—well, a cup of Cabernet—though color was not our main consideration. This is a delicious meaty borscht, bortsch, or even barszcz—with the California sparkle of Cabernet. We admit, as Helen Evans Brown wrote in the West

Coast Cook Book of her Jellied California Borscht, that "Quite certainly the first Russians on our Coast did not bring this recipe with them. . . ."

1 pound stewing beef, fat removed, cut into 1-inch chunks	7 cups beef stock*
	3 tablespoons chopped fresh parsley
3 large beets, peeled and diced	salt and pepper
1 carrot, peeled and diced	3 medium potatoes, peeled and cut into ½-inch cubes
1 onion, chopped	2 cups shredded cabbage
2 celery stalks, sliced	1 cup Cabernet wine
2 tomatoes, seeded and coarsely chopped	1 egg yolk
	¼ cup raspberry vinegar**

In a 6-quart pot place meat, beets, carrot, onion, celery, and tomatoes and cover with beef stock. Bring to a boil and add the parsley, salt and pepper. Simmer, covered, for about 1¼ hours.

Add potatoes, cabbage, and Cabernet, and continue to cook until potatoes are tender, about 20 minutes.

Beat yolk with about ½ cup of the hot broth and pour back into soup, stirring constantly. Do not allow to boil. Stir in vinegar just before serving.

Serves 8 to 10

Spicy Lamb and Lentil Soup with Cilantro Cream

Because of their growing popularity, lentils are now available in more colors and types than ever before. The hardy brown ones, sometimes called German, are generally considered less flavorful than the more delicate, light green French "lentilles de Puy." These are more expensive and available only in special stores. However, "Few people," says Jane Grigson in her <u>Vegetable Book</u>, "at a blind tasting could tell the difference."

Actually there are at least fifty varieties of lentils, though few of them are available to American cooks of Indian and Middle Eastern background who want to re-create old family recipes. With soups, the universal solvents, there is less concern for particular types of lentils.

The Pennsylvania Dutch make Linsensuppe, usually adding the leftover bones of pork or ham or, if all else fails, a few new frankfurters. The Italian Zuppa di lenticchie may either be perfumed with sage or combined with chestnuts and herbs. And in the Spanish-influenced American Southwest, Sopa de lentejas often contains a good jolt of chorizo. Therein lies a certain inspiration for this soup, with its spicy sausages and tender bits of lamb. But it's really the final swish of cilantro-flavored sour cream that makes this soup so memorable.

3 tablespoons butter
2 medium onions, chopped
1 cup chopped fresh parsley
2 tablespoons chopped celery leaves
1 tablespoon freshly ground pepper
1 teaspoon turmeric
½ pound lamb shoulder, cubed
½ pound spicy sausage, sliced

4 tomatoes, pureed
4 cups beef stock*
4 cups water
2 cups washed lentils
½ cup fresh cilantro leaves
1 teaspoon salt
½ cup sour cream or plain yogurt
thin lemon slices dipped in paprika for garnish

In a 6-quart saucepan melt butter and sauté onions, parsley, celery leaves, pepper, and turmeric just until tender, about 5 minutes. Add the lamb and sausage and sauté for another 5 minutes, turning mixture frequently. Add the tomatoes, stock, water, and lentils and bring to a boil. Lower heat, cover, and cook for 1 hour.

Puree cilantro leaves with salt and sour cream in a food processor or blender. Swirl into soup.

Float a lemon slice on top of each serving.

Serves 10 to 12

Guacamole Soup

Aficionados of the avocado might appreciate Poor Man's Breakfast, an intriguing-sounding avocado dish from the West Indies. Although the entire breakfast is nothing more than a single avocado, the custardy green fruit of that area customarily weighs from three to four pounds. That certainly is enough avocado to last most people until lunch; but true addicts may prefer to take a midmorning break of toast slathered with "midshipman's butter," another name given to the navy-pleasing fruit. Another possibility is avocado ice cream, a dish that Somerset Maugham, among others, claims to have invented.

Other famous people have also had their fingers in avocados. Novelist-playwright Richard Harding Davis purportedly brought some from Caracas to have them handled professionally by the chef at Delmonico's restaurant. With them the chef created exotic salads and many elaborations on guacamole, a recipe which his enthusiastic New York society patrons gave him credit for inventing.

All makers of guacamole have proprietary feelings about their particular recipe; but the dish is originally Aztec, as is the word ahuacatl (avocado). In transforming this beloved buttery dip into a cumin-scented soup, we wanted to conserve as much of its original enchantment as possible, tortillas and all.

4 tablespoons vegetable oil
2 corn tortillas, cut into
  strips
1 onion, chopped
2 cloves garlic, minced
2–3 jalapeño peppers,* seeded
  and cut into slivers
2 large ripe tomatoes, seeded
  and coarsely chopped

1 tablespoon ground cumin
  salt and pepper
6 cups chicken stock*
½ cup chopped fresh
  coriander leaves
2 avocados, peeled and cut
  into small cubes (see Note)
  juice of 1 lime
  sour cream for garnish

In a 4-quart saucepan heat oil and sauté tortilla strips until lightly browned. Add onion, garlic, and jalapeños, and cook until soft. Stir in tomatoes, cumin, salt and pepper, and cook for 8 minutes over medium-high heat. Add the stock and coriander and bring to a boil.

Meanwhile, sprinkle the avocados with the lime juice. Reduce heat to simmer and add the avocados.

Remove from heat and allow to sit for about 10 minutes. Top each serving with a dollop of sour cream. May be served hot or cold.

Serves 6

AVOCADO NOTE: Since avocados never soften on the tree, they are almost always rock-hard in the market. Leave them at room temperature, or warmer, to ripen—you can even wrap them in paper to hasten the process. Resist the temptation to poke, which can cause bruises. Instead, squeeze them gently in the palm of your hand to test their ripeness. When ready, store them in the refrigerator, preferably on the top shelf, the least cold spot.

Strawberry-Melon Soup with White Zinfandel

Although fruit soups may be new to some, Americans of German and Scandinavian ancestry enjoy them often, served either before dinner or after, hot or cold. This one should be made from the freshest, most fragrant cantaloupes you can find. The flavor of some other melons, such as honeydews, is too light to contribute successfully here.

Cantaloupes are most demonstrative about when they are ready for picking. When perfectly ripe, they form a layer of cells to seal themselves from further nourishment and growth. This layer often breaks their link to the vine, so that they literally pick themselves. Cantaloupes get their name from the papal residence, Cantalupo, where they were once extensively cultivated. In this country, their popularity incited Pennsylvanians to institute an annual Melon Frolics. California's Imperial Valley is the main supplier of what we call cantaloupes; technically speaking, however, they are French netted (musk)melons. In any case, pureed with ripe, succulent strawberries, this sweet orange fruit makes an extravagantly wonderful summer first course.

1 large very ripe cantaloupe (see Note)	juice of 1 lime
2 boxes (24 ounces) strawberries, washed and hulled	½ cup fresh or frozen orange juice
2–3 tablespoons brown sugar	½ cup white Zinfandel or light dessert wine
3 tablespoons chopped fresh mint leaves (reserve several whole leaves)	½ cup plain yogurt
	¾ cup heavy cream

Cut melon in half, remove seeds, and slice each half into thirds. Remove rind and chop melon into chunks. Halve strawberries, reserving 6 whole berries for garnish.

Place berries, melon, sugar, chopped mint, and lime juice into a food processor and puree while adding orange juice and wine.

In a large bowl, combine the yogurt and cream, stirring well until blended. By hand stir in the fruit puree to make a marbleized mixture.

Pour into chilled bowls and garnish each with a whole berry and mint leaf.

Serves 6

MELON NOTE: To test for ripeness, use your nose. If the melon smells "cantaloupey" held 6 inches away, it's probably ripe.

Seafood Gazpacho

For many people, gazpacho may have been the first excursion into the once-exotic realm of cold soups. Sometimes served with chunks of ice floating in it, gazpacho transcended the known categories. It was the first hint that there was probably more out there than a whole childhoodful of school-lunch soups had led us to believe. It was a surprise. Even more surprising was the second gazpacho experience because, more likely than not, it was also completely different. The combination of ingredients, the thickness, tartness, texture—what is this thing called gazpacho? we may have asked, and kept on eating.

Sooner or later someone went to Spain and returned with The Recipe. Straight from Spain, The Recipe had a special ingredient, certainty, the assurance that its origins proved its authenticity. No sooner was that settled when new claims and counterclaims arose, all insisting on equal validity for rival gazpachos. Finally we realized, Solomon-like, that the wisest thing to do was taste them all.

According to the Herters' Bull Cook cookbook, no mystery surrounds the soup. "Gazpacho soup was invented by a poor Andalusian farmer in Spain named Xavier Fernandez in 1861," the authors state categorically. "Mr. Fernandez was visited by his friend Juan Diagre one evening. When the time came to serve his friend a meal, he had to apologize to him because he had no wood to warm his vegetable soup. The two good friends ate the soup cold and both liked it very well."

At any rate, we have tried to introduce a hint of mystery into this California version, which tastes wonderful cold and even more wonderful the next day. For that reason alone, you may want to take the advice of M. F. K. Fisher: "I always see to it that I have made too much gaspacho."

1 cucumber, peeled, seeded, and chopped	2 large ripe tomatoes, seeded and chopped

1 green bell pepper, seeded,
  deveined, and chopped
1 large red onion, chopped
¼ cup chopped fresh parsley
4 cloves garlic, minced
4 cups tomato juice
1 8-ounce bottle clam juice
1 tablespoon good-quality
  mustard

¼ cup olive oil
4 tablespoons balsamic
  vinegar**
1 tablespoon Worcestershire
  sauce
dash Tabasco
salt and pepper
½ pound tiny bay shrimp,
  cleaned and cooked

In a blender or food processor make a coarse puree of all ingredients except the shrimp.

Pour gazpacho into a large bowl and stir in the shrimp. Cover and refrigerate for at least 4 hours before serving.

Because gazpacho will thicken due to the gelatin in the shrimp, you might want to add some more tomato juice to mixture before serving. Soup may be garnished with any of the above chopped vegetables or with garlic croutons.

Serves 6 to 8

Cool Cucumber and Hot Mustard Soup

It may be true, as Waverley Root says, that the taste of cucumbers is as neutral as anything can be "without ceasing to exist." But attitudes toward this most ancient of vegetables have been anything but neutral. Introduced to Haiti by Columbus in 1494, cucumbers were soon brought under extensive cultivation in the Americas, especially by the Pueblos of the Southwest. The cucumber's previous high point of popularity may have to be traced back to the time of the Roman emperor Tiberius, who had cucumbers grown in carriages that were wheeled out for a daily stroll in the sun so they would flourish, even in the off-season. Today, cucumbers are available all year, though their squirty refreshing character seems most welcome during the summer.

Cold soups and salads, paired with an assertive taste such as that of yogurt, are the legacy of Russian, Turkish, Indian, and Near and Middle Eastern cuisines, to name a few. Here we use an unexpected and provocative flavoring, hot-sweet mustard, in a true summer special: It is not only served cold but requires no cooking to begin with.

1 small onion
2 cucumbers, peeled and
   seeded
4 sprigs parsley
2 tablespoons hot-sweet
   mustard**
½ cup fresh lemon juice

1½ cups heavy cream or half
   and half
   salt and pepper
1 tablespoon sugar
   chopped fresh dill for
   garnish

Put onion, cucumbers, parsley, and mustard into a food processor and chop finely. Add the lemon juice, cream, salt and pepper, and sugar and process until fairly smooth.

Chill for at least 2 hours before serving, as this soup tastes best icy cold. Serve garnished with chopped dill.

Serves 4 to 6

APPETIZER SALADS

The eating of salad in America raises many questions, but none so provocative as "When?" Whether 'tis nobler to have one's salad after the main course (usually considered European and therefore correct) or before the meal (usually dismissed as American and un-sophisticated), or, dare we mention, <u>with</u> the entrée (permissible in family-style meals only): Those are the questions. There are a few interesting answers, each with its own sort of integrity.

Proponents of serving salads "before" muster the dignity of history to their defense. They claim that when the first Europeans came to this fresh and fertile land, they were overwhelmed by the goodness and variety of vegetation. In fact, while they waited for their chunks of meat to cook over open fires, they could never resist nibbling away at the nearest greenery. These wilderness habits persisted, transformed somewhat into an attraction to crudités and first-course salads. Sometimes premeal salads are linked to the arrival of Italians and their antipasto, or to Scandinavians with their cold tables and the traditions of the Swedish smorgasbord. Some more cynical theorists have blamed restaurants for using premeal salads to stuff their hungry customers with inexpensive lettuces. An extension of this modus operandi is the ubiquitous, though often boring, salad bar.

On the other hand, those who would have their salad postprandially seem to assume that there is prestige in the very preference. Actually the fact that people want salads at all is a fairly recent phenomenon. As recently as a hundred years ago, salads were not only unpopular, they were feared. People distrusted anything raw. This was partly because, with increasing urbanization, people no longer grew their own vegetables nor did they know where they came from. Cookbooks advised boiling vegetables to oblivion, dropping sliced cucumbers immediately into cold water, throwing away the water that potatoes were cooked in. Tomatoes were rare and considered dangerous. Some of this fear was linked to epidemics that ran rampant at the same time fresh vegetables were in season, an association that was coincidental rather than causative. People were also suspicious of olive oils, which were often laced with cheaper, often rancid oils. Vinegars, adulterated with all manner of insalubrious acids, were always suspect. Boiled dressings and bottled condiments were the common solution. People did eat composed salads, however, made with assorted cooked ingredients. German Americans turned the potato salad into an American institution. The Dutch contributed coleslaw to the sweet-sour category of salads, and soul-food cooks made "hog maw" from celery and peppers, with results that hinted at chicken salad. But only the upper classes had green, leafy salads, or even wanted them.

The difficulties of farming on the American frontier encouraged the planting of only the hardiest of roots, potatoes, cabbages, and pumpkins. Farm people subsisted on corn bread, pork, and salted fish, with few, if any, vegetables. The average American at that time (according to Richard Hooker's History of Food and Drink in America) "probably did not eat salads at all." Then, in the late 1800s, salads started to become, in Hooker's words, the "plaything of the adventurous."

As people moved to the cities, which meant more sedentary living, they became interested in less substantial meals, more appropriate to urban life. The new Fannie Farmer cookbook of 1906 was advising that salads could be made from "watercress, chiccory, cucumbers, etc." which contain "little nutriment, but are cooling . . ." Her recipe for East India Salad, which begins "Work two ten cent cream cheeses until smooth," indicates dietary as well as economic distance: It seems a bit heavy for current tastes, and it's hard to imagine two packages of anything for twenty cents. A recipe for French dressing sounds familiar enough, but her variation, called "Parisian French Dressing," adds several pinches of powdered sugar. Another cookbook of that era warns that dressings must be made with "a silver or wooden fork, a large soup plate, which should be very, very cold." Maximilian De Loup, the foresightful author of the American Salad Book, predicted in 1900 that Americans would someday accept salads and even prefer them over "heavy bulky materials." He exhorted his countrymen to be proud of the variety and abundance of vegetables and not to feel intimidated by the less bountifully endowed French nor by the English, whom he called "still barbaric" in their dealings with salads.

Meanwhile, back at the gold mines, Californians by contrast had early recognized that the value of salads could be monetary as well as nutritional. Those who pioneered in produce realized considerable profits from the cultivation and marketing of "green gold." This early exposure probably explains why Californians have always been more experimental about salads than just about anybody outside the Mediterranean. "To my knowledge, California is the only place where truck drivers eat fresh salads without fear of being considered effete," says Jonathan Leonard in American Cooking: The Great West. San Diego patrons reportedly beat a path to the door of Caesar Cardini's Tijuana restaurant when he created the now-famous Caesar Salad. Credit for Crab Louis is in dispute, but

San Francisco's St. Francis Hotel and the old Solari restaurant have the most plausible claims to authorship. The Palace Hotel in San Francisco celebrated the presence of George Arliss touring in the play The Green Goddess by creating an appropriately named salad dressing in his honor.

Traveling west to California one hundred years ago, a visitor asserted that the avocado and shrimp salads of San Francisco "made the trip worthwhile" and dubbed California the "land of salads." It seems even more appropriate today when the plethora of "makins" means that the salad can often be the most colorful part of a meal.

This chapter offers a selection of green salads and composed salads meant to accompany a meal (either before, after, or, yes, even during). The recipes for Basic Vinaigrette and Basic Mayonnaise are followed by variations using herbs, spices, and various condiments.

All salads in this chapter—and everywhere else, for that matter —taste best at room temperature, unless otherwise noted. If you do make the salad ahead, take it out of the refrigerator an hour or so before serving and, even more important, taste. The high water content of salad ingredients will dilute the dressing, making it necessary to adjust seasonings just before serving.

Throughout, blanching refers to a very fast, preliminary plunge into boiling water for no longer than two minutes (unless otherwise noted), followed by refreshing the vegetable in cold water.

For more substantial salads, the "Littlemeals" chapter has a section called Event Salads, a whole array of buffet, picnic, pasta, and main-course salads.

———————
———————

Dilled Baby Cucumbers and Sour Cream
Rutabaga Remoulade
Mixed Mushrooms with Vermont Cheddar

Salad of Green and Gold
Balsamic Broccoli with Golden Raisins and Toasted Walnuts
Garden Greens with Goat Cheese Dressing
Sunchoke and Spinach Salad with Brandy and Walnut Oil
Comice Pear Wedges and Endives Julienne on Watercress
Tomato, Onion, and Cucumber Salad Ribboned with
Ricotta Pesto Cream
Potato, Carrot, and Leek Salad in Mustardy Vinaigrette
Fresh Peas in Cumin Yogurt with Mint
Salad Scheherazade
Marinated Mexicali Eggplant Salad
Parsnip-Carrot Salad in Raspberry Vinaigrette with Walnuts
and Currants
Green Bean, Corn, and Red Pepper Salad
Napa Cabbage in Garlic-Dill Cream
Chilled Asparagus with Smoked Salmon and Horseradish Cream
Asparagus with Orange-Sherry Vinaigrette
Broccoli-Jicama Salad
Coriandered Carrot Coins
Baby Green Beans, Sun-dried Tomatoes, and Pine Nuts in
Basil Vinaigrette
Curried Radicchio, Endive, and Golden Delicious Apple Salad
Artichokes and Mushrooms with Country Ham
Black Bean, Cranberry, and Roasted Pepper Salad
Vinaigrette and Variations
Mayonnaise Medley

Dilled Baby Cucumbers and Sour Cream

In many of today's more artistically arranged produce departments, baskets of tiny cucumbers are often decoratively framed
by lacy sprays of fresh dill. This seems especially appropriate in a

country where "preserved cucumbers" are practically synonymous with "dilled pickles." Americans of German, Scandinavian,
and Russian background have traditionally made use of dill in
cabbage, salmon, and cucumber dishes, and now the frilly-
leaved herb is becoming as commonly used as it is commonly
available. When we find it fresh, we feel the Pavlovian urge to
locate some nearby cucumbers so we can enjoy them together
in this crisp, lively salad.

2 pounds young firm cucumbers	1 cup sour cream
	salt and pepper
1 tablespoon lemon juice	½ cup chopped red onion for garnish
1 tablespoon olive oil	
2 tablespoons chopped fresh dill	

If cucumber skins are waxy, peel off entirely, Otherwise, peel skin off
for a striped effect. Cut cucumber in half lengthwise, seed, cut into
thin slices, and place slices in a bowl.

In a separate bowl mix lemon juice, olive oil, and dill and pour over
cucumbers. Allow to marinate for about 1 hour.

Add sour cream and mix gently. Add salt and pepper to taste.
Garnish with chopped red onion.

Serves 6

Rutabaga Remoulade

In the Plains States, rutabagas were once a life-sustaining food,
being the first root crop of the season. From the Swedish rot-
bagga, meaning ram's root, the rutabaga's culinary possibilities
have until now been best explored by Scandinavian Americans,
whose example is beginning to inspire a whole litany of delicious
rutabaga dishes.

Capers are the pickled buds of a wild plant that grows in the crannies of old walls—never new walls—around the Mediterranean and in deserts. They are costly because of the time-consuming effort of gathering the few buds which are ready each day. Drying and pickling the small crop is also a long and ultimately expensive process. Although some European marketplaces sell capers raw, their "goaty" taste comes through only after pickling. Pickled capers are sometimes available loose, but they must be covered with salted vinegar if not used immediately. Salt-dried capers are best left ignored.

Capers play a vital role in classic sauces (ravigotes, gribiches) and in our tartly sweet dressing, tempered with some good, pebbly whole-grain mustard. Since the bright orange slivers of rutabaga also derive from the mustard family, this makes a visually poetic combination.

2 pounds rutabagas, peeled and julienned*
water
½ cup Basic Mayonnaise (see page 120)
3 tablespoons whole-grain mustard

½ teaspoon cayenne
2 tablespoons capers, rinsed and drained
2 tablespoons lemon juice
½ cup chopped fresh chives or green onions for garnish

Cook rutabaga in a pot of boiling water for 4 minutes. Drain rutabaga in a colander while running cold water over it to stop the cooking. Drain well and set aside.

In a bowl mix mayonnaise, mustard, cayenne, capers, and lemon juice. Combine with cooled rutabaga.

Serve garnished with chopped chives.

Serves 6

Mixed Mushrooms with Vermont Cheddar

From the Greek word meaning "vase," the chanterelle mushroom has the form and often the color of a flaring, polished trumpet. The close, narrow gills begin under its broad and floppy cap, and cover most of the stem "like fine vaulting," according to Jane Grigson's Mushroom Feast. Chanterelle mushrooms can be any color from vermilion to ochre to blue-black, but the one most delicious and prized (Cantharellus cibarius) looks, smells, and even tastes like ripe apricots. This particular rich yellow, fleshy chanterelle is considered eminently edible both for its texture and its fruity flavor. Louis Charles Christopher Krieger, the famous American artist-mycologist, made beautiful and scientifically accurate paintings of the chanterelle, one of his favorite subjects. It is also one of ours, for reasons most obvious in this strikingly handsome, three-mushroom salad.

½ pound very fresh, cultivated mushrooms (see Note)
¼ pound fresh chanterelles
¼ pound fresh shitake mushrooms, stemmed
2 teaspoons lemon juice

¼-pound wedge of Vermont cheddar
½ cup good olive oil
3 tablespoons good white wine vinegar, preferably Chardonnay vinegar

salt and pepper   4 tablespoons chopped fresh
                                        parsley for garnish

Clean mushrooms and slice thinly before placing in a serving bowl. Sprinkle with lemon juice.

With a swivel vegetable peeler, peel thin strips of cheese and add to bowl.

In a separate bowl combine oil, vinegar, and salt and pepper; pour over mushrooms and cheese and toss gently. Sprinkle with parsley and serve immediately.

Serves 6

MUSHROOM NOTE: Gills are the ridges and lines under the mushroom cap. For salads, or whenever you plan to use mushrooms raw, check that the gills are tight and closed. This is less important in cooking, in which case the mushrooms should be firm and healthy looking.

Salad of Green and Gold

The papaya is a vegetable and a fruit. Its leaves can be cooked like spinach and the rest of it has many possibilities, both cooked and raw. Cooks have recently been exploring its many virtues by baking the halved fruit like squash, sautéing its thin golden slices with ginger (a spectacular combination), making it into pickles, and substituting it in just about any melon recipe. Papaya is also paired with pork and other meats, possibly because of the dramatic tenderizing effect of its special enzyme, papain.

Tossed into a salad, papaya leaves contribute a flavor similar to that of bitter greens. Even the papaya's pearly black seeds, which look like caviar but taste like mustard, often serve as a condiment. (They are annoyingly disappointing, however, if one is expecting their costly and elegant look-alike.)

When Columbus found this tropical fruit in the Caribbean, he thought it was something to write home about; when he did, he called it "the fruit of the angels."

In this unusually attractive salad, the muted colors of avocado and papaya contrast with shiny shreds of red onion and deep green romaine. The short marination also works wonders.

2 avocados
1 large ripe papaya
1 small red onion, cut into rings
2 tablespoons chopped fresh mint leaves (reserve some whole leaves)

2 tablespoons raspberry vinegar**
⅓ cup vegetable oil
salt and pepper
2 cups shredded romaine lettuce

Cut avocados and papaya with a melon baller and put in a bowl. Mix onion rings and mint.

In a separate bowl combine vinegar, oil, and salt and pepper and pour over avocado mixture. Toss gently and allow to marinate for 1 hour at room temperature.

Arrange a bed of shredded lettuce on each plate and top with marinated mixture. Garnish with mint leaf.

Serves 6

Balsamic Broccoli with Golden Raisins and Toasted Walnuts

In Consuming Passions, anthropologist Peter Farb uses broccoli to prove his assertion that no society chooses its food based on nutritional value. Although broccoli contains more nutrients than any other plant consumed in this country, it is still only twenty-first in frequency of consumption. Even so, this is a big improvement over the first century and a half of our culinary history, when broccoli was virtually unknown. It was the Italians from Calabria who popularized the flavorful, green "little sprouts," which is what broccoli means in Italian; actually, in some Italian dialects, calabrese means broccoli. In adopting this Western vegetable, Chinese cooks have become as adept as their Italian counterparts in conserving its characteristic crispness and flavor.

Even more than the balsamic vinegar and Parmesan cheese, our recipe reflects an Italian heritage most strongly in its use of the whole broccoli. Like Italian cookbook author Marcella Hazan, we too have seen people snip off the flowerets and throw out the stalk, thinking they are eating the choicest part. "Actually," says the all-wise Marcella, "it is just the other way around."

½ cup golden raisins
3 tablespoons balsamic vinegar**
water
1 bunch broccoli, peeled and ends trimmed
2 teaspoons lemon juice
½ cup coarsely chopped toasted walnuts*

1 shallot, thinly sliced
⅓ cup olive oil
1 clove garlic, finely minced
2 tablespoons grated Parmesan cheese
1 teaspoon anchovy paste
salt and pepper

Soak raisins in balsamic vinegar for about 1 hour.

Meanwhile, in a pot filled with boiling water cook broccoli until barely tender, about 5 minutes. Run cold water over it to stop cooking and intensify green color. Cut stems into ¼-inch sticks and break heads into small flowerets. Place in a bowl and sprinkle with lemon juice.

Drain raisins, reserving vinegar. Add raisins, walnuts, and shallot to broccoli.

In a cup or jar make a dressing of reserved vinegar, oil, garlic, cheese, anchovy paste, and salt and pepper. Pour over the ingredients in the bowl and toss well to coat.

Serves 6

Garden Greens with Goat Cheese Dressing

The diversity of interesting greens available today demands a recipe that accommodates the best of whatever is available. This one will be full of flavor with just about any mix of greens you decide on. Some of the more popular greens, along with their aliases and more salient characteristics, might include:

Bibb or Limestone Lettuce. Crispy leaves, small heads.

Boston or Butter Lettuce. Loose-leafed, delicate green.

Chicory or **Curly Endive.** Green, feathery leaves, slightly bitter.

Cos or **Romaine.** Crunchy midribs, dark green elongated leaves, famous in Caesar's Salad.

Dandelions. Tangy, flavorful leaves from the plant that has been called this country's most neglected free food, since the whole thing is edible. (This attribute was not lost on members of the Shaker religious communities, who once advised: " . . . have the children gather these succulent plants. This furnishes you with a tasty dish and at the same time rids your dooryard of weeds.")

Endive. Ivory colored, delicate, crisp.

Escarole. Heavier than chicory with less frilly leaves and a tougher texture.

Leaf Lettuce. Tender, delicate leaves.

Mache, Corn Salad, Lamb's Lettuce, or **Field Lettuce.** A tangy, dark-green rosette of leaves, mild but stimulating, delicious with cooked beets.

Radicchio. An Italian magenta-colored, bitter-leafed plant which has a local California counterpart called Tallarosa.

Rocket, Arugula, Rugula, Roquette, or **Rocket Cress.** An unmistakable relative of the cabbage with a pungent taste, slightly hot and peppery.

Salad Burnet. Has the smell and taste of cucumber, once revered as a privileged member of Napoleon's daily salad, often paired with wild chicory (though he preferred dried haricot beans).

Watercress. Dark green, mildly peppery, refreshing.

These are only a few of the possibilities; there are also the chards, red and green; several sorrels; spinach; frisée; various other cresses; and a thousand herbs.

a variety of the freshest lettuces and greens, enough for 6 people
1 bunch fresh chives, chopped
¼ pound goat cheese**
½ cup olive oil
1 tablespoon lemon juice

2 tablespoons good white wine vinegar
½ teaspoon dried thyme, or 1 teaspoon chopped fresh thyme
salt and pepper
½ cup toasted pine nuts* for garnish.

Wash greens and dry thoroughly. Toss with chives in a bowl.

In a separate bowl mix remaining ingredients except pine nuts until smooth.

Pour over greens, toss well, and garnish with pine nuts.

Serves 6

Sunchoke and Spinach Salad with Brandy and Walnut Oil

Sunchokes resemble a cross between a scrawny Idaho potato and fresh ginger. Originating in North America, this vegetable is also called Canadian potato, Jerusalem artichoke, and topinambour. The last name is perhaps the most curious: Topinambour was the name of a Brazilian Indian tribe, several members of which were introduced to Paris society at the same time as the sunchoke.

The sunchoke's most vital culinary role in the American past was possibly as part of the diet of the Lewis and Clark expedition in 1804. The forty-member team survived their two-and-one-half-year transcontinental journey partly through a knowledge of the wild or easy-to-find edibles they stalked along the way.

The sunchoke's papery skin, which is sometimes easier to peel after parboiling, protects its sweet, nutty taste and tempting crunchiness. Captured in our salad, these wonderful qualities mingle well with brandy, walnut oil, red threads of onion, and the bright green accent of spinach.

½ pound sunchokes, peeled
   and sliced ⅛ inch thick
1 tablespoon lemon juice
1 bunch fresh spinach,
   washed, dried, and
   stemmed
½ small red onion, cut into
   thin rings

3 tablespoons good white
   wine vinegar
2 cloves garlic, put through
   garlic press
1 tablespoon brandy
2 tablespoons walnut oil
¼ cup vegetable oil
   salt and pepper

Place chokes in a bowl and sprinkle with lemon juice (see Note). Toss with spinach and red onion.

In a separate bowl mix remaining ingredients until well blended. Add to bowl of sunchokes and toss well.

Serves 6

CHOKE NOTE: The lemon juice keeps the sliced vegetable from turning black.

Comice Pear Wedges and Endive Julienne on Watercress

The development of Belgian endive is a true story of a mom-and-pop operation. Sometime in the 1840s, a gardener at the Brussels botanical gardens planted only the roots of his chicory plants in hopes of producing a hardy winter crop. The result was the elongated, silvery white, spindle-shape salad star which we call "Belgian endive." Because the gardener and his wife so closely guarded his techniques, the family still operates a flourishing Belgian endive business today in the city of Brabant.

The Belgians call this vegetable witloof (waterleaf). The French call it endive, but in England and Germany, it's called chicory. Using its Latin scientific name, Cichorium intybus, is about the only way out of this dilemma, but in the grocery store, pointing may be a more practical alternative.

In this salad, the endive's light, barely bitter taste is a delicious contrast to the delicately sweet Comice pear.

2 large Comice pears, peeled and cored	3 tablespoons raspberry vinegar**
1 tablespoon lemon juice	¼ cup vegetable oil
2 endives, julienned*	2 tablespoons walnut oil
2 bunches watercress leaves, coarsely chopped	salt and pepper
1 clove garlic	½ cup chopped walnuts for garnish

Slice pears into thin wedges and sprinkle with lemon juice. Arrange with endive on a bed of watercress in a bowl or on a platter, reserving 2 tablespoons of cress for dressing.

In a food processor or blender puree garlic with reserved cress. Add vinegar, oils, and salt and pepper. Process until smooth.

Pour over vegetables and mix gently. Garnish with walnuts.

Serves 6

Tomato, Onion, and Cucumber Salad Ribboned with Ricotta Pesto Cream

"Fried for breakfast and dinner, raw for lunch." This was the usual procedure for onion eating about a century ago in this country, when onions were often the only vegetable available in many areas for much of the year. They were also the cowboys' favorite, the essence of their colorfully named Son-of-a-Bitch Stew. In that melange, onions had the even more colorful name "skunk eggs." Legend has it that a native American wild variety, called "nodding" onions, once grew in profusion on the shores of Lake Michigan and kept Father Marquette from starvation. On the southern shores of that same lake, a city was actually named after the Indian word for the haunting and ever-present smell of onion: Chicago.

The best onions for eating raw in salads should be fresh and firm. Yellow globes (Spanish), big white Bermudas, Walla Walla sweets, Maui sweets, Vidalia, red Italian, or Creole—all work beautifully with the contrasting, mellowing touches of ricotta, cream, and pesto.

2 large ripe tomatoes, seeded and sliced
1 English cucumber, seeded and sliced
1 large sweet onion,** cut into rings
3 tablespoons pesto*

½ cup whole-milk ricotta
1 teaspoon lemon juice
2 tablespoons heavy cream
salt and pepper
½ cup chopped fresh basil for garnish

On a flat platter arrange tomatoes, cucumber, and onion slices in alternating pattern.

Mix pesto, ricotta, lemon juice, and cream in a blender or food processor until smooth. Add salt and pepper to taste.

Pour dressing down center of vegetable slices and sprinkle with chopped basil. Serve immediately.

Serves 6

Potato, Carrot, and Leek Salad in Mustardy Vinaigrette

Anyone who has cleaned leeks will find merit in the theory that their popularity coincides with the advent of running water. The success with which mud hides out in leeks is equaled in few other vegetables, with the possible exception of spinach. Once clean, however, the sweet and satiny leek is like no other member of the onion family, to which it belongs.

The Scottish soup cock-a-leekie is one of the leek's most famous elaborations; but the Welsh are even fonder of leeks, though not just for cooking. A symbol of wartime victory, leeks are worn on the lapel as the national emblem of Wales. Leeks are essential in French cooking as a vegetable in themselves, as a flavoring element, and often as part of bouquet garni. Raw grated leeks have been used in salads since Roman times.

New Orleans cooks make quichelike pies using leeks or bunches of closely related scallions. Appalachia has its wild leeks, also known as "ramps"; but leeks have no substitute in the most American of leek dishes, vichyssoise. Reportedly the 1910 creation of Louis Diat, the chef at New York's Ritz-Carlton, vichyssoise was the chilled version of his French mother's potato-leek soup. Vichyssoise has survived two threats to its existence: The first was a move during World War II to change the name to crème Gauloise because of the widespread opposition to the Vichy government; the second was being included, through no fault of its own, on lists of the "in" dishes of our times. This recipe might be seen as a warm salad version of Louis Diat's chilled soup version of his mother's hot potage. But we certainly hope not!

Leeks have a few alleged magical properties as well: They keep the hair from turning gray, improve the voice, cure coughs. But mainly they taste good, as everyone will agree who enjoys this warm and pretty salad, which is also delicious cold.

water

4 new potatoes, scrubbed and
cut into ¼-inch sticks

2 carrots, peeled, halved
horizontally, and sliced
into ¼-inch sticks

2 small leeks, white part
only, julienned*

1 tablespoon good-quality
mustard

2 tablespoons good white
wine vinegar

1 tablespoon chopped fresh
dill

salt and pepper

½ cup olive oil

In a large pot of boiling water, cook vegetables for 4 minutes, then
run under cold water. Let drain in colander.

Meanwhile, in a bowl mix remaining ingredients until well
blended.

Remove still-warm vegetables to a separate bowl and pour dressing
over them. Toss well. Serve warm or cold.

Serves 6

Fresh Peas in Cumin Yogurt with Mint

Farmers' markets and outdoor produce stands have suddenly
become popular in this country, even though patronizing them
often means getting up at dawn. Those located in and near large
cities offer fresh produce from nearby growers and many delicacies that are never mass-marketed in the larger outlets. According to the late James Beard, this outdoor-market movement
may portend the biggest changes in American food habits in
decades.

The street criers who sold peas and beans through New York
City streets in the early 1800s bought their wares from eight
open-air markets. Wheeling their carts and barrows through
neighborhoods far from the markets, the criers would announce
their arrival by repeating rhythmic calls such as this one, from
about 1825:

BEANS, PEAS, &c. &c.

Here's nice Beans or Peas,
 Only ten pence a peck!
Come buy if you please,
 I've an excellent stock.

from New York Street Cries in Rhyme
by Mahlon Day

If you decide to spare ten pence for a whole peck of peas, as the crier urges, you'll have to increase the dressing proportions by a couple of gallons. Since a peck is eight dry quarts, we think that just might be too much of a good thing. Otherwise we usually can't get enough of this brightly herbed, pea-studded salad.

3 cups fresh peas	½ cup plain yogurt
1 cup thinly sliced celery	1 teaspoon lemon juice
1 cup fresh coriander leaves	1 tablespoon vegetable oil
½ cup mint leaves	1 tablespoon brown sugar
½ cup fresh parsley	1 tablespoon ground cumin

Place peas and celery in a bowl.

In a food processor, chop coriander, mint, and parsley. Add remaining ingredients and process until well blended.

Pour over peas and celery and mix well.

Serves 6

Salad Scheherazade

From personal experience, we can assert that children growing up in Brooklyn have little contact with wild animals of any sort, least of all camels. Yet we knew about dromedaries from our earliest days, thanks to grandmothers and their ever-present caches of dromedary-decorated boxes of dates. Fresh dates contain seven percent protein and fifty-four percent sugar. They are an excellent high-energy food for children, as well as for hikers, joggers, and other nutritionally aggressive types, but they are most highly recommended for people who love to "discover" ancient wonders.

The date palm thrives only in the intense, dry heat of desert air, but also requires plenty of water for its roots. These "oasis" conditions are met in few places in the world, one of which is California's Coachella Valley, the source of virtually the entire U.S. commercial crop. Date cuttings were brought to California by government experts who visited the Babylonian and Arabian date palms at the turn of the century. The prospect of a competitive date industry in the United States did not appeal to the Arabian date keepers, who were reportedly ungenerous in handing over date cuttings. So, according to Helen Evans Brown, in her West Coast Cook Book, the aforementioned cuttings may not have been "purchased" but rather transported "in the dead of night." However they arrived, California's crop includes just about every variety known, but the three main varieties are the exotically named Khadrawi, Golden Saidy, and the most precious and profuse Deglet Noor, which means "beautiful maiden."

These fresh dates, far different from the dried and shriveled specimens of yore, are now an important California crop and the main enterprise of Indio, California, the date capital of the country. Each year, the area sponsors a ten-day date celebration, including such regal trappings as the crowning of an annual Queen Scheherazade. She reigns over the festivities, which center around enactment of tales from the Arabian Nights and the consumption of innovative date dishes.

Many new recipes take advantage of the date's lovely compatibility with butter, cream, cheese, and yogurt, as in various Indian preparations or with nuts and/or rice, as used in Middle Eastern—style stuffings for fish and meat. Here we plant the chopped fruit into a buttery nest of avocado and sprinkle dry roasted nuts over all for texture and contrast. It's a combination that has provoked, on more than one night, a thousand and one compliments.

4 tablespoons good red wine
vinegar, preferably
Cabernet vinegar

½ teaspoon sugar
salt and pepper

2 tablespoons vegetable oil

½ pound pitted dates,
quartered

1 large red onion, quartered
and slivered

½ cup chopped fresh parsley

3 avocados, halved and seeds
removed

4 tablespoons chopped dry-
roasted peanuts

Combine vinegar, sugar, salt and pepper, and oil, and stir until sugar dissolves.

Put dates, onion, and parsley in a bowl and pour vinegar dressing over them, mixing to coat well.

Fill avocado halves with mixture and top with chopped peanuts.

Serves 6

Marinated Mexicali Eggplant Salad

On a recent eggplant hunt in preparation for this book, we discovered an amazing specimen. Called "Chinese eggplant," it was iridescent, purple-white, and elongated, with the curve of a ballet slipper and all its grace. But we could not find what we were looking for: a pearly white eggplant, small and oval-shaped, like a hen's egg, the kind of eggplant that could provide full justification for the name of this not very egglike plant. Though we have seen white eggplant, nothing that day confirmed the stories that somewhere, some time, enough small opalescent, ivory-colored spheres existed to inspire the name of an entire vegetable group. We did, however, find purple ones in abundance, a tribute to their ever-rising popularity.

Eggplant, in fact, has become something of a passion in current California cookery. Often it is simply grilled with or without herbs and olive oil. Or it might be buried in coals to smolder away until its skin is charred and wrinkled. It is then slit open, the smoky, cream-textured flesh anointed with lemon, olive oil, and little else. Some of the more traditional preparations are also popular, such as Greek moussaka; Provençal ratatouille; and various Middle Eastern, Turkish, and Syrian dishes.

New York's once-renowned Delmonico's has been falsely credited with introducing the eggplant in the late 1800s to America—it actually made its debut in American cookbooks a half-century before the restaurant was founded. The first Fannie Farmer cookbook, in 1896, contained only two halfhearted suggestions. The number increased to a dozen by the 1946 edition.

Eggplants were once denounced as "apples [with] a mischievous quality," just as tomatoes were disparaged as suspicious love apples. Eggplants are, in fact, related to tomatoes—both are from the deadly nightshade family—and both make their appearance in this salad. This wonderfully flavorful recipe, a sort of Hispanic caponata, also makes a fine topping for baguettes.

2 pounds Chinese, Japanese
   or young eggplants
1 fresh jalepeño pepper,*
   seeded, deveined, and cut
   into slivers
1 large tomato, seeded and
   coarsely chopped
3 green onions, cut into
   rings
½ cup chopped fresh
   coriander leaves

3 tablespoons lime juice
1 tablespoon balsamic
   vinegar**
1 teaspoon sugar
½ teaspoon ground cumin
½ teaspoon ground coriander
   salt and pepper
⅓ cup olive oil

Roast eggplants in preheated 375°F oven for 40 to 45 minutes, until skins are dark and flesh feels soft. Allow to cool and cut into thin strips. Place in a bowl with jalapeños, tomato, onions, and coriander leaves.

Make marinade by combining remaining ingredients in a bowl until well blended. Pour into the bowl with eggplant mixture and toss. Cover and refrigerate for at least 12 hours. Pour off excess dressing. Taste before serving and adjust seasonings. Serve only slightly cold or at room temperature.

Serves 6

Parsnip-Carrot Salad in Raspberry Vinaigrette with Walnuts and Currants

After centuries of associating Vinland with grapes, we may now have to swallow a conflicting bitter (or at least acidic) truth: Vinland was probably not named for rambling grape vines, which Waverley Root claims would not have survived that far north, but more likely for currants. The tiny, black, dried currants, soaked in raspberry vinegar for this salad, are themselves named for Corinth, west of Athens, where they were known two thousand years ago. Although Greece is a major exporter of currants, few of the little grapes ever found their way into Hellenic kitchens. The English, on the other hand, have used currants in their cookery since the seventeenth century. Scandinavian, German, and Russian cooks include them in desserts as well as in main dishes and, of course, in jams.

There are over one hundred species of currants. The two main colors (red and white) are really one and the same, the white being a less acidic, and consequently sweeter, albino of the red.

½ cup currants soaked in 4 tablespoons raspberry vinegar** for 1 hour (see Note)

3 large carrots, peeled and grated

3 medium parsnips, peeled and grated

½ cup coarsely chopped toasted walnuts*

2 tablespoons walnut oil

3 tablespoons vegetable oil

1 teaspoon ground coriander

salt and pepper

4 tablespoons chopped fresh chives for garnish

Drain currants and reserve vinegar for dressing.

In a bowl combine currants, carrots, parsnips, and walnuts.

In a separate bowl mix reserved vinegar with oils, coriander, and salt and pepper until well blended.

Pour over ingredients in salad bowl and toss well. Sprinkle with chopped chives.

Serves 6

CURRANT NOTE: Unlike raisins, which they resemble, currants must always be soaked before being incorporated into any dish or they will be much too dry.

Green Bean, Corn, and Red Pepper Salad

A U.S. Senate resolution a few years ago proposed that the corn tassel be adopted as the country's national flower. Currently, every state in the Union produces corn, which has been called "the grain that built a hemisphere" for its life-sustaining role in the American past. This New World plant is grown on three quarters of our farms, supplying half the world's corn.

Of the many ways to eat corn, there is no disagreement over the best method, as suggested by Mark Twain. Set a pot to boil over a fire in the middle of the cornfield, shuck the warm, tender ears, and plunge them immediately into the boiling water. Alternatively, you can "walk down the garden path to cut your corn," advises Andre Simon (A Concise Encyclopedia of Gastronomy), "but you must run back." The point, of course, is always to cook and devour corn quickly after picking. For this brilliantly colored, meadow-fresh salad, you'll only have to run back with one or two cobs.

1 pound green beans, washed, trimmed, and blanched*	3 tablespoons lemon juice
	1 tablespoon good white wine vinegar
1 cup fresh corn kernels, blanched* (see Note)	1 teaspoon honey
	salt and pepper
2 red bell peppers, seeded, deveined, and cut into strips	3 tablespoons chopped fresh dill
2 small shallots, peeled and chopped	¼ cup vegetable oil
	¼ cup olive oil

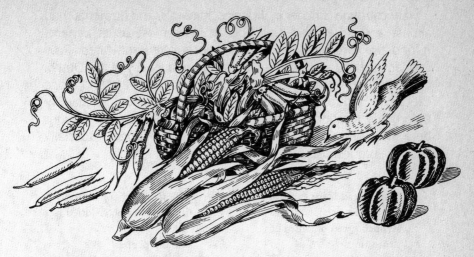

Cut beans into 2-inch pieces and place in a bowl with corn and peppers.

In a blender or food processor mix remaining ingredients until thick and creamy.

Pour over vegetables and toss until well coated.

Serves 6

KERNEL NOTE: There are several types of corn-kernel cutters on the market—and there are sharp knives, which is really all you need. Stand the cooked or uncooked corn on end and slice downward to remove a few rows at a time.

Napa Cabbage in Garlic-Dill Cream

Contrary to the obvious assumption, Napa cabbage comes from just about everywhere—except Napa, California. This Oriental cabbage has a taste and texture perfect for salads. Also called Tientsin, Peking, Chinese, or celery cabbage, the Napa is reportedly a Japanese word for the type of cabbage used for kim chee, spicy salt-fermented pickled cabbage.

Raw cabbage is richer in vitamins, minerals, and nutrients than almost any other vegetable, but it loses most of its benefits during the long cooking to which it is often subjected. Raw cabbage salads, accompanied by beer, are a legacy of the Dutch, who began emigrating to New Netherland in 1624. And, since cabbage is reputed to stave off drunkenness if eaten in quantity before any feasting begins in earnest, this cabbage salad might be a most practical, as well as nutritious first course, especially for certain guest lists.

1 large head Napa cabbage, shredded	3 tablespoons chopped fresh dill, or 2 teaspoons dried dill
1 bunch green onions, cut into rings	salt and pepper
½ cup Basic Mayonnaise (see page 120)	¼ cup plain yogurt
3 cloves garlic, put through garlic press	

Place cabbage and green onions in a large bowl.

Mix remaining ingredients together in a separate bowl until well blended. Pour over cabbage mixture and toss well.

Serves 6

NAPA NOTE: Because the leaves of Napa cabbage are sweeter when wilted, you might leave this cabbage unrefrigerated for 24 hours before preparing the salad.

Chilled Asparagus with Smoked Salmon and Horseradish Cream

According to legend, anyone who wants to play with snakes should wash both hands thoroughly in horseradish juice. These ablutions guarantee immunity to every kind of poison, though they may lead to a reputation for somewhat eccentric behavior. Eating horseradish in quantity has at least one known unfortunate side effect: It occasionally strips all the enamel off the teeth. This drawback is dismissed by horseradish buffs as a small price to pay for all the other benefits.

German and English cooks embraced horseradish early on as the perfect accompaniment to beef, smoked fish, and hard-cooked eggs. Much appreciated as a salt substitute, grated horseradish may also be mixed with butter for a versatile and pungent spread. Horseradish should be incorporated only into uncooked sauces, since heat destroys its volatile oils.

The grated fresh root gives the best flavor, but if it is unavailable, the bottled sauce works nicely in this fluffy cream, which accentuates the clearly defined flavors of asparagus and smoked salmon.

1 cup heavy cream
1 tablespoon lemon juice
  salt and pepper
1 teaspoon sugar
2 tablespoons prepared
  horseradish

1½ pounds asparagus, peeled
  and blanched*
¼ pound smoked salmon,**
  cut into thin strips

In a bowl beat cream with lemon juice until soft peaks form. Mix in salt and pepper, sugar, and horseradish.

Place 2 tablespoons of cream mixture on each of 6 plates. Top with asparagus and most of the smoked salmon strips. Nap with remaining cream, and garnish with remaining smoked salmon.

Serves 6

Asparagus with Orange-Sherry Vinaigrette

For something that has so brief a season, asparagus gives rise to quite a bit of controversy. There is the debate over color: One faction asserts that white asparagus are the finest of all because they are never subjected to the harshness of sunlight; proponents of the greens and purples argue that these colorful contenders have more nutrients and better taste precisely because of the time they spend in the sun. Temperature is another touchy subject: Serve asparagus either cold or warm, never hot, demand some; vice versa, scoff their opponents.

And then there's size. "I know that the sensitive and sensible among you will be shocked to hear this," warns the pseudonymous Vladimir Estragon of the Village Voice, "but there are some people who actually like thin asparagus." He prefers the plump stalks for the rare quality of what he calls "a substantial tenderness."

Finally, though we offer this recipe as one which interferes as little as possible with the glory of asparagus, we are not unaware of Richard Olney's proscription (in Simple French Food) against serving any sort of vinaigrette "however pure, with asparagus." Even after all this, there is one point upon which most people do agree: Whenever possible, eat asparagus with your fingers—preferably dressed with some good walnut oil and sherry vinegar.

1½ pounds asparagus, peeled and blanched*	salt and pepper
1 small egg yolk	2 teaspoons chopped fresh chives
2 tablespoons good sherry vinegar**	¼ cup walnut oil
2 tablespoons fresh or frozen orange juice	½ cup vegetable oil
1 teaspoon mild mustard	½ cup coarsely chopped toasted walnuts* for garnish

Arrange whole asparagus on a flat dish, or cut stalks on the diagonal in 2-inch pieces and place in a bowl.

In a separate bowl break up yolk with whisk or fork and add vinegar, orange juice, mustard, salt and pepper, chives, and oils. Whisk until well blended.

Pour dressing over asparagus and toss gently until well coated. Garnish with chopped walnuts.

Serves 6

Broccoli-Jicama Salad

The same sesame seeds that are used in Greek hummus, Turkish halvah, Middle Eastern tahini, and the Indian leavened bread nan, are also practically a trademark of the American South. To South Carolina, Virginia, and Georgia, slaves brought their beloved "benne seeds," planted them where they could (secretly and methodically at the end of rows of cotton), and made them into the famous Charleston Good Luck Cookies, Savannah Benne Seed Candy, Sesame Catfish, and seed-sprinkled chicken. They also mashed the seeds and mixed the resulting paste with hominy; and they often used toasted seeds to create a nutty-flavored cream of oyster soup.

Sesame seeds were also known for their special powers in attracting good luck and discouraging ants. The high oil content of these seeds—fifty percent—is important for cooking in Oriental and Indian cuisines, and in Mexico, where it is called "gingelly oil."

From South America, our salad also borrows the crunchy tuber, jicama, which has a crisp texture similar to that of fresh water chestnuts. The gleaming whole snow peas add beauty and flavor. Popular among Chinese cooks, snow peas have also been a long-time favorite in Pennsylvania. Around Bethlehem, Lancaster, and Allentown, they are called "Mennonite pod peas," the prize vegetable of the Pennsylvania Dutch.

1 bunch broccoli, peeled and blanched* for 2 minutes

¼ pound snow peas, strings removed and blanched* for 30 seconds

1 small jicama, peeled and cut into ¼-inch sticks

1 bunch green onions, cut into rings

1 red bell pepper, seeded and cut into strips

2 cloves garlic, put through garlic press

3 tablespoons good rice wine vinegar

1 tablespoon good sherry vinegar**

1 tablespoon honey

1 teaspoon dry Chinese mustard

1 tablespoon soy sauce

1 teaspoon ground ginger

1 tablespoon Oriental sesame oil

½ cup vegetable oil

½ cup toasted* sesame seeds for garnish

Cut broccoli heads into flowerets, stems into pieces on the diagonal, and place in a bowl with other vegetables.

In a separate bowl mix together all remaining ingredients except sesame seeds until well blended. Pour over vegetables and toss.

Sprinkle with sesame seeds.

Serves 6

Coriandered Carrot Coins

Only a teaspoon of ground cumin is mixed into the marinade for this carrot salad, but its spicy presence is strongly felt. One of the principal ingredients of Indian curry mixtures, cumin is used in rice dishes and unleavened breads, and is often paired with coriander. Cumin also defines the flavor of many Spanish meat dishes and sauces, Mexican beans and enchiladas, all of which have brought cumin into the American lexicon of currently popular spices, where its unusual taste adds character and interest.

Sometimes mistaken for caraway, cumin seeds take on a

slightly different, nutlike personality when toasted. Black cumin seeds are often used in place of pepper.

1 pound carrots, peeled and thinly sliced	1 teaspoon ground coriander
salted water	1 teaspoon honey
3 tablespoons lemon juice	½ cup olive oil
1 tablespoon balsamic vinegar**	½ cup coarsely chopped fresh coriander leaves
1 teaspoon ground cumin	salt and pepper

Blanch carrots by plunging in boiling salted water for 1 minute, refresh under cold water, and drain thoroughly. Place in a bowl.

In a separate bowl mix remaining ingredients until well blended and toss with carrots. Allow to marinate, covered, a few hours before serving.

Serves 6

Baby Green Beans, Sun-dried Tomatoes, and Pine Nuts in Basil Vinaigrette

N. B. Keeney of Leroy, New York, made a major, largely unheralded contribution to world gastronomy when he developed the stringless green bean early in this century. And yet green beans are often associated with the French. Obviously haricots verts, as some green beans are often listed on restaurant menus, have an attractive French name. However, further investigation reveals that haricot comes from the Aztec word for bean, ayacotyl. But despite their New World origins, green beans were eaten but rarely at the American table, where they were referred to as French beans. Their unpopularity in this country can be traced to the habit of picking them too late, way past their tender prime, and then cooking them to an off-colored pulp. The French, by contrast, gather young beans at the peak of their characteristic sweetness and cook them as lightly as possible. French horticulturists have developed many varieties, including mangetout (eat all), which never need to be topped or tailed.

Now that we are finally getting to know our beans, the early, tender ones are well appreciated in all-bean salads and lightly cooked dishes. Cookbook author Elizabeth David considers young green beans more "worthwhile" than asparagus and counsels that they should rightfully be served as a separate course. In this salad, toasted pine nuts are especially successful in bringing out the flavor of the beans . . . and vice versa.

1½ pounds very young green
    beans, trimmed and
    blanched*
8 sun-dried tomatoes,** cut
    into strips, plus 2
    tablespoons oil from
    tomato jar
½ cup toasted pine nuts*

½ cup fresh basil leaves
2 cloves garlic, minced
1 tablespoon grated
    Parmesan cheese
2 tablespoons good white
    wine vinegar
⅓ cup olive oil
    salt and pepper

In a bowl toss green beans, tomato strips, and pine nuts.

Place remaining ingredients in a blender or food processor and puree. Pour over vegetables and toss, coating well.

Serves 6

Curried Radicchio, Endive, and Golden Delicious Apple Salad

In Italy they call it the flower you can eat (fiore che si mangia). Radicchio, a winter lettuce, is really a garnet-red chicory, with white streaks and a slightly bitter taste, which is a natural companion to walnut oil. These days, any of the three main types of radicchio may find their way to the market: the tulip-shaped Rossa di Trevisso; the round, roselike Rossa di Verona; and a dark ruby chicory, with a long narrow shape similar to Belgian endive. Red is the predominant color, but there is also a beautiful snow-white radicchio that occasionally comes to market.

In traditional Italian recipes, the whole head is stuffed with anchovies and olive oil–soaked bread crumbs. Grilled radicchio is a growing favorite among inventive American cooks. But the brilliant red color—in her Vegetable Book Jane Grigson calls it the color of a "bishop's robe in a Titian painting"—is unfortunately lost in the cooking, though the taste is worth the visual deprivation.

Tossed with bone-white endive, green parsley, and sticks of yellow apple, this radicchio is dazzling to both eye and palate.

2 medium heads endive, julienned*	½ teaspoon dry mustard
1 head radicchio, julienned*	2 tablespoons lemon juice
2 medium Golden Delicious apples, skin left on, cored and cut into thin sticks	2 tablespoons good red wine vinegar
1 large shallot, chopped	1 tablespoon honey
½ cup coarsely chopped toasted walnuts*	½ teaspoon ground cumin salt and pepper
1 teaspoon curry powder dissolved in 1 tablespoon boiling water	½ cup walnut or olive oil
	½ cup chopped fresh parsley

In a large bowl combine endive, radicchio, apples, shallots, and walnuts.

Make dressing by combining remaining ingredients in a separate bowl. Pour over endive mixture and toss well.

Serves 6

Artichokes and Mushrooms with Country Ham

In 1868, artichokes formed part of a special menu honoring Charles Dickens at New York's Delmonico's, then a relatively new restaurant. These artichokes were probably imported, since domestic artichokes were very rare. Any artichoke was considered a special treat affordable only for honored guests. Not long afterward, Pierre Caron, the restaurant's widely esteemed chef, included a recipe for Artichokes Vinaigrette in the Delmonico cookbook, published in 1886. Twenty years later, even Fannie Farmer discussed them in her ninth edition, noting that they were starting to be transported to that area (Boston) from California. They were slightly cheaper than the imported French ones, which cost about forty cents apiece, an astonishing amount at the time.

California continues to be virtually the only producer of artichokes in the country. The recent harvest yielded over 73 million pounds, or about one third of an artichoke per person in the United States. But, in France and Italy, per capita consumption is over two hundred times as great and includes several varieties. California specializes in the globe, which is cultivated virtually year-round. Most of the crop still comes from thirty-seven growers and seven packing houses around Castroville, the city whose main street is draped with the banner: "Welcome to Castroville, The Artichoke Capital of the World."

Just a few tender artichokes define the character of this salad, in which they mingle with strands of Smithfield or any country ham, and firm, al dente mushrooms.

5 tablespoons olive oil
½ pound small mushrooms, cleaned and quartered
½ pound fresh artichoke hearts* (or frozen, thawed), quartered
1 small red onion, chopped

½ cup heavy cream
1 tablespoon lemon juice
1 tablespoon good white wine vinegar
1 teaspoon good-quality mustard
salt and pepper

| 3 tablespoons chopped fresh parsley | ¼ pound country ham,** julienned* |

In a large skillet heat 3 tablespoons oil and sauté mushrooms and artichoke hearts for about 3 minutes. (If using fresh artichokes, sauté for an additional 3 minutes before adding mushrooms.) Place in a bowl with red onion.

In another bowl combine cream with lemon juice, vinegar, mustard, and salt and pepper. Beat until slightly thickened and then add 2 tablespoons olive oil gradually, while continuing to beat until fairly stiff.

Pour over mushroom mixture and toss to coat well. Sprinkle with parsley and ham.

Serves 6

Black Bean, Cranberry, and Roasted Pepper Salad

The first time one hears the name of the classic American Three Bean Salad, one is struck with a logical and disappointing vision: an almost empty plate. Neatly arranged in the center, perhaps, sit three beans, mute examples of the strictest possible interpretation of nouvelle cuisine. This austere specter dissolves as the salad is served and, not three beans, but three different types of beans—millions of them—come tumbling onto the plate.

Bean salads have been continuously popular since the Spaniards brought the first black beans, or "turtle" beans, from the Caribbean to Florida. Even then, a native American dish of cold cooked beans was already a widespread form of salad. The Florida custom of cooking the black beans in rum assured their popularity there. Further west, Texas Caviar became fashionable. In this Lone Star bean salad, the cooked dried legumes marinate for a day or so in a spicy oil-and-vinegar dressing. In the Southwest, green chiles and cumin entered the picture. Californians serve their version on a bed of greens. Known as Ranch Salad, it became for a while a kind of national rage.

Our boldly colored interpretation is an array of ruby cranberries, red pepper strips, and a generous number of sparkly black beans.

2 cups black beans	1 cup cranberries
water	3 red bell peppers, roasted*
1 bay leaf	1 cup chopped fresh parsley
1 whole carrot	4 shallots, chopped
1 stalk celery	⅓ cup sherry vinegar**
salt and pepper	
2 tablespoons plus ½ cup	
olive oil	

Soak beans in a pot of water to cover for 3 hours. Discard any beans that rise to the top. Pour in another 2 inches of water and add bay leaf, carrot, celery, and salt and pepper. Simmer for 30 minutes. Drain beans and vegetables and place in a bowl with 2 tablespoons oil.

Cook cranberries in ½ cup water for 4 minutes. Drain and add to beans.

Chop roasted peppers and add to bowl along with parsley and shallots.

Mix vinegar and ½ cup oil in a jar and pour over bean mixture. Toss well and taste for salt and pepper.

Serves 6 to 8

Vinaigrette and Variations

For your own salad combinations, here are basic recipes for vinaigrette and mayonnaise dressings and some delightful variations.

Basic Vinaigrette

1 teaspoon salt
½ teaspoon freshly ground
   pepper
3 tablespoons red or white
   wine vinegar
½ cup olive or vegetable oil

Stir salt and pepper into vinegar in a small bowl. Gradually stir or whisk in the oil.

Makes ¾ cup

Mustard Vinaigrette

1 teaspoon salt
½ teaspoon freshly ground
   pepper
1 teaspoon good-quality
   prepared mustard
pinch sugar
2 tablespoons red or white
   wine vinegar
½ cup vegetable or olive oil

In a bowl stir salt, pepper, mustard, and sugar into vinegar until well blended. Gradually stir or whisk in the oil.

Makes ¾ cup

Creamy Vinaigrette

2 tablespoons heavy cream
salt and pepper
2 tablespoons lemon juice
2 tablespoons red or white
   wine vinegar
½ cup vegetable oil

Combine cream, salt and pepper, lemon juice, and vinegar in a small bowl. Gradually stir or whisk in oil.

Makes approximately 1 cup

Variations

Herbed Vinaigrette: Add to Basic Vinaigrette 1 or 2 tablespoons chopped fresh herbs, such as parsley, chives, dill, mint, basil, tarragon, or whatever you like.

Garlic Vinaigrette: Stir in 1 large clove garlic put through a garlic press with the vinegar before adding the oil.

Lemon Vinaigrette: Substitute freshly squeezed lemon juice for all or some of the vinegar.

A word about unusual vinegars and oils: Sherry, raspberry, champagne, and balsamic vinegars are just a few of the never-ending variety one might find on the shelf today. (See "Pantry Fancies.") Olive, walnut, hazelnut, and almond oils are the most frequently found varieties of oil. Which ones to use? Light olive and vegetable oils should dress light greens; fruity olive and nut oils are wonderful on tangy, bitter greens. Extra-virgin olive oil and nut oils are too delicate and expensive to be used for cooking. (Heat can break down the composition of the oil.) Fruit-flavored vinegars marry well with salads that contain fruit and hearty greens. A highly acidic vinegar blends tastefully with a strongly flavored oil such as the combination of balsamic vinegar with walnut oil. Experiment and enjoy!

Mayonnaise Medley

Basic Mayonnaise

2 egg yolks
1 teaspoon good-quality mustard

2 teaspoons fresh lemon juice
salt and pepper
1–1½ cups olive or vegetable oil

Blender or processor method: Combine all ingredients except oil in a bowl of a food processor or blender. While machine is still running, pour in oil in a slow steady stream. For a light mayonnaise, use 1 cup oil. For a stiffer, thicker mayonnaise, use 1½ cups oil.

By hand: In a bowl whisk together all ingredients except oil. Whisking constantly, add the oil drop by drop at first. When sauce starts to thicken, pour in remaining oil in a thin, steady stream, still whisking constantly.

Makes 1–1½ cups

Variations

Herb Mayonnaise: Add ¼ cup chopped fresh herbs to Basic Mayonnaise.
Garlic Mayonnaise: Combine 2 or 3 garlic cloves put through a garlic press with yolks, mustard, lemon juice, salt and pepper, before adding oil.
Sherry Mayonnaise: Substitute 1½ tablespoons sherry vinegar** for the lemon juice.
Green Mayonnaise: Make a puree of ½ cup fresh watercress leaves and ¼ cup fresh parsley and add it to the thicker version of Basic Mayonnaise.
Tomato Mayonnaise: Add 2 tablespoons tomato puree.
Mustard Mayonnaise: Add 2 tablespoons good-quality mustard of your choice.
Mint Mayonnaise: Add 2 tablespoons chopped fresh mint leaves.
Mayonnaise-Yogurt Dressing: Use a ratio of 1 to 1 of any of the above mayonnaises to plain yogurt and stir well to combine.

LITTLEMEALS

For this section, we have assembled a group of informal, uncomplicated dishes, each of which can serve as a complete meal in itself.
We might have called them the 1980s California version of the old-
fashioned one-dish meal; but they have none of the old-fashioned
leaden qualities and overly homogeneous taste that usually characterized those long-cooking melanges. There are a variety of styles
here, from pizza to warm salads, vegetable meals to fish pies.

Because they fit no existing category, we just call them what they are: Littlemeals.

Most of them are light and herby, straightforward but soul-satisfying. They take full advantage of the powers of contrast (chunks of chopped artichokes in a pebbly, barley-shaped pasta; ribbons of leeks and meltingly molten goat cheese); the earthy satisfaction of unpretentious ingredients (Cajun sausage and black beans huddled in a yeasty calzone); the lure of the almost unadorned (strips of chicken fragrant with basil). Some things are simply wild with delights: the Wild, Wild Pasta with Watercress, for example, with its combination of wild rice and wild mushrooms. And some Littlemeals are tempting transformations of small amounts of chicken, fish, and lamb, leftover or otherwise. Many rely on an unexpected, slightly exotic touch, such as a dollop of caviar or a strip of smoked trout, to convey a sense of occasion.

Littlemeals make great little suppers, but can also be excellent brunch food or last-minute lunches. Preparations are neither time-consuming nor difficult; most of them can be prepared entirely in advance, they keep very well, and often improve in flavor with the wait. Many also travel well, making them good choices for picnics or pot-luck contributions. Often these dishes are as good when served at room temperature as they are when piping hot; they fit right into an atmosphere of flexible or unpredictable schedules.

If you plan to prepare any of these Littlemeals for guests, consider your diners' personalities: Littlemeals appeal to lovers of informality; to people who welcome the unconventional; and to people who would really rather order all the appetizers on a menu than any one of the main courses. Littlemeals are for those who appreciate what Julia Child meant when she said she would rather have one teaspoon of chocolate mousse than a bowlful of Jell-O. Littlemeals are not Sunday dinners with uncles and everything; rather they are something you don't have to wait until the weekend to make.

This chapter is divided into four parts: Hot Plates and Warm Dishes, Event Salads, Pizza and Calzone, and Pasta. In addition to the recipes in this chapter, you can make a Littlemeal from many of the soups, the heartier dishes in the vegetable chapter, and many of the "Specials of the Day."

HOT PLATES AND WARM DISHES

Reuben Quiche
Leeks and Goat Cheese in a Flaky Drum
Three Peppers Pie
Smoked Salmon and Sweet Onion Pie
Corn Crepe Cake with Chicken-Chile Filling
Green Risotto
Baked Cornmeal Wheels with Herbed Tomato Sauce
Vermont Cheddar and Leek Soufflé
Golden Caviar—Mascarpone Roulade
Palace Chile

EVENT SALADS

Pasta Shells with Smoked Salmon and Fresh Chives
Shrimp Pasta Salad with Crumbled Feta, Olives, and Oregano
Tortellini and Artichokes in Fresh Tomato and Sun-dried Tomato
Vinaigrette
Asparagus and Toasted Almonds with Oriental Noodles
Melon Seed Pasta with Saffroned Mussels
Curried Rice Salad with Cashews and Snow Peas
Sushi Salad
Lentil, Parsley, and Goat Cheese Salad
Smoked Trout, Red and White Radish, and Watercress
Macédoine of Monkfish
Curried Tuna and Mango Chutney on Garden Lettuces
Tarragon-Walnut Chicken Salad
Potato Pesto Chicken with Red Pepper Strips
Triple Onion and Red Potato Salad
Warm Spinach and Sausage Salad
Duck Liver and Orange Salad with Curly Endive and Pecans
Duck and Sweet Potato Salad
Marinated Lamb, Corn, and Baby Bean Salad with Cherry
Tomatoes

PIZZA AND CALZONE

Basic Pizza Dough and Variations
Herb Crust Pizza with Three Cheeses and Pesto

Whole-Wheat Pizza with Pancetta and Artichokes
Pizza Jalisco
Three Mushroom Pizza with Sun-dried Tomatoes
Pizza Y'All
Calzone with Chard and Mozzarella
Calzone with Eggplant, Garlic, and Teleme Cheese
Hot Cajun Sausage Calzone

PASTA

Basic Egg Pasta and Variations
Fettuccine with Shrimp in Saffron Cream Sauce
Pasta Verde with Tomato-Pecan Sauce
Red Pepper Pasta with Tapenade
Herbed Tagliarini with Creamy Wild Mushroom Sauce
Tomato Linguine with Broccoli Flowers and Goat Cheese
Buckwheat Pasta with Endive, Smoked Chicken, and Fontina
Basil Pasta with Two Salmons
Pasta Shells with Smoked Trout and Red and Yellow Peppers
Pasta Bows in Walnut-Zucchini Sauce
Wild, Wild Pasta with Watercress
Melon Seed Pasta with Artichokes and Feta Cheese

HOT PLATES AND WARM DISHES

Reuben Quiche

With the publication of Eliza Leslie's <u>Directions for Cookery</u> in 1837, the sandwich received its first honorable mention in an American cookbook. Sandwiches soon became so fashionable that travelers carried them in special silver cases designed for that purpose. Even peanut butter sandwiches were considered elegant enough to warrant mention in certain cookbooks, one of which directed that they be tied up in brown ribbons "having the same tint as the paste." The sandwich must have been quite firmly institutionalized by 1887, because The Successful House-keeper appeared that year with recipes for "school lunch sandwiches."

Some of the most famous American sandwiches have been around since the early 1900s—grilled cheese, deviled ham, and the Club among them. The exact origin of most sandwiches is lost in obscurity, even those with especially intriguing names: hoagies, heroes, submarines, grinders, Sloppy Joes, Poor Boys. The hot dog is an exception, its birthplace being the St. Louis World's Fair of 1904. New Orleans claims both the oyster-filled French loaf, called the "Peacemaker," and the Italian-Cajun-Creole amalgamation known as "Muffeletta," an invention of the Central Grocery of that city. The Reuben can be traced back directly to New York's legendary but now defunct Reuben delicatessen at Madison Avenue and Fifty-ninth Street.

Our California Reuben is really a sandwich in quiche clothing, but it is full of the requisite corned beef, Swiss cheese, and cabbage. We think it holds up to James Beard's characterization of the beloved Reubens of his childhood: "rather stupendous" as a "summer meal and . . . also well fitted for a picnic."

1 recipe pâte brisée*	¼ pound cooked corned beef,
3 tablespoons vegetable oil	cut into strips
1 large onion, chopped	¼ pound imported Swiss
½ head cabbage, shredded	cheese, grated
salt and pepper	2 eggs
1 tablespoon caraway seed	1 cup heavy cream
2 tablespoons good-quality	
mustard	

Preheat oven to 400°F.

Roll out dough to fit a 10-inch tart pan with a removable bottom. Place dough in pan lined with parchment* or foil and fill with weights (rice, beans, or aluminum shot). Bake for 10 minutes, remove paper and weights, and continue baking at 375° for another 8 minutes, or until lightly browned. Allow dough to cool while preparing filling. Keep oven on.

In a medium skillet heat oil and sauté onion and cabbage until wilted, about 10 minutes. Season with salt and pepper and caraway. Spread mustard on bottom of baked quiche shell, top with onion mixture, corned beef, and cheese.

In a bowl combine eggs and cream. Pour over other ingredients and bake at 375° for 30 minutes. Allow to cool 10 minutes before serving.

Serves 8

Leeks and Goat Cheese in a Flaky Drum

<u>Spitiko</u> is the Greek word for homemade phyllo dough. It is not a word which gets much use these days since few people make phyllo at home. Commercial bakers produce machine-made phyllo but this is considered unacceptable by the handful of family-run San Francisco bakers who still make their phyllo by hand. Each of these small bakeries uses its own traditional methods, though they begin with the same basic ingredients.

After mixing the flour, salt, water, and sometimes other ingredients (olive oil, eggs, vinegar, and salt), the baker separates the dough into balls and allows it to rest. One method proceeds with the rolling of the dough ball into a flat circle about two feet in diameter. Two people then stretch the dough, which rests on their knuckles, tossing it around, constantly lifting and turning, until it becomes as large as a bed sheet. This purposeful ballet takes only about two very rhythmic minutes. In another method, a rolling pin is used to flatten the circles of dough, twenty of which are piled on top of each other and rolled out simultaneously by hand. Both of these methods produce diaphanous tissues of dough that you can actually read through.

Silky leeks, goat cheese, and ricotta are turned into the voluptuous filling in these butter-dribbled leaves of phyllo, which acquire their melting flakiness from the springform method used here.

3 tablespoons olive oil
1 bunch leeks, white part
   only, sliced
   salt and pepper
½ pound goat cheese**
½ pound whole-milk ricotta
2 tablespoons chopped fresh
   tarragon, or 1 tablespoon
   dried tarragon

2 eggs plus 2 yolks
12 sheets of phyllo dough
   (available in the freezer or
   deli section of your
   supermarket)
¼ pound butter, melted

In a small skillet heat oil and sauté leeks until very soft, about 20 minutes. Season with salt and pepper and allow to cool.

In a bowl blend cheeses together until smooth and add tarragon and eggs, beating until well combined.

Preheat oven to 350°F and, using a pastry brush, grease an 8-inch springform pan with some of the melted butter.

Brush 1 sheet of phyllo sparingly with butter; fold in half, buttered side in. Place in springform, allowing some of the dough to overhang the pan. Continue in the same manner with tne next 5 sheets of dough, placing them in pan in a spokelike fashion.

Spread leek mixture in bottom of phyllo-lined pan and pour cheese mixture over leeks.

Fold overhanging phyllo over filling and brush well with melted butter. Butter and fold the remaining sheets of phyllo and place also in pan in spokelike fashion. Tuck overhanging phyllo inside of pan, lifting bottom crust and gently pushing leaves underneath. (This may seem like a very delicate procedure but the dough has been strengthened by the layering and is no longer fragile. Long fingernails are the greatest danger in this operation.)

Brush top very liberally with melted butter and bake for 35 minutes. Remove sides of springform, invert "drum" on cookie sheet, remove bottom of springform, which now is on top, and continue to bake 15 to 20 minutes longer. Allow to cool 15 minutes before serving.

Serves 8

Three Peppers Pie

During the Gold Rush days in California, fresh eggs were a precious commodity. At eighteen dollars per dozen, they were worth more than their weight in any legal tender, and recipes made with even a few scrambled eggs became legendary for their extravagance. Cookbooks explained how to preserve eggs: First their pores were sealed by varnishing the shells and greasing them with suet; then the eggs were packed in salt or bran, always with the small ends down. In this way an egg could keep for three months. The frugal omelette lover could also be assured of freshness by using the Krepps family's egg-tester which, fortunately, came with complete instructions. Unfortunately, the instructions have been lost in obscurity, along with the device itself.

By the 1950s California's egg industry was centered in Petaluma, north of San Francisco, where many small producers earned the town its title of "Egg Basket of the World." As Helen Evans Brown describes in her West Coast Cook Book, you knew you were in Petaluma because the air suddenly became "loud with proud cacklings, and white with feathers." Today, egg production is a far more corporate enterprise located in places like Egg City, in Moorhead Park, California, where 2½ million chickens produce over a million eggs every day.

You need only two eggs for this pepper pie, with its ribbons of colorful peppers baked into a cheese-rich custard, fragrant with fresh herbs.

1 recipe pâte brisée*
4 tablespoons olive oil
1 large onion, thinly sliced
1 red bell pepper, seeded, deveined, and cut into strips
1 green bell pepper, seeded, deveined, and cut into strips
1 yellow bell pepper, seeded, deveined, and cut into strips

salt and pepper
1 teaspoon thyme
1 teaspoon oregano
1 teaspoon rosemary
¼ cup fresh chopped basil leaves
2 tablespoons imported tomato paste**
1 cup whole-milk ricotta
2 eggs
¼ cup grated Asiago cheese

Preheat oven to 400°F.

Roll out dough to fit a 10-inch pie plate. Place dough in pan, line with parchment* or foil, and fill with weights (rice, beans, or aluminum shot). Bake for 10 minutes, remove paper and weights, and bake at 375° for another 8 minutes. Allow to cool while preparing filling.

In a large skillet heat oil and sauté onion and peppers over low heat for 20 minutes, or until vegetables are very soft and jamlike. Add salt and pepper, herbs, and tomato paste and cook for another 3 minutes. Allow to cool before placing in bottom of partially baked pie shell.

Combine ricotta, eggs, and Asiago in a bowl until smooth. Pour into pie shell.

Bake in preheated 375° oven for about 30 minutes. Allow to cool 10 minutes before cutting.

Serves 8

Smoked Salmon and Sweet Onion Pie

Lox, the Russian word for salmon, seldom appears on the breakfast table without a full complement of cream cheese. Strictly speaking, a dozen bagels should also be in proximity, or at least a good Jewish rye bread. For one of us, an early experience instilled a lifelong affection for the combination. The first time we were served lox, we eyed the glistening pink strips suspiciously for a moment. Noting this hesitation, the hostess was moved to immediate action: "Eat that," she commanded. "It's very expensive."

This dish, which looks like a platter of lox and cream cheese, is a warm bagel-less version of the New York deli breakfast. With a little imagination, the encircling rim of pâte brisée might serve as an image, or perhaps a mirage, of the absent bagel. For those who insist that you can't get a good bagel outside New York, this won't help. For everyone else, this Sweet Onion Pie makes a nice little meal, even for breakfast, certainly for brunch.

1 recipe pâte brisée*
3 tablespoons olive oil
3 large sweet onions,**
   thinly sliced
   salt and pepper
1 teaspoon thyme

8 ounces cream cheese
2 tablespoons chopped fresh
   dill
2 eggs
¼ pound smoked salmon**
   (lox), cut into strips

Preheat oven to 400°F.

Roll out pâte brisée to fit a 10-inch ungreased pie pan. Place dough in pan. Line with parchment* or foil and weights (rice, beans, or aluminum shot), and bake for 12 minutes. Remove paper and weights, lower temperature to 375°, and bake for another 8 minutes. Allow to cool while preparing filling. Keep oven on.

In a large skillet heat oil and sauté onions until very soft, about 10 to 15 minutes. Season with salt and pepper and thyme.

While onions are cooling, beat cream cheese, dill, and eggs together in a bowl until smooth.

Place onions in the pie shell, cover with cream cheese mixture, and arrange smoked salmon strips in a spokelike design on top. Bake at 375° for 25 minutes. Allow to cool 10 minutes before serving.

Serves 6 to 8

Corn Crepe Cake with Chicken-Chile Filling

The word "crepe" is related to the word "crisp," a clue to how it was originally made. With lacy crinkled edges, early crepes were much too delicate to be rolled or folded, unlike the sturdy-battered varieties that came along later. Colonial cooks served their crepes in the English style, spread with a filling, piled up and sliced in wedges, like a cake. For this similarly constructed version, both sweet corn and cornmeal are processed into a smooth batter. The cumin-scented crepes are spread with chile-coriander sauce, chunks of chicken, and two cheeses, and baked as twin, stacked cakes. You can, if you wish, make only one crepe cake and keep the remaining crepes to serve another time, when only a generous smear of butter transforms them into an easy treat.

Crepes

2 eggs

½ cup milk

½ cup water

½ cup fresh, frozen, or canned corn kernels

½ cup flour

¼ cup cornmeal

2 tablespoons vegetable oil

salt and pepper

2 teaspoons sugar

1 teaspoon ground cumin

shortening for pan

Filling

2 tablespoons olive oil

2 cloves garlic, minced

1 small onion, chopped

¼ cup chopped fresh coriander leaves

1 cup chopped fresh or canned tomatoes

1½ pounds skinned and boned chicken breast, cooked and diced

2 jalapeño peppers,* seeded, deveined, and cut into very thin slivers

½ cup grated dry Jack cheese mixed with 1 cup shredded Monterey Jack cheese

1 bunch green onions, sliced

4 tablespoons sour cream

To make crepes: Mix eggs, milk, water, and corn in a food processor or blender until smooth. Add remaining ingredients and mix again. Refrigerate, covered, for about 1 hour before using.

Heat crepe or omelette pan with a bit of shortening. Pour about ¼ cup crepe batter into center of pan and swirl off heat until batter covers bottom evenly. Cook for about 1 minute or until crepe seems dry. Turn crepe over and cook very briefly on other side. Continue in this manner until batter is used up, stacking crepes between sheets of paper towels. Crepes are now ready to fill, refrigerate, or freeze. You should have about 12.

In a medium skillet heat oil and sauté garlic and onion until wilted. Add coriander and tomatoes. Cook over medium-high heat until sauce begins to thicken slightly, about 10 minutes.

Preheat oven to 400°F and oil two 8- or 9-inch cake pans. Place 1 crepe at the bottom of a pan.

Spread about 1½ tablespoons sauce over the crepe. Sprinkle with chicken, jalapeños, both cheeses, and onions. Cover with another crepe and continue until you have used 6 crepes. The last crepe should be spread with 2 tablespoons sour cream and the cheeses. Repeat the process in the other pan, using remaining crepes and filling.

Bake for about 15 minutes, then let cool about 5 minutes before removing from baking dish. Do not invert but slide onto serving plate. Cut into wedges.

Serves 6 to 8

Green Risotto

Risotto, a nice dish cooked in flavorful stock, was introduced widely in this country following World War II. The response was almost as enthusiastic as that shown for the all-time Italian favorites, pasta and pizza. Like them, risotto is a wonderful medium in which to set a collection of summertime vegetables, a dense savory sauce, or both. Because today's cooking emphasizes using ingredients at their flavorful peak, rice, pasta, and pizza make successful vehicles for tastes since they neither compete nor interfere. A handy example is the following Green Risotto, fragrant with the tender greens of early spring.

But the ways of risotto are probably infinite. An even more monochromatic dish than ours is Black Risotto, tinted with the dark ink of calamary. Chopped chicken is the main ingredient in the mysteriously named Risotto alla Sbirraglia, after the word for the Austrian police (sbirri) who once ruled Venice. Rice wrapped in flattened veal scallops bears the enigmatic name Mexicans with Risotto, possibly because of its visual resemblance to the tortilla.

True risotto aficionados insist that there is a vast difference between the first sublime spoonful taken from the pot of ready risotto and the last, which will already be past its peak. If this is true, the best time to eat risotto, whichever the recipe, is when it's ready.

2 quarts chicken stock*	2 young zucchini, coarsely
¼ pound butter	chopped
4 green onions, sliced	2 tablespoons chopped fresh
2 cups Italian Arborio rice**	parsley
salt and pepper	2 tablespoons chopped fresh
2 ounces snow peas, strings	chives
removed	1 cup grated Parmesan cheese
½ pound asparagus, peeled	
and cut into 1-inch pieces	

Bring stock to a boil in a pot and keep it on a slow simmer.

In a skillet melt half the butter and sauté the green onions. When onions are wilted, add the rice and stir until well coated with butter. When rice becomes shiny, start adding the stock, 1 ladle at a time. Allow the first ladle of stock to be absorbed into the rice before adding the next, but never allow rice to become completely dry. Add salt and pepper to taste.

When rice is half done, about 12 minutes, add the vegetables. Continue to add the stock, stirring continuously (you may not have to use all the stock). After another 12 minutes test the rice by biting into a grain. It should be firm but not hard. At this point add the parsley, chives, Parmesan cheese, and remaining butter. Serve immediately or the rice will continue to cook and become mushy.

Serves 6 to 8

Baked Cornmeal Wheels with Herbed Tomato Sauce

Until recently, few elegant restaurants would have offered a course of Cornmeal Mush. But now this classic American dish has enough charm in name alone to qualify as fashionable in any quarter. Traditionally, cornmeal was boiled in a heavy pot over a fire and served immediately; or it was cooled, cut into slices, and browned in fat or butter until crisp. Molasses or maple syrup, dried fruits, or berries often accompanied the dish, which might have been breakfast or supper and was very often both. Equally traditional accompaniments of wild animal fats and greases have failed to regain their frontier popularity.

The aroma of bubbling, hot cornmeal excites both the appetite and the imagination. Here the cooked, now-chic mush is cut into rounds and baked under a mantle of bubbling brown Fontina cheese and fresh tomato sauce.

Wheels

6 cups water
2 cups cornmeal
1 tablespoon salt

2 tablespoons chopped fresh
   basil leaves
1 teaspoon oregano

Sauce

2 tablespoons olive oil
2 cloves garlic, minced
2 pounds tomatoes, seeded
   and finely chopped
1 bay leaf
1 teaspoon oregano

2 tablespoons chopped fresh
   basil leaves
salt and pepper
¼ pound Fontina cheese,
   shredded

In a large pot bring water to a boil and very gradually add the cornmeal and salt, stirring constantly to prevent lumping. Turn heat down and simmer about 20 minutes, stirring every so often to make sure cornmeal is not lumping or sticking. Add herbs during last 2 minutes of cooking. Cornmeal should pull away from sides of pan when done.

Pour a ½-inch-thick layer of cooked cornmeal onto a wet marble slab or greased cookie sheet. Let cool completely. (It will harden as it cools.)

To make sauce: In a medium skillet, heat olive oil and sauté garlic until wilted. Add remaining ingredients except cheese and cook until thickened, about 10 minutes.

Preheat oven to 400°F. and butter a shallow 10-inch baking dish.

With a 2-inch round cookie cutter, cut firm cornmeal into rounds. Arrange half the rounds in an overlapping layer in baking dish and pour half the sauce over them. Sprinkle with half the cheese. Repeat with remaining cornmeal rounds, sauce, and cheese.

Bake for about 20 minutes. Allow to cool 10 minutes before serving.

Serves 6 to 8

Vermont Cheddar and Leek Soufflé

Made in every dairy state, cheddar cheese is the most widely consumed cheese of its type in this country. Vermont was one of the first states to develop a fine, perfectly balanced cheddar, and some cheesemakers there still follow the century-old ways of hand-tended aging in old farmhouse sheds. Yesterday's cheddars were tinted with carrot juice, but today's cheesemakers often add food coloring to achieve the same effect. We still favor the natural look, that healthy, yellow-white that looks so bland but tastes so lively, especially in this cloud of puffy cheddar and glossy leeks.

¼ pound Vermont cheddar,
finely grated
3 tablespoons butter
3 tablespoons flour
1 cup milk
5 egg yolks

6 egg whites
3 leeks, white part only,
finely chopped and sautéed
until wilted
salt and pepper

Butter a 1½-quart soufflé dish and sprinkle it with 2 tablespoons cheddar. Set aside.

In a heavy saucepan, melt butter and add flour, stirring constantly with a whisk until bubbling. Turn heat to low and stir in milk. Continue to cook until thick and smooth, about 5 minutes.

In a small bowl, stir yolks to break them up and add some of the milk mixture to warm them. Add yolks to milk mixture in saucepan and cook until thick, about 2 minutes, stirring continuously. Remove from heat and allow to cool for about 5 minutes.

Preheat oven to 375°F. Beat egg whites in a bowl until stiff peaks form and they are no longer sliding around bowl. Add one quarter of the whites to the yolk mixture along with the leeks, cheese, salt and pepper. Stir lightly to blend and fold in remaining whites, one quarter at a time. Fold quickly but gently. Pour into prepared soufflé dish, set on a preheated metal cookie sheet (see Note), and bake for about 25 minutes until top is browned and soufflé seems firm when gently shaken. Serve immediately.

Serves 6 to 8

SOUFFLÉ NOTE: Since Americans tend to prefer their soufflés rather firm, the use of a preheated cookie sheet will assure a smooth and thoroughly cooked center. As the heat is transferred to the bottom of the soufflé dish, it causes the soufflé to rise quickly, cooking it through. Also, it helps if the sides and bottom of the soufflé dish are sprinkled with something for the soufflé to climb on: sugar or ground nuts are common for sweet soufflés, while grated cheese, bread crumbs, and ground nuts work well for savory dishes. All such ingredients should be finely chopped so that they do not break down the whites during rising.

Golden Caviar–Mascarpone Roulade

Mascarpone is a soft Italian cheese with the texture and spread-ability of Devon clotted cream. It is often served as a separate course, dusted with cinnamon or chocolate, accompanied by brandied berries or even spread like buttercream over a plain chocolate cake. Cheese shops often sell Mascarpone torta, a block of Mascarpone and Gorgonzola sandwiched together in alternating layers.

In this Parmesan-scented, rolled soufflé, the creamy cheese is especially luxurious in the exalted company of both caviar and sour cream.

Roulade

3 tablespoons butter
3 tablespoons flour
1 cup milk
5 egg yolks
2 tablespoons finely chopped
    fresh parsley

3 tablespoons grated
    Parmesan cheese
6 egg whites
    pinch salt

Filling

6 ounces Mascarpone cheese,
    room temperature
3 tablespoons sour cream
½ cup chopped onion

4 ounces golden caviar**
    chopped fresh parsley for
    garnish

In a heavy saucepan melt butter and add flour, stirring constantly with whisk about 3 minutes. Remove from heat and stir in milk. Return to heat and cook about 5 minutes, or until thick and smooth. Remove from heat and stir in yolks, whisking until very smooth. Stir in parsley and cheese and let cool.

Preheat oven to 350°F. In a bowl beat egg whites with salt until stiff. Add one quarter of the whites to yolk mixture and fold lightly. Add remaining whites one fourth at a time, folding gently.

Pour mixture into a parchment*-lined 11"-×-16" jelly-roll pan and bake for about 20 minutes or until sides start shrinking away from pan. Turn out on towel (flat weave), remove parchment, and roll up with towel. Let cool in towel.

For the filling: Beat Mascarpone with sour cream in a bowl until very smooth and spreadable. Unroll roulade and spread cheese on it. Sprinkle with onions and caviar and roll up again.

Place on serving dish and sprinkle with chopped parsley. Each slice may be served with some additional sour cream.

Serves 8

Palace Chile

The question of whether chickens or eggs came first is a simple one to solve in comparison to the "chile" question. Which state can truly claim chile as its own creation: Texas, Arizona, New Mexico, Louisiana, California, Ohio? What is chile anyway: beans with meat, meat with beans?; should it be made with cheese, tomatoes, noodles, or all of the above?

The record is clear that McKinney, Texas, had a full-blown chile parlor by 1890. Jesse James reputedly left this whole town un-robbed because of his affection for its particular version of chile. At about the same time, San Antonio was the site of the travel-ing chile booth. Itinerant chile makers, known as "chile queens," would wheel their carts into the town square and set up shop for the night, selling their chile from cauldrons. At Chicago's Columbian Exposition of 1893 the San Antonio "Chilley Stand" was a center of attraction. Due to Cincinnati's eastern European influences, chile was served there on a big pile of noodles.

Further west, California also qualified as a budding chile state. At San Francisco's Palace of Art (actually a "saloon" with a lot of paintings on the walls), the copious Free Lunch included two different kinds of chile as well as thirty other items. These ranged from Bolinas Bay Clams and Crab Salad to Veal Croquettes or Popcorn, any and all included in the price of a beer. California now hosts an annual World Championship Chile Cookoff. In all honesty, it must be mentioned that this one is modeled after a similar competition begun in 1967 in Terlingua, Texas. Chile recently became an official concern of the U.S. Congress. In a spirit of unity, a New Mexico congressman urged that, no matter what its origins, chile be declared the "official food" of the United States because it so perfectly "embodies the robust and indomitable American spirit."

Our version nominally recalls its San Francisco predecessor from the very bygone Free Lunch era. To avoid any entanglement in the chile debate, we claim only that it is authentically delicious.

4 tablespoons vegetable oil	2 tablespoons green
2 large onions, chopped	peppercorn mustard** or
3 cloves garlic, minced	any strong mustard
2 pounds coarsely ground	1 cup beef stock*
beef chuck	1½ cups fresh, canned, or
2 tablespoons ground cumin	frozen corn kernels
2 tablespoons chile powder	1 cup cooked pinto beans
(see Note)	1 cup cooked black beans
4 large tomatoes, seeded and	2 small oranges, peeled,
coarsely chopped	pithed, and sectioned
3 tablespoons imported	
tomato paste**	

In a large saucepan heat oil and sauté onions, garlic, and beef until onions are wilted and beef begins to lose raw color. Add remaining ingredients except oranges and bring to a boil. Turn down flame and simmer, uncovered, about 1½ hours.

Add orange sections just before serving. Most satisfying accompanied with our Chile-Cornmeal Biscuits (page 307).

Serves 8

CHILE NOTE: Chile powder has been around since 1902, when the pulp was first extracted from the pods. The dried powder is often mixed with cumin, oregano, and other dried seasonings and marketed as chile powder. However, for true flavor and unadulterated taste, pure unseasoned chile powder is best.

EVENT SALADS

Pasta Shells with Smoked Salmon and Fresh Chives

The wild chives of the northeastern United States probably started out in Siberia. Making their way across by the polar route, chives were known in North America before they ever got to Europe. Slender green herbs of the onion family, chives are now commonly used in salads, soups, and egg dishes. With chervil and parsley and sometimes tarragon or basil, chives are essential to traditional Fines Herbes combinations. They may be mixed with parsley to make chive butter, which is delicious with cooked chicken. Because of their delicacy, they should be clipped into cooked dishes only at the last minute.

Chives are the civilizing principle in the strong horseradish cream that often accompanies roast beef; and they serve a similar function in this two-salmon salad. By the way, should you discover tiny blue flowers on your chives, throw them right in. Their intense chive taste is as sensuous as their color.

12 ounces small pasta shells, cooked
½ cup chopped red onion
½ cup chopped fresh chives
3 ounces smoked salmon,** cut into strips
½ pound fresh salmon, cooked, skinned, boned, and cut into cubes
2 ripe plum tomatoes, peeled, seeded, and coarsely chopped
4 tablespoons fresh lemon juice
3 tablespoons prepared white horseradish
½ cup heavy cream
¼ cup mayonnaise
salt and pepper

In a large bowl, toss pasta with red onion, chives, both salmons, and tomatoes. In a separate bowl whisk remaining ingredients until well blended and slightly thick. Pour over salmon mixture and mix well.

Serves 6 to 8

Shrimp Pasta Salad with Crumbled Feta, Olives, and Oregano

Americans are the world's largest consumers of shrimp. We eat more of it than any other seafood, perhaps because the world's most abundant shrimp fisheries flourish in the Gulf of Mexico.

The cooking of that region reflects this bounty in dishes like Shrimp Creole, Jambalaya, and Southern Shrimp Paste. A nice healthy Georgia breakfast might well include a dish of boiled or deep-fried shrimp, always served with grits. In Savannah, they make their Southern Shrimp Pie with rice; Charleston cooks do it with bread crumbs.

The baby shrimp in our recipe might come from the Pacific coast, Maine, or Alaska, where small shrimp abound. Small is determined by the "count," or the number of shrimp per pound, which is thirty-five to forty-five for these babies. Holland has even tinier specimens, three hundred to the pound! But Devil's River, Texas, holds the record for the largest shrimp ever recorded, a three-pounder.

Turned into a paste and spread on bread, tiny shrimp can become Rejemad, a Danish open-faced sandwich. The act of dropping live shrimp directly into the mouth is an exalted Japanese delicacy. Some argue that the shrimp are not really alive at this point, since their little heads have been chopped off; nevertheless, they are wriggling perceptively from the neck down. "Brushwood Shrimp," a Chinese dish offered on some restaurant menus, is worth noting especially because it is actually made with grasshoppers.

With crumbly feta cheese and black olives, this shrimp salad has a Grecian air, heightened by the scent of oregano, the only herb, according to Richard Olney, that has more flavor dried than fresh.

½ pound small pasta shells, cooked
½ pound baby shrimp, cleaned, shelled, and cooked
½ cup crumbled feta cheese
½ cup black olives,** pitted and halved
¼ cup chopped fresh parsley

2 tomatoes, seeded and coarsely chopped
3 tablespoons lemon juice
1 teaspoon oregano
1 teaspoon good-quality mustard
½ cup olive oil
salt and pepper

In a large bowl combine pasta, shrimp, feta, olives, parsley, and tomatoes.

In a separate bowl or jar combine remaining ingredients; pour into pasta bowl, and toss well.

Serves 6

Tortellini and Artichokes in Fresh Tomato and Sun-dried Tomato Vinaigrette

This cold pasta salad is not simply sprinkled with grated cheese at the end, it is tossed with the highly flavored Romano, the oldest and most venerable cheese of Italy. When grated it is more powdery than Parmesan and contributes a sharper flavor. Consequently, it is not used interchangeably with Parmesan, but is reserved for spicy pastas and bean dishes.

Pecorino Romano is made from whole sheep's milk which, after cooking, is molded into a cylindrical shape and aged eight months or more. This white or delicate gold cheese is named for pecora, the Italian word for sheep. Most American Romano cheese is made exclusively from cow's milk, yet is often marketed under the name Pecorino, and usually aged only four months. Piccolo Romano is a Wisconsin cheese produced in the shape of flat small wheels. Romanello, or "Little Romano," might be from Italy, the United States, Australia, or Canada.

Needless to say, should you be making this cold pasta salad in Italy, buy your Romano on the spot where, Italian cooking teacher and cookbook author Marcella Hazan advises, "It is likely to be the best cheese you will ever eat." If you are on home ground, search out a friendly honest cheese shop to guide you.

1 pound tortellini, cooked	8 sun-dried tomatoes,** cut
1 pound fresh or frozen	into strips
artichoke hearts,* cooked	1 large ripe tomato, seeded
and quartered	and chopped

4 tablespoons good white wine vinegar	1 teaspoon oregano
½ cup olive oil	½ cup chopped fresh basil leaves
salt and pepper	¼ cup grated Romano cheese

In a large bowl mix tortellini, artichoke hearts, and dried and fresh tomatoes.

In a separate bowl or jar combine vinegar, oil, salt and pepper, and oregano. Add to pasta bowl and toss with basil leaves and grated cheese.

Serves 8 to 10

Asparagus and Toasted Almonds with Oriental Noodles

Gingerbread men, which originally represented various English personages, may have led to an early affection for ginger in this country. It was a coveted spice in New England where it was basic to cranberry sauce and where, even today, Ginger Ice Cream has its only sizable following. In the South, ginger and ginger confections were the special treat of pre-election feeds given to sway voters at election time. During the Revolutionary War, ginger was listed as a standard military ration.

Fresh ginger is stir-fried into many Chinese dishes and chopped into cooked Indian chutneys. Much Italian food contains ginger, especially in those areas of Italy once under Saracen rule; there, food described as "strong" contains a goodly amount of ginger.

The stimulating nature of raw ginger has elevated this ancient spice to current popularity in California. In this recipe, its power and distinction flourish in the midst of asparagus, almonds, Italian vinegar, and Oriental oils.

1 pound Chinese egg noodles, cooked and cooled
1 cup slivered toasted almonds*
½ pound asparagus, cooked until barely tender, sliced diagonally
1 bunch green onions, white part only, cut into rings
2 cloves garlic, crushed
1 teaspoon minced fresh ginger
2 tablespoons balsamic vinegar**

4 tablespoons Oriental sesame oil
4 tablespoons black soy sauce (available at Oriental markets)
2 tablespoons brown sugar
¼ teaspoon Chinese mustard powder
1 tablespoon Chinese chile oil (available at Oriental markets)
½ cup fresh coriander leaves for garnish

In a large bowl combine noodles, almonds, asparagus, and onion.

In a bowl or food processor mix remaining ingredients except coriander leaves until sugar is dissolved (a food processor makes fast work of this) and toss with noodle mixture.

Garnish with coriander leaves. For a true explosion of flavors, allow to stand at room temperature about 2 hours before serving.

Serves 8-10

Melon Seed Pasta with Saffroned Mussels

Most people associate saffron with bouillabaisse ("the indispensable condiment for bouillabaisse," according to <u>Larousse Gastronomique</u>), or with Cornish saffron buns or various dishes of Spain. But saffron has a distinct American identity too. The Pennsylvania Dutch have been growing their own saffron since 1734, when a German religious sect, the Schwenkfelders, emigrated to Pennsylvania's Perkiomen Valley, bringing with them years of experience in the saffron business.

Because they harvest and process the spice themselves, the

Pennsylvania Dutch use saffron freely in their cooking, unconcerned that it is the most expensive spice in the world. The cost is due to the labor involved in removing the two or three little stamen, or saffron threads, from the purple crocus blossoms. But at the Kutztown Folk Fair in Pennsylvania Dutch country, chicken casseroles, noodle dishes, and breakfast buns and breads are fragrant with the rust-color spice. It is also an essential flavoring of the traditional Schwenkfelder wedding cake.

For some, the melon seed pasta in this mussel-rich salad may evoke the saffroned rice dish, Paella Valenciana. It is an especially beautiful salad, gleaming with mussels, red peppers, and saffron, colorfully mingled with peas and artichokes.

2 shallots, chopped
1 clove garlic, minced
½ teaspoon saffron threads
½ cup white wine
2 pounds mussels, debearded and scrubbed
6 ounces melon seed pasta,** cooked
1 cup fresh peas (or frozen, thawed)

8 fresh or frozen artichoke hearts, cooked* and quartered
1 red bell pepper, roasted* and cut into strips
2 tablespoons lemon juice
salt and pepper
⅓ cup olive oil
½ cup chopped fresh parsley

In a large pot bring shallots, garlic, saffron, and wine to a boil. Add mussels, cover, and cook until all mussels have opened. This should take about 5 minutes. With a slotted spoon remove mussels and allow to cool before removing from shells (reserve shells for garnish). Return wine mixture to heat and reduce* to about ⅓ cup.

In a bowl combine mussels with pasta, peas, artichoke hearts, and red pepper.

In a separate bowl mix reduced wine-saffron mixture with lemon juice, salt and pepper, and oil. Add to pasta mixture, along with parsley, and mix well. May be garnished with mussel shells.

Serves 6

Curried Rice Salad with Cashews and Snow Peas

The Sacramento Valley is California's major rice-growing area. It boasts the highest rice yield per acre in the world, though other places, particularly Italy, make similar claims. Having begun in 1912, the California commercial rice industry is still comparatively new. Actually, rice has been grown in California since 1760, but at that time, Carolina rice was getting all the attention.

Eventually Louisiana, Texas, and Arkansas began to grow rice, much of it also called "Carolina" or, equally often, "American." Almost all this rice is now exported. Even so, ninety percent of the world's rice is produced and consumed in Asia's monsoon regions, where over ten thousand varieties are known.

Short-, medium-, and long-grain varieties of both white and brown rice constitute the California crop, along with special new strains of California wild rice. Every year, the Sacramento Valley hosts a rice festival complete with rice tastings, giveaway bags of the latest rice, and cooking contests. Winners are included in the annual cookbook of the Farmers Rice Cooperative, which recently showed an interest in rice salads. Like pasta, cooked rice can become a salad with a moment's thought; mixing in leftovers gives the rice a chance to resonate with the already mellowed ingredients. In this double-rice salad, speckled with clips of green snow peas and glints of lavender shallot, everything comes under the seductive spell of curry.

1½ cups cooked white rice
1½ cups cooked wild rice**
¼ pound baby shrimp, cleaned, shelled, and cooked

1 cup snow peas, blanched* and cut into thirds
1 cup coarsely chopped toasted cashews*
½ cup golden raisins

3 tablespoons chopped shallot	2 tablespoons curry powder dissolved in 2 tablespoons boiling water
½ cup mayonnaise*	½ teaspoon cayenne
⅓ cup plain yogurt or sour cream	salt and pepper
juice of 1 medium lemon	

Combine both kinds of rice, shrimp, snow peas, cashews, raisins, and shallot in a large bowl.

In a separate bowl mix remaining ingredients until blended, then toss with rice mixture.

Serves 6 to 8

Sushi Salad

The Japanese characters for "happiness" and "occasion" make up the word sushi, the thousand-year-old national dish of Japan. There, this festive rice is served at marriages, births, and other celebratory occasions where tradition richly embellishes its preparations. Sushi is made from vinegared rice and bits of fish or vegetables rolled up together in a thin sheet of nori, a seaweed. Among the condiments customarily accompanying the bite-sized rolls might be shredded cucumber, carrots, onions, and daikon, a Japanese white radish. Referred to as tsuma, meaning "wife," these garnishes always include wasabi, a green horseradish powder mixed to a paste. A small sampling of the pungent paste reveals why wasabi means "tears."

Our salad takes inspiration from the artistry and splendor of this ancient creation. We have been told there is a venerable custom of treating the sushi chef, called the shokunin (actually, "artisan") to a special drink after the meal. This may be worth recounting to guests, especially if you happen to be the "shokunin" in the house.

1 cup freshly cooked rice
1 tablespoon rice wine or
  sherry
  salt and pepper
¼ cup rice wine vinegar or
  light white wine vinegar
¾ teaspoon wasabi or 2
  tablespoons very strong
  mustard
1 teaspoon honey
⅓ cup vegetable oil
1 carrot, peeled and shredded
1 6-inch piece daikon, peeled
  and shredded

1 small cucumber, vertically
  halved, seeded, and thinly
  sliced
1 avocado, peeled, pitted,
  and cut into small chunks
2 green onions, thinly sliced
½ pound very fresh raw fish
  such as tuna, salmon, or
  sole, cut into thin strips
¼ pound baby shrimp,
  cleaned, cooked, and
  shelled

Place rice in a large bowl.

In a separate bowl combine rice wine, salt and pepper, vinegar, wasabi, honey, and oil. Pour over rice and mix well. Allow to stand at room temperature until completely cool.

Add remaining ingredients and toss gently. Serve on a bed of crisped greens.

Serves 6

Lentil, Parsley, and Goat Cheese Salad

The growing popularity of goat cheese is probably due to its greater availability, as well as to its range of styles. From creamy and mild to dry and almost acrid, there's a goat cheese (chèvre) to exhilarate every cheese lover. The varieties are interesting to look at as well: some wrapped in walnut or grape leaves; some of them dusty from the characteristic ash and salt that helps them ripen more quickly toward their special tang; others packed in herb-infused olive oil. Shaped like small logs or pyramids or fat cylinders, they are known under many names—

Bûcheron, Montrachet, Chabis, Cabécou, Crottins—all traditionally imported from France and now also made in California and
New York.

In this dish, the cheese invests the cumin-scented lentils with
an earthiness all its own.

12 ounces lentils	1 teaspoon ground cumin
salted water	salt and pepper
2 carrots, peeled and grated	½ cup olive oil
1 cup chopped fresh parsley	3 ounces goat cheese,** cut
½ cup fresh lemon juice	into small cubes or
2 cloves garlic, put through	crumbled
garlic press	

Cook lentils in boiling salted water to cover, about 10 minutes. Drain
and mix with carrots and parsley in a bowl.

In a separate bowl combine lemon juice, garlic, cumin, and salt and
pepper with olive oil. Pour over lentil mixture, toss well, and sprinkle
with goat cheese.

Serves 6 to 8

Smoked Trout, Red and White Radish, and Watercress

Because neither of us had parents who swore very much, if at
all, we learned very few really potent curse words at home. With
one exception: one of us had a father who said that, if he did
swear, he would undoubtedly do it with the word rabanos. With
its trilled initial r and rolling, lip-curling force, "rabanos" always
seemed like a fierce and effective substitute for whatever he
wasn't saying instead. As it turned out, rabanos is the Spanish
word for radishes. The other of us had a father whose fateful

curse promised a naughty child would grow up like a radish, if she didn't behave. The word radish actually means "easily raised" because radishes are ready to eat very soon after planting.

Radishes are an extraordinary palate cleanser, either before the meal, with buttered triangles of brown bread; or as part of a taste-provoking salad; or as a refreshing conclusion to the meal, as reflected in the Japanese custom of serving bits of the pickled white radish, daikon.

The Romans loved radishes and brought them to public debates where, during moments of disagreement, they were hurled in the direction of any unpopular pronouncements. They were picked up afterward and served, salad style, with a little oil and vinegar.

Whatever functions they might otherwise serve, radishes endow this salad with their peppery crispness, especially pleasant in the company of the smoked trout.

¼ pound smoked trout,** skinned and boned
1 cup red radishes
1 cup white radishes
1 bunch watercress leaves
1 cucumber, peeled, seeded, and julienned*
2 tablespoons fresh lemon juice

1 tablespoon balsamic vinegar**
1 egg yolk
½ teaspoon thyme
2 teaspoons good-quality mustard
salt and pepper
½ cup vegetable oil
½ cup chopped fresh chives

Cut trout into thin strips. Cut radishes into thin rounds and mix with watercress, cucumber, and trout in a bowl.

In a separate bowl combine lemon juice, vinegar, egg yolk, thyme, mustard, and salt and pepper with oil until well blended. Add to trout mixture and sprinkle with chopped chives.

Serves 6

Macédoine of Monkfish

The "Sidney Greenstreet of the ocean" is how Julia Child described the monkfish, by which she meant big. Many newly converted monkfish lovers first witnessed the giant fish's American debut on Ms. Child's television cooking program, where she good-heartedly whittled away at its massive frame. Although a monkfish may weigh as much as fifty pounds, virtually the only edible portion is the tail. Since these fillets represent about twenty percent of the monkfish's total body weight, the tail is often the only part of the fish that returns with the fisherman to shore.

Also called angler, baudroie, lotte de mer, goosefish, molligut, and, most appropriately, allmouth, monkfish has a solid texture somewhat like lobster. It makes a sublime bouillabaisse, and works wonders in both cold and hot pâtés. Cooked with tomatoes and brandy, it can successfully replace lobster in Lobster à l'Américaine. Because of its mild taste, it goes well with assertive seasonings like the sherry vinegar and Tabasco in our marinated fish salad. The carrots and sweet peas, recalling the sparkling pea salads of Iowa, offer textural counterpoint to the plump, ivory-white chunks of fish.

1 pound monkfish, poached for 8 minutes and cut into bite-size chunks

1 cup fresh peas, cooked until tender

2 medium carrots, peeled, diced, and cooked until tender

1 large tomato, seeded and coarsely chopped

4 green onions, cut into rings

2 tablespoons good sherry vinegar**

dash Tabasco sauce

½ cup mayonnaise*

2 tablespoons capers, rinsed and drained

4 tablespoons chopped fresh parsley

salt and pepper

Combine fish and vegetables in a bowl. Toss with vinegar, and allow to marinate, covered, for about 1 hour in refrigerator.

Add remaining ingredients and mix well. May be served in avocado halves or lettuce leaves.

Serves 6

Curried Tuna and Mango Chutney on Garden Lettuces

Chatni, a Hindi word referring to highly seasoned foods, is the root of the word chutney. Like pickles, relishes, and jams, chutneys are preserves of any number of fruits, vegetables, and/or spices, often including the traditional ginger. Strictly speaking, in India chutney refers to a paste of raw ingredients. What we call chutney, the bottled sweet condiment, is more like a relish.

If we think of chutney in the same breath as curry, it is because they appeared simultaneously on our culinary horizons as part and parcel of Indian food. Chutney's popularity eventually resulted in such combinations as Corned Beef with Chutney on white bread, a once-popular sandwich at Schrafft's restaurant in New York. A jar of homemade chutney is a coveted gift, since a mere dollop can add magic to an otherwise ordinary dish.

Comprehensive cookbooks include recipes for chutneys made from peaches, apples, pears, and even green tomatoes. Mango chutney is the Indian classic in many people's minds, but the fruit tends to be expensive, since, except for a small Florida crop, it is all imported. Consequently, we were surprised to find a recipe in Mrs. Rorer's late nineteenth-century cookbook for "Mangoes." As it turned out, however, her mangoes were actually cabbage-stuffed sweet peppers covered with vinegar and preserved upright in stone jars. "Mangoes are also made from peaches and small melons," she explains.

Mango chutney and aromatic spices add a teasingly exotic element to this simple salad.

2 7½-ounce cans good-
   quality tuna fish, drained
1 large red apple, cored and
   coarsely chopped
½ cup green onion rings
½ cup mayonnaise*
1 tablespoon lemon juice
2 tablespoons mango
   chutney**

1 tablespoon curry powder
   dissolved in 1 tablespoon
   boiling water
½ teaspoon ground cumin
   red and green lettuce leaves
½ cup coarsely chopped dry-
   roasted peanuts, for garnish

In a bowl mix tuna, apple, and onion rings.

In a separate bowl combine mayonnaise with lemon juice, chutney, curry infusion, and cumin and add to tuna mixture. Line plates with lettuce leaves, top with tuna salad, and garnish with chopped peanuts.

Serves 6

Tarragon-Walnut Chicken Salad

California produces virtually all the walnuts grown for human consumption in this country. Although first planted in the south and east, the favored Persian walnut survived nowhere until grown in California and Oregon. As a result, walnuts are featured in many California dishes today, especially salads, where they are likely to be tossed in a dressing made with walnut oil. Many cooks mash walnuts into a fine paste as a sauce base for meats, pasta, or vegetables. For soups, walnuts may be roasted and pulverized with cream and stock. Or they are chopped, mixed with herbs, and used as a stuffing for chicken or ravioli.

These combinations are born of a multiplicity of influences: Chinese, Italian, Iranian, French. In our salad we may even have a touch of Arizona, famous for its vegetable-laden, conical-shaped chicken dish called "Topopo Salad." Here the tastes of fresh tarragon and cayenne suffuse the juicy chunks of chicken and bright broccoli flowerets, all strewn with California walnuts.

3 whole skinned and boned
chicken breasts, cooked
(see Note)
½ head broccoli, peeled and
blanched*
¾ cup coarsely chopped
walnuts
2 tablespoons fresh tarragon
leaves, or 1 teaspoon dried
tarragon

2 tablespoons fresh lemon
juice
¾ cup mayonnaise*
¼ cup sour cream or plain
yogurt
¼ teaspoon cayenne
salt and pepper

Cut chicken into ½-inch cubes. Cut broccoli into small pieces. Mix broccoli and chicken with walnuts and tarragon in a large bowl.

In a separate bowl mix remaining ingredients until well blended and stir into bowl with chicken mixture.

Serves 6

CHICKEN BREAST NOTE: To cook skinned and boned chicken breasts: Cover breasts with a light coating of yogurt and put them on a baking sheet at 375°F for 25 minutes. Allow to cool, scrape off yogurt, and proceed. The yogurt imparts little of its flavor but all of its properties to tenderize and moisten. For salads, always use fresh breasts, never frozen. There is a tremendous difference in both taste and texture.

Potato Pesto Chicken with Red Pepper Strips

To many people, a salad that contains even one small potato is, quite simply, potato salad. To determine more about a salad's ethnic identity, we must look at its accompanying ingredients. With mayonnaise or salad dressing, in both hot and cold versions, the potato salad is associated with German Americans, who all but invented the dish in this country. Needless to say, the Irish have also contributed a fair share of potato salads ever since Irish Presbyterians planted their first crop of the white tubers in Londonderry, New Hampshire, in the 1720s. Cold potatoes with aioli have French-Italian roots, and those in saffron or peppery dressings are usually Hispanic.

The culinary heritage behind this potato salad, with its oregano, Parmesan, and pesto, seems obvious enough. It is made with new potatoes, so called because they are harvested when still slightly immature. This waxy, low-starch variety is especially delicious here if slightly undercooked.

1 pound small new potatoes, cooked and cooled
3 skinned and boned chicken breasts, cooked
1 red bell pepper, seeded and cut into strips
½ cup fresh basil leaves
2 cloves garlic
3 tablespoons grated Parmesan cheese
½ teaspoon oregano
4 tablespoons good white wine vinegar
½ cup olive oil
salt and pepper

Cut potatoes and chicken into 1-inch cubes. Toss with red pepper in a large bowl.

Place remaining ingredients in a food processor and puree. Toss with chicken-potato mixture.

Serves 6

Triple Onion and Red Potato Salad

Even as children, we knew potatoes were important. We would clench our fists to make them look like potatoes. Then we began one of those eternal, continuous childhood chants—"One potato, two potato, three potato, four..."—the purpose of which, as far as we can now remember, was the establishment of some sort of short-lived supremacy in choosing up teams.

But potatoes had other functions as well. At dinner, potatoes were the only root vegetable eaten with enthusiasm almost every day. They were lunch or snacks for people who bought them, piping hot, from street vendors who roasted them over glowing coals. This custom presaged the current style of serving potatoes as a separate course; in elegant restaurants, they are sometimes embellished with ingredients almost antithetical to their earthiness, like caviar or chopped truffles. This seems particularly poetic since the potato, when first discovered by the conquistadores in Spanish America, was originally considered a strange new form of truffle.

Another reason for the revival of interest in potatoes may be their high nutritional content, especially when eaten, as in our recipe, unpeeled. James Beard once said in unabashed praise, "Whoever thought of boiling potatoes in their jackets—probably the Irish or the English—has my gratitude." Here we are also grateful to three kinds of chopped onions and the splash of vermouth for making this vivacious combination.

2½ pounds small red potatoes, scrubbed but not peeled	1 leek, white part only, sliced and separated into rings
water	1 small red onion, diced
3 tablespoons good white wine vinegar, preferably Chardonnay vinegar	2 tablespoons chopped shallots
¼ cup dry vermouth	2 tablespoons chopped fresh parsley
2 cloves garlic, put through garlic press	1 tablespoon chopped fresh dill
salt and pepper	
½ cup olive oil	

Cook potatoes in boiling water to cover for about 18 minutes. Drain and rinse briefly under cold water. While still warm, cut the potatoes in quarters.

In a bowl mix vinegar, vermouth, garlic, and salt and pepper with oil, and pour over the still-warm potatoes. Allow to cool and toss with remaining ingredients.

Serves 6 to 8

Warm Spinach and Sausage Salad

Because the sausage has so long been an American institution, no one can claim to have invented it, though of course everybody does. The Pennsylvania Germans have been famous for their smoked beef sausages, originally made in and named after Lebanon, Pennsylvania. At the annual autumn "metzel," hogs were butchered and sausages made to be hung for the winter. Similar activities characterize the Cajun boucherie, or pig slaughter, in Louisiana's bayou country. The resulting sausages are called "boudin blanc," from the Latin botulus, meaning sausage. Distantly related to the French boudin, the Louisiana versions are fiery hot from strong spices and cayenne pepper

In other parts of the South, sage is a common flavoring for milder sausages, which can be seen hanging in cool and airy places, wrapped in corn husks. In the Southwest, Arizona's and New Mexico's chorizos owe their "picante" personality to chile peppers and their Spanish heritage.

Nor could anyone dispute the powerful Italian claim to sausagery. Italian butchers in the Northeast often provided their customers with instructions and recipes for making sausages from less costly cuts of meat. Near Provincetown, Massachusetts, Portuguese fishing villages became famous for Sausage-stuffed Squid and, even more so, for Quahog Pie, a combination of linguiça sausage and clams. But no one seems to know who deserves the credit for the once famous beef-and-oyster sausages, flavored with cloves and mace, that were all the rage a century ago.

California cooks today are creating sausages from mixtures of Pacific fish and seafood, from assortments of wild and cultivated mushrooms bound with eggs and crumbs, from purees of almost any ingredients. Our warm salad, with juicy orange sections and golden egg strips, takes on all the gusto of the thick chunks of sausage with every drop of their spicy pan juices. But the faint hint of Pernod is the salad's true secret.

1 pound spicy sausage of your choice, cut into ¼-inch-thick slices
1 red onion, sliced
3 tablespoons vegetable oil
2 eggs, beaten
2 bunches spinach leaves, room temperature, washed and torn into bite-size pieces

2 oranges, room temperature, peeled and sectioned
3 tablespoons good sherry vinegar**
1 teaspoon tarragon mustard**
1 teaspoon Pernod
salt and pepper
2 tablespoons olive oil

In a skillet cook sausage until all or most of the fat is rendered. Remove sausage and set aside. In same skillet cook onion until just barely wilted. Remove and add to sausage. In same skillet, add vegetable oil and fry eggs on both sides. Remove and cut into strips.

While rendered fat and oil are still hot pour over spinach leaves in a large bowl. Toss well to coat. Add reserved sausage slices, onion, oranges, and eggs.

Mix remaining ingredients together in a separate bowl, then pour over spinach mixture. Toss and serve immediately.

Serves 6 to 8

Duck Liver and Orange Salad with Curly Endive and Pecans

The late James Beard called sage "the herb that traveled the covered-wagon trail." As a flavoring for pork and game, it has been held in high regard since pioneer days. This favoritism probably can be explained by its heritage, since English dishes of duck, sausages, leek pies, and cooked tomatoes were full of the pungent herb. Sage cheese has always been popular with the English, and sage-flavored stuffings have by now found their way into almost everybody's Thanksgiving turkey at least once. From the French, we have inherited a tradition of sage-flavored vinegars, chestnuts boiled with sage, and sage-wrapped thrushes roasted over an open fire.

Some species of sage make interesting teas or honey; others supposedly whiten teeth brushed vigorously with its leaves. One species, obviously to be used with caution, is reputed to revive the dead.

Whatever its other miracles, sage gives this salad a lovely balance in company with the plush tastes of duck liver and juicy orange slices.

7 tablespoons vegetable oil	grated zest* of 1 small
1½ pounds duck livers, cleaned and halved	orange
	2 cloves garlic, put through
salt and pepper	garlic press
½ teaspoon dried sage	1 cup coarsely chopped
1 teaspoon fresh lemon juice	toasted pecans*
1 tablespoon chopped fresh parsley	1 large head curly endive, torn into bite-size pieces
1 bunch green onions, cut into rings	2 small oranges, peeled, seeded, and thinly sliced
3 tablespoons walnut oil	for garnish
3 tablespoons raspberry vinegar**	

In a medium skillet heat 4 tablespoons oil and sauté livers until they lose their red color, about 4 minutes. Sprinkle with salt and pepper, sage, and lemon juice, and cook for another minute. Add chopped parsley and allow livers to cool in pan.

With a slotted spoon remove livers from pan, reserving pan drippings. Slice livers and mix with green onions in a bowl.

In a separate bowl combine pan drippings with 3 tablespoons vegetable oil, walnut oil, vinegar, zest, and garlic. Pour over liver mixture along with pecans and mix well.

Arrange endive on plates, top with livers, and garnish with orange slices.

Serves 6

Duck and Sweet Potato Salad

A steaming hot roasted sweet potato and a glass of milk made a fine dessert in the Virginia of the 1850s. Sweet Potato Pie was even better. For the main course, ham, chicken, and possum were often surrounded by, or draped on top of, sweet potatoes, which were always favored over white potatoes in the South. Elsewhere, Thanksgiving would be downright disappointing without the traditional candied sweet potatoes, a dish so sweet it is sometimes considered more an accompanying relish than a vegetable.

The Indians of northern Florida and eastern Carolina cultivated sweet potatoes and roasted them in hot ashes, a method the colonists later imitated. When Columbus discovered the vegetable, he sent it back to Spain, where it met instant acceptance and wide distribution. It soon reached the court of Henry VIII, whose enthusiasm over Sweet Potato Pie was already legendary by 1509. Oddly enough, many colonists did not taste this New World vegetable until they imported it back from England and Spain.

Fried Sweet Potato Chips, Custard Meringue Sweet Potato Pie, and Sweet Potato Bread, made with oven-roasted sweet potatoes, had already appeared in American cookbooks by the 1800s. Now produced in Louisiana, North Carolina, and Georgia, sweet potatoes are high in vitamin C and carotene. Their sweetness is inviting and mature, rather than overpowering. These virtues, plus a newly appreciated American identity, may help explain their current rise in popularity.

In our recipe, the sweet potatoes, nestled among ribbons of roast duck and crisp green beans, make a flamboyantly colorful salad.

1 duck, roasted, skinned, boned, and cut into strips	2 medium sweet potatoes, peeled, cubed, and boiled until tender

½ pound green beans,
blanched* and cut into
2-inch pieces

2 large shallots, peeled and
sliced

1 tablespoon hot-sweet
mustard**

3 tablespoons good red
wine vinegar

salt and pepper

6 tablespoons olive oil

1 teaspoon chopped fresh
rosemary leaves, or ½
teaspoon dried rosemary

3 tablespoons chopped fresh
parsley

1 teaspoon chopped fresh
tarragon

Combine duck, potatoes, green beans, and shallots in a bowl.

In a separate bowl mix remaining ingredients together until blended and pour over duck mixture. Toss well.

Serves 6 to 8

Marinated Lamb, Corn, and Baby Bean Salad with Cherry Tomatoes

As they once were in the past, meat salads have become popular, if not downright trendy. Corned beef and chicken salads were homestyle favorites, sausage and cervelas salads were German and Dutch specialties, and sophisticated beef salads became "de rigueur" in some dining circles. Veal, once much less expensive than chicken, was often suggested as a substitute because, with a deft hand, it could be made to taste just like chicken. One of Mrs. Rorer's recipes from the late 1800s is a dressed salad of cooked, thin-sliced sweetbreads served on top of—not mixed with—a single sliced onion. (It thus guaranteed "only the faintest suspicion of onion.")

As has become preferable today, meat salads make use of relatively small quantities of meat, enhanced with light saucings and an exotic ingredient or two. Chunks of smoked pheasant, strips of rare cooked breast of duck, or, as in this salad, slices of marinated spring lamb, can make an exciting creation. The cornichons, those midget pickles whose name means "little horn," join an all-American troop of corn, young beans, and red potatoes and contribute a characteristic Gallic flair.

1 pound lamb, cooked and julienned*
4 small red potatoes, cooked and julienned*
1 cup cooked fresh or frozen corn kernels
½ pound very young green beans, blanched*
¼ cup chopped cornichons
1 small red onion, diced

6 cherry tomatoes, halved
2 tablespoons good strong mustard
1 tablespoon good red wine vinegar
⅓ cup olive oil
salt and pepper
3 cloves garlic, put through garlic press

In a large bowl combine lamb, potatoes, corn, green beans, cornichons, onion, and tomatoes.

Make marinade by mixing remaining ingredients in a bowl until well blended. Add to lamb mixture and refrigerate for 12 hours before serving.

Serves 6

PIZZA AND CALZONE

Pizza has made a tremendous contribution in educating the American palate: It has taught Americans to like, in almost any combination, anchovies, garlic, Italian sausages, and oregano. Equally significant, it has encouraged a national passion for cheese, now evident in the proliferation of small-scale cheesemakers in many dairy regions and the construction of large-scale cheese shops in every shopping mall. Although pizza now flourishes throughout the country—James Beard called it the "pizza epidemic"—it should come as no surprise that the food has strong Italian connections.

Naples has been the undisputed world capital of pizza for several centuries, though the concept of hot yeasty crusts, laden with savory toppings, is as old as ancient Rome, where "bread with a relish" was a favorite breakfast dish. Neither mozzarella nor tomatoes were added until the Middle Ages. In fact putting tomatoes on pizza might have been the device that helped people overcome the strong fear of tomatoes which had accompanied that vegetable's introduction from the New World.

Plain old "American"-style pizza—a tenderly puffed, crisp-bottomed crust layered with herbed tomatoes and molten mozzarella—didn't become institutionalized until the nineteenth century, when it was reportedly named for Italy's pizza-ravenous monarch, Queen Margherita. However, there are many variations on the basic pizza theme.

For example, Seven-Eyed Pizza, a specialty of Abruzzi, is made with pizza dough, but is sweetened and braided in a long tress with seven holes peeking through. Pizza Pasqualina is an Easter cake with ricotta, honey, and eggs. Pizza casalinga, or "homemade" pizza, is a savory pie with a pastry crust. Pizza rustica is, in various forms, the deep-dish pizza of Abruzzi, Apulia, and Chicago, but in some places it can be a dessert, made with puff pastry and spilling over with unexpected grapes and sweet salami.

When traditional pizza dough is folded over to enclose its ingredients, it becomes a calzone. Calzones are another Neapolitan specialty, supposedly named after "trouser legs" because their shape was once more tubular and elongated. They can be either baked or deep-fried. The word may also refer to a small type of ravioli, filled with meat, then both boiled and baked. In this country calzones fit so neatly into the category of turnovers, right along with South American empanadas, Russian pirogi, and Cornish pasties, that almost everyone finds them comfortably familiar.

The popularity of pizza and calzone has led some people to

make proprietary claims that transcend all factual foundation. In New Haven, Connecticut, up and down Wooster Street, the menus of several restaurants explain in emotional detail how they came to "invent" the pizza, calzone, or both. The more modest establishments may claim merely to be the first to serve calzone with a sauce, or with a certain filling, or as dessert. One family-run place insists that it was absolutely the first place to serve calzone "in a Restaurant Atmosphere."

Those who prefer eating their pizza standing up at dollar-a-slice pizza counters all over Greenwich Village and environs would take strong exception to these Connecticut claims. After all, the first pizzeria in this country opened in New York in 1895 at 53½ Spring Street. A safe distance away, in Berkeley, California, or in the North Beach section of San Francisco, delighted eaters munch away unconcerned, believing that some of the new or long-beloved West Coast versions may not be the first but are unquestionably the best.

In all this we cannot overlook the claim of Italian cookbook author Marcella Hazan, though we can accept her challenge. She says, unequivocally, "There is no way to improve upon . . . the taste of genuine Neapolitan pizza." Well, it's worth a try. In fact, it's worth several tries, presented here in both pizza and calzone forms: one with Cajun sausage, one with three kinds of wild mushrooms, another with hot chile pepper, and a few wonderful others.

A WORD ABOUT HEAT: Few of us have home ovens constructed of volcanic rock from Mount Vesuvius, like the great Neapolitan pizza ovens, where air penetrates the underside of the baking surface and the high heat removes the moisture from the dough. Only pizza baked on such porous rock or in brick ovens at very high temperatures has a chance at the pizzaic Platonic ideal of a crisp undercrust supporting a pillowy-rimmed, firm top. To approximate the optimum oven conditions as much as possible, line your oven shelf—not the floor of the oven—with an unglazed baking tile (fired at 1500°F) or with a number of unglazed, one-inch-thick quarry tiles. You can also buy a pizza stone made for this purpose, though it is more expensive than the other suggestions.

If you have a gas oven, set it on the highest setting. Electric ovens can be set on "broil," which is usually hotter than the highest "bake" setting. Always let the oven preheat before sliding your pizza onto the hot stone. The best way to do this, by the way, is with a "pizza peel," a large wooden spatula made for this purpose. It does take an experienced hand, but the more you use the peel the more seasoned it becomes, and the easier it will be to use. You can also form the pizza on a cookie sheet and put the sheet directly on the tiles. Then again, you can just put your old cookie sheet in the oven and accept the fact that serving a pizza in your very own house is going to be one of the best ideas you ever had. Just ask anyone in your kitchen at the time.

Basic Pizza Dough and Variations

Basic Pizza Dough

1 tablespoon dry yeast	1 tablespoon olive oil
pinch sugar, or 1 teaspoon	2½ cups flour
honey or malt extract	½ teaspoon salt
¾ cup warm water (about	
110°F)	

By hand: Mix yeast and sugar with water in a bowl and let proof* about 10 minutes. Add oil to yeast mixture.

In another mixing bowl place flour and salt and stir in yeast mixture until dough holds together (dough will be slightly sticky). Turn out onto a floured board and knead lightly until smooth and springy, about 3 minutes. Place in oiled bowl, cover, and let rise for 1 hour, or until doubled in bulk. Punch down and allow to rest for 10 minutes before rolling out.

Food processor method: In a small bowl mix yeast and sugar with water and let proof* about 10 minutes. Add oil to yeast mixture. Place dry ingredients in the bowl of a food processor and process briefly to combine. With machine running, pour yeast mixture through feed tube and process until a ball of dough forms on the blade. Remove dough from processor and knead lightly for about 3 minutes. Proceed as in hand method.

Makes one 15-inch pizza or two calzones

Variations

Herb Pizza Dough: Add to flour in Basic Pizza Dough recipe ¼ cup chopped fresh basil leaves; 1 tablespoon chopped fresh parsley; 1 tablespoon oregano; and 2 cloves garlic, minced.

Whole-Wheat Pizza Dough: Substitute ½ cup whole-wheat flour for ½ cup all-purpose flour and proceed as for Basic Pizza Dough.

Cornmeal Pizza Dough: Substitute ½ cup cornmeal for ½ cup all-purpose flour. Add 1 teaspoon ground cumin to flours and proceed as for Basic Pizza Dough.

Herb Crust Pizza with Three Cheeses and Pesto

1 recipe Herb Pizza Dough (see above)	2 ounces Jarlsberg cheese, grated
2 tablespoons cornmeal	2 ounces Asiago cheese, grated
3 tablespoons olive oil	½ cup chopped red onion
2 ounces Fontina cheese, grated	½ cup pesto*

Preheat oven to 500°F.

Roll out dough to fit a 15-inch pan that has been sprinkled with cornmeal. Place dough in the pan and crimp edges slightly.

Brush dough with olive oil and sprinkle with cheeses and onion.

Bake for 10 minutes, distribute pesto by spoonfuls over cheeses, and place back in oven for 3 more minutes. Serve immediately.

Serves 8

Whole-Wheat Pizza with Pancetta and Artichokes

4 tablespoons olive oil
2 cloves garlic, peeled
¼ pound pancetta, slivered
   (an uncured bacon,
   available in Italian
   delicatessens)
5 artichoke hearts,* cooked
   and quartered
1 small onion, chopped
1 recipe Whole-Wheat Pizza
   Dough (see page 168)

2 tablespoons cornmeal
4 ounces imported Swiss
   cheese, grated
2 ounces Romano cheese,
   grated
1 teaspoon chopped fresh
   rosemary leaves, or ½
   teaspoon dried rosemary
3 tablespoons chopped fresh
   parsley

Preheat oven to 500°F.

In a medium skillet heat olive oil and sauté garlic cloves until golden brown. Remove and discard. Sauté pancetta, artichokes, and onion in same oil for about 5 minutes. Remove and reserve.

Roll out dough to fit a 15-inch pan that has been sprinkled with cornmeal. Place dough in the pan and crimp edges slightly.

Brush dough with oil from skillet and arrange pancetta, artichokes, and onion on dough, cover with cheeses, and sprinkle with rosemary and parsley. Bake for about 13 minutes. Serve immediately.

Serves 8

Pizza Jalisco

4 large, ripe tomatoes,
  seeded and chopped
2 jalapeño peppers,* seeded,
  deveined, and slivered
¼ cup chopped fresh
  coriander leaves
½ onion, chopped
1 clove garlic, minced
  salt and pepper
  pinch sugar

1 recipe Cornmeal Pizza
  Dough (see page 168)
2 tablespoons cornmeal
1 avocado, peeled and sliced
  into thin wedges
½ pound chorizo sausage,
  cooked and crumbled
4 ounces Monterey Jack
  cheese, grated
1 teaspoon oregano

Preheat oven to 500°F.

In a medium bowl combine first 7 ingredients to make the salsa.

Roll out dough to fit a 15-inch pan that has been sprinkled with cornmeal. Place dough in the pan and crimp edges slightly.

Arrange avocado and sausage on dough, spread with salsa, and sprinkle with cheese and oregano. Bake for 13 minutes. Serve immediately.

Serves 8

Three Mushroom Pizza with Sun-dried Tomatoes

1 ounce porcini
  mushrooms,** soaked in 1
  cup hot water 30 minutes
3 tablespoons butter
3 ounces fresh shitake
  mushrooms, washed,
  stemmed and sliced

6 ounces fresh mushrooms,
  washed and sliced
  salt and pepper
3 tablespoons olive oil
2 onions, peeled and thinly
  sliced

1 recipe Basic Pizza Dough
(see page 167)
2 tablespoons cornmeal
¼ pound Monterey Jack
cheese, shredded
½ teaspoon oregano
½ teaspoon basil

6 sun-dried tomatoes,**
coarsely chopped, plus
2 tablespoons oil from
tomato jar
¼ pound Parmesan cheese,
grated

Preheat oven to 500°F.

Drain porcini and reserve water, straining through fine strainer or cheesecloth.

In a medium skillet melt butter and sauté all mushrooms over high heat, about 4 minutes. Add salt and pepper to taste.

In a separate skillet heat olive oil and sauté onions until very soft. Add ½ cup of reserved mushroom liquid to onions and continue to cook until water has evaporated. Allow onions and mushrooms to cool to room temperature.

Roll dough out to fit a 15-inch pizza pan that has been sprinkled with cornmeal. Place dough in the pan and crimp edges slightly.

Spread dough with onions, then top with mushrooms. Sprinkle with Jack cheese and herbs. Place dried tomatoes over cheese and dot with tomato oil. Bake for 8 minutes, sprinkle with Parmesan, then bake another 4 minutes.

Serves 8

Pizza Y'All

¾ pound tomatoes, peeled,
seeded, and chopped
1¾ cups ricotta cheese
⅓ cup shredded Smithfield
ham**
⅓ cup grated Parmesan cheese
¼ cup chopped fresh basil
leaves

freshly ground pepper
6 ounces goat cheese**
1 recipe Basic Pizza Dough
(see page 167)
2 tablespoons cornmeal
¼ cup olive oil
¼ cup chopped pecans
(optional)

Preheat oven to 475°F.

Put tomatoes in a potato ricer or strainer and press to remove excess moisture. In a bowl mix drained tomatoes with ricotta, ham, Parmesan, basil, pepper, and half the goat cheese.

Roll out pizza dough to fit a 15-inch pan that has been sprinkled with cornmeal. Place dough in the pan and crimp edges slightly.

Brush dough with olive oil and spread with tomato mixture. Crumble remaining half of goat cheese on top, sprinkle with optional pecans, and bake until crust is golden, about 12 to 15 minutes.

Serves 8

Calzone with Chard and Mozzarella

4 tablespoons olive oil
2 cloves garlic, minced
1 small bunch chard, stems
   and leaves, chopped
2 medium red potatoes,
   cooked and diced
¼ pound prosciutto,
   julienned*

¼ pound whole-milk
   mozzarella, shredded
¼ cup chopped fresh parsley
1 recipe Basic Pizza Dough
   (see page 167)
2 tablespoons cornmeal

Preheat oven to 500°F.

In a medium skillet heat oil and sauté garlic and chard until wilted. Let cool and mix with next 4 ingredients.

Divide dough in half. Roll out one half into an 8-inch circle. Mound half the filling on lower half of the circle, leaving a ½-inch margin. Fold top half over filling and crimp edges well to seal. Repeat with other half of dough and filling.

Place calzones on a baking sheet sprinkled with cornmeal and bake for about 13 minutes. Let stand about 5 minutes before cutting.

Makes 2 calzones

Calzone with Eggplant, Garlic, and Teleme Cheese

5 tablespoons olive oil
3 cloves garlic, minced
1 onion, chopped
1 small eggplant, unpeeled, cut into 1-inch cubes
½ red bell pepper, seeded, deveined, and cut into thin strips
1 yellow summer squash, sliced
2 medium tomatoes, seeded and coarsely chopped
1 teaspoon oregano
¼ cup chopped fresh basil leaves
salt and pepper
¼ pound whole-milk ricotta
¼ pound Teleme cheese, shredded or cut into small dice
1 recipe Basic Pizza Dough (see page 167)
2 tablespoons cornmeal
3 tablespoons grated Parmesan cheese

In a large skillet, heat 3 tablespoons oil and sauté garlic, onion, and eggplant until slightly wilted, about 4 minutes. Add bell pepper, squash, and tomatoes and cook another 5 minutes. Add oregano, basil, salt and pepper. Cook 1 minute longer. Allow mixture to cool, then stir in cheeses and preheat oven to 500°F.

Divide pizza dough in half. Roll out one half into an 8-inch circle. Mound half the filling on lower half of circle, leaving ½-inch margin. Fold upper half over filling, crimping edges well to seal. Repeat with other half of dough and filling.

Place on a baking sheet that has been sprinkled with cornmeal and bake for 13 minutes.

Remove from oven, brush with 2 tablespoons olive oil, and sprinkle with Parmesan cheese. Let stand 5 minutes before cutting.

Makes 2 calzones

Hot Cajun Sausage Calzone

2 tablespoons olive oil
1 pound hot Louisiana
   sausage, cut into ¼-inch-
   thick slices
1 large onion, thinly sliced
1 red bell pepper, seeded,
   deveined, and sliced
1 teaspoon thyme

1 teaspoon oregano
1 teaspoon sweet paprika
   salt and pepper
1 cup cooked black beans
1 recipe Basic Pizza Dough
   or Cornmeal Pizza Dough
   (see pages 167–68)
2 tablespoons cornmeal

In a medium skillet heat oil and sauté sausage until cooked, about 8 minutes. Remove and reserve.

In same skillet cook onion and pepper over low heat until very soft, about 15 minutes. Meanwhile, preheat oven to 500°F. Mix onion and pepper with reserved sausage and remaining filling ingredients.

Divide dough in half. Roll out one half into an 8-inch circle. Mound half of filling on lower half of circle, leaving ½-inch margin. Fold upper half over filling and crimp edges well to seal. Repeat with other half of dough and filling.

Place calzones on a baking sheet sprinkled with cornmeal and bake for 13 minutes. Let stand 5 minutes before cutting.

Makes 2 calzones

PASTA

"In this country, it is a sort of luxury among the upper classes," Sarah Rorer wrote in 1886. She was not talking about caviar or truffles; she was talking about pasta.

As Mrs. Rorer was writing these words (in *Mrs. Rorer's Cookbook*), she could not have known what was about to happen: that within four years, a vast Italian immigration to this country would begin and would continue for twenty years; that a depression in the 1890s would dictate a need for economically made meals, including noodle dishes of all descriptions from every ethnic group; or that a Department of Agriculture agronomist named Dr. Mark Carleton would persuade American farmers to begin growing durum wheat. This last achievement removed the necessity of importing hard-wheat pasta from Italy, which would have ceased anyway when trade with Italy was curtailed during World War I. These events popularized pasta and made it more widely available, but they by no means introduced the food to this country.

By 1886, pasta had already been around for a hundred years, brought to our shores by none other than Thomas Jefferson. When he visited Naples in 1786, Jefferson was impressed by the sheets and ribbons of pasta hanging over the roadways and alleys throughout the town. On every street corner, he could see the maccheronaro selling dried macaroni or cooking it on the spot, presumably al dente. In his notes, Jefferson recorded his fascination with a pasta-making machine, which he arranged to import, along with quite a few crates of "maccarony," some olive oil, Parmesan cheese, and anchovies. Once back in Monticello, he developed his recipe: two eggs, a wine glass measure of milk, a pinch of salt, and enough hard flour to make a firm dough, a formula perfectly serviceable today. Using his own spaghetti die, he made pasta for his guests.

In this distinguished company, pasta acquired an early reputation for "luxury among the upper classes," but by the time of the Gold Rush, pasta was a common meal at Italian restaurants in almost every California mining town. By this century, "spaghetti joints" everywhere began attracting people in droves because of the generous quantity of food offered and also because the meal generally included a bottle of Chianti. In Greenwich Village, San Francisco, and other urban areas, Italian neighborhoods grew up next door to artist communities whose Bohemian element reveled in the earthiness of spaghetti, handmade pastas, and imported cheeses bought from shops with comfortable, foreign ambiances. Chicago developed a special noodle dish around 1912 consisting of ground beef, tomatoes, onions, and peppers. It was originally called "German Chop Suey" but was changed, during World War II, to just plain chop suey. Of course, there were also plenty of dishes with real Chinese noodles and real German noodles. In the twenties, incoming Greek populations added to the already plentiful pasta menus. St. Louis created a distinctively American variation called Toasted Ravioli unknown anywhere else.

Perhaps it is this very range of possibilities that accounts for the current ardor over pasta. We can follow a traditional pasta recipe from the many that make up our rich culinary heritage; or we can mix different ethnic or regional elements, combining whatever is most intriguing or appealing. In this country, pasta is almost synonymous with innovation. A hundred years after Mrs. Rorer, this informality and versatility are pasta's true luxury.

As interesting as are the ingredients and sauces, pasta can also be fascinating for its shapes, which usually determine its name. Our recipes include "little tongues" (linguine), "conch shells" (conchiglie), and "bows" or "butterflies" (farfalle). If you can't find any "little ribbons" (fettuccine) or "narrow cuttings" (tagliarini), you can always use some "string" (spaghetti).

Preceding the recipes are directions for homemade pasta, another luxury worth treating yourself to. Of all commercial pastas, we recommend those made from hard durum wheat, or semolina, because they absorb very little water when cooked and have good taste and bite. We have had best results with the imported brands Agnesi and DeCecco. Or try to find a market that sells different shapes from open bins so you can buy only what you need and experiment with various types.

Finally, we should like to quote someone who claims, and indeed possesses, no expertise whatever on the subject of pasta. Woody Allen, in a mock-restaurant review, called pasta "an expression of Italian Neo-Realistic starch" with a "wry and puckish" nature useful "as an instrument of social change." This approach to pasta is consistent with ours: in other words, don't take it too seriously. Have fun with it. Try these sauces, make up your own, substitute one shape or type of pasta for another.

With pasta, especially homemade pasta, you can be adventurous, take chances. No matter what you do, or what else you serve with it, people will usually tell you the pasta was the best part of the meal.

Basic Egg Pasta and Variations

Basic Egg Pasta

1¾ cups all-purpose flour plus
½ cup semolina,** or 2¼
cups all-purpose flour

½ teaspoon salt
3 large eggs
1 tablespoon olive oil

By hand: In a large bowl mix flours and salt. Add eggs and olive oil and mix well until a smooth dough is formed. Wrap and rest at room temperature about 30 minutes before rolling out.

With food processor: Place flours and salt in a food processor bowl and process briefly to combine. With machine running add eggs and olive oil and process until a ball of dough is formed.

Roll out by hand and cut into desired shapes or use pasta machine following manufacturer's directions.

Makes about 1½ pounds pasta, enough for 6 to 8 people

NOTE: Recipe may be halved, doubled, tripled, et cetera. If making ahead, sprinkle a flat towel with flour, spread pasta on towel, and sprinkle with additional flour, tossing occasionally. Allow to sit at room temperature until ready to use.

Variations

Pasta Verde: In Basic Egg Pasta recipe, substitute ¼ pound fresh spinach, pureed, for 1 egg.

Red Pepper Pasta: Substitute ¼ cup roasted red bell pepper* puree for 1 egg.

Herbed Pasta: Add 1 teaspoon each chopped fresh oregano, rosemary, and thyme, or ½ teaspoon each dried, to flour.

Basil Pasta: Add ¼ cup finely chopped fresh basil leaves to flour.

Tomato Pasta: Substitute 4 tablespoons imported tomato paste,** for one egg.

Buckwheat Pasta: Substitute ½ cup buckwheat flour (available at health-food stores) for ½ cup all-purpose flour.

Fettuccine with Shrimp in Saffron Cream Sauce

2 tablespoons butter
2 shallots, chopped
½ cup dry vermouth
½ cup fish stock* or clam juice
1 cup heavy cream
½ teaspoon saffron threads
1 pound shrimp, shelled and cleaned

salt and pepper
1 recipe Basic Egg Pasta (see page 177), cut into fettuccine
salted water
4 tablespoons chopped fresh parsley for garnish

In a large skillet melt butter and sauté shallots until wilted. Add vermouth and fish stock and cook about 5 minutes, until syrupy. Pour in cream and saffron, and cook until thick, about 8 minutes. Add shrimp and cook just until pink.

Remove three-quarters of the shrimp and set aside.

Puree shrimp-cream sauce until smooth in a food processor or blender, and reheat gently with salt and pepper.

Cook pasta in a large pot of boiling salted water for about 3 minutes and drain. Toss with shrimp sauce, garnish with reserved whole shrimp, and sprinkle with parsley.

Serves 6 to 8

Pasta Verde with Tomato-Pecan Sauce

3 tablespoons olive oil
1 small onion, chopped
1 clove garlic, minced
1 cup finely chopped toasted
   pecans*
½ cup Zinfandel or hearty red
   wine
1 pound ripe tomatoes,
   seeded and pureed
2 tablespoons imported
   tomato paste**

pinch sugar
1 teaspoon chopped fresh
   rosemary leaves, or ½
   teaspoon dried rosemary
1 bay leaf
   salt and pepper
½ cup heavy cream
1 recipe Pasta Verde (see
   page 177), cut into
   fettuccine or linguine
   salted water

In a medium skillet heat oil and sauté onion, garlic, and pecans. Add remaining ingredients except cream and cook over medium-high heat, uncovered, until thickened, about 10 minutes. Add cream and cook another 3 minutes.

Cook pasta in a large pot of boiling salted water for 3 minutes, drain well, and toss with sauce.

Serves 6 to 8

Red Pepper Pasta with Tapenade

4 ounces imported black
   olives,** pitted
4 ounces green olives, pitted
¼ cup capers, rinsed and
   drained
1 7½-ounce can albacore
   tuna, drained
1 1-ounce can anchovy fillets,
   rinsed and drained
2 cloves garlic

1 ripe tomato, seeded
½ cup chopped fresh parsley
¼ cup fresh lemon juice
   salt and pepper
1 tablespoon brandy
½ cup olive oil
1 recipe Red Pepper Pasta
   (see page 177), cut into
   fettuccine
   salted water

Puree all sauce ingredients in a food processor until smooth and thick.

Cook fettuccine in a large pot of boiling salted water for about 3 minutes. Drain and mix with tapenade sauce. Wonderful hot or cold.

Serves 6

Herbed Tagliarini with Creamy Wild Mushroom Sauce

2 tablespoons butter
2 tablespoons olive oil
2 shallots, chopped
1 clove garlic, minced
1 ounce porcini mushrooms,** soaked in 1 cup hot water for 30 minutes
½ pound mushrooms, washed and sliced
¼ pound chanterelles, washed and sliced
1½ cups heavy cream
salt and pepper
½ cup chopped fresh parsley
1 recipe Herbed Pasta (see page 177), cut into tagliarini
salted water

In a large skillet heat butter and oil and sauté shallots and garlic until wilted.

Meanwhile, drain porcini and reserve soaking liquid. (Strain liquid if it seems sandy.) Chop porcini. Add all mushrooms to the skillet and cook until they release liquids. Continue cooking until all liquids are evaporated. Add ½ cup of reserved soaking liquid along with cream. Cook over high heat until thickened, about 8 minutes. Add salt and pepper and parsley.

Cook pasta in a large pot of boiling salted water for 3 minutes. Drain, mix with sauce, and serve immediately.

Serves 6 to 8

Tomato Linguine with Broccoli Flowers and Goat Cheese

1 bunch broccoli, stems
  peeled and ends cut off
4 quarts water
4 tablespoons butter
1 tablespoon minced garlic
1 cup heavy cream

¼ pound goat cheese**
1 recipe Tomato Pasta (see
  page 178), cut into
  linguine
salted water

Cook broccoli in 4 quarts boiling water for 3 minutes. Drain in colander and run under cold water until broccoli is no longer hot to the touch. Cut stems into 3-inch matchsticks and flowerets into small pieces. Set aside.

In a medium skillet melt butter and sauté garlic until soft. Add cream and bring to a boil. Lower heat to medium and add goat cheese, cooking until cheese melts into cream and is very hot. Add broccoli and stir well. Remove from heat.

Cook pasta in a large pot of boiling salted water for 3 minutes. Drain and toss with sauce.

Serves 6

Buckwheat Pasta with
Endive, Smoked Chicken, and Fontina

4 tablespoons olive oil
2 cloves garlic, halved
2 heads Belgian endive,
  julienned*
¼ pound smoked chicken (or
  smoked turkey breast), cut
  into strips
1 recipe Buckwheat Pasta
  (see page 178), cut into
  thin noodles

salted water
¼ pound Fontina cheese,
  shredded
½ cup chopped fresh parsley
salt and pepper

In a medium skillet heat olive oil and sauté garlic until brown. Remove garlic and discard.

In the same pan sauté endive until slightly wilted, about 3 minutes. Add chicken and heat through.

Meanwhile, cook pasta in a large pot of boiling salted water for 4 minutes. Drain pasta and toss with endive-chicken mixture, adding more oil if pasta seems too dry. Sprinkle with Fontina and parsley and toss gently again. Season to taste with salt and pepper.

Serves 6

Basil Pasta with Two Salmons

3 tablespoons butter
1 pound salmon, skinned,
  boned, and cut into 1-inch
  pieces
2 shallots, chopped

1 clove garlic, minced
2 ripe tomatoes, seeded and
  coarsely chopped
¼ cup vodka
¼ cup white wine

¼ cup fish stock* or bottled
  clam broth
1 cup heavy cream
½ cup chopped fresh basil
  leaves
¼ pound smoked salmon,**
  cut into thin strips

salt and pepper
1 recipe Basil Pasta (see page
  178), cut into fettuccine
salted water
chopped parsley for garnish

In a large skillet melt butter and sauté salmon until it starts to lose its raw color, about 3 minutes. Remove and reserve.

In the same skillet sauté shallots, garlic, and tomatoes until wilted, about 4 minutes. Add vodka, wine, and fish stock, bring to a boil, and cook for about 8 minutes, until liquid becomes syrupy. Add cream and basil and cook for 5 minutes, until cream begins to thicken.

Return salmon to sauce, add smoked salmon, and heat through. Taste before seasoning with salt and pepper, since smoked salmon can be rather salty.

Cook pasta in a large pot of boiling salted water for 3 minutes. Drain well and toss with salmon sauce. Sprinkle with chopped parsley and serve immediately.

Serves 6 to 8

Pasta Shells with Smoked Trout and Red and Yellow Peppers

2 tablespoons butter
1 tablespoon olive oil
1 bunch green onions, white
  part only, chopped
1 red bell pepper, seeded,
  deveined, and cut into thin
  strips
1 yellow bell pepper, seeded,
  deveined, and cut into thin
  strips

1 cup heavy cream
½ cup half and half
¼ pound smoked trout,**
  skinned, filleted, and cut
  into strips
1 pound small pasta shells
salted water
½ cup chopped fresh chives
  for garnish

183

In a skillet heat butter and oil and sauté green onions and peppers until wilted. Add cream and half and half and cook over high heat until slightly thickened, about 10 minutes. Reduce heat, add smoked trout to cream and cook another 2 minutes.

Cook pasta in a large pot of boiling salted water for about 8 minutes, then drain. Toss sauce with pasta and sprinkle with chopped chives.

Serves 6 to 8

Pasta Bows in Walnut-Zucchini Sauce

½ cup olive oil
½ cup vegetable oil
2 cups toasted walnuts,* plus
　½ cup coarsely chopped
　toasted walnuts
½ cup grated Parmesan cheese
2 tablespoons chopped fresh
　parsley
¼ cup chopped onion

2 cloves garlic
1 cup sliced zucchini,
　blanched,* plus 1 small
　zucchini, finely grated
½ teaspoon oregano
　salt and pepper
1 pound pasta bows or
　butterflies
　salted water

In a food processor puree oils, 2 cups walnuts, cheese, parsley, onion, garlic, sliced zucchini, and seasonings. Transfer sauce to a pot and heat gently but do not boil.

Cook pasta in a large pot of boiling salted water for about 8 minutes. Drain and toss with sauce. Garnish with chopped walnuts and grated zucchini.

Serves 6 to 8

Wild, Wild Pasta with Watercress

4 tablespoons butter
½ pound assorted fresh, wild mushrooms (such as shitake, chanterelles, morels), slivered
¼ pound domestic mushrooms, thinly sliced
¾ cup chicken stock*
2 cloves garlic, peeled and halved
1½ cups heavy cream
3 ounces Muenster cheese, shredded

2 tablespoons grated Parmesan cheese
½ teaspoon freshly ground nutmeg
salt and pepper
8 ounces freshly cooked pasta, homemade or good-quality commercial
1½ cups cooked wild rice**
1 bunch watercress, leaves only, coarsely chopped

In a large skillet melt butter and sauté mushrooms over medium-high heat for about 8 minutes. Pour in stock, bring to a boil, reduce heat, and cook until slightly syrupy, about 5 minutes. Add garlic and cream and simmer for 8 minutes (cream will have thickened slightly). Remove garlic and discard. Add cheeses, nutmeg, salt, and pepper, and cook just above a simmer until cheeses melt.

In a large pot or bowl toss sauce with pasta and wild rice, sprinkle with watercress, and mix again.

Serves 6

Melon Seed Pasta with Artichokes and Feta Cheese

2 tablespoons olive oil
1 pound fresh or frozen
   artichoke hearts,* cooked
2 cloves garlic, minced
2 leeks, white part only,
   chopped
1 red bell pepper, seeded,
   deveined, and diced
1 pound melon seed pasta,**
   cooked 4 minutes
3 tablespoons butter

3 tablespoons flour
2 cups milk
3 tablespoons minced fresh
   tarragon, or 1 tablespoon
   dried tarragon
¼ cup chopped fresh parsley
   pinch cayenne
   salt and pepper
½ pound California or
   imported feta cheese,
   crumbled

Preheat oven to 350°F.

In a medium skillet heat oil and sauté artichoke hearts, garlic, leeks, and red pepper for about 4 minutes. Toss with cooked pasta in a large bowl.

In a small pan melt butter and stir in flour. Cook this roux over low heat for about 3 minutes, stirring constantly. Remove pan from heat and pour in milk, stirring until smooth. Return to heat and cook until thick. When mixture starts to boil, remove from heat and add tarragon, parsley, cayenne, salt and pepper, and half the feta.

Toss feta mixture with cooked pasta, then place pasta in a 9″-×-13″ baking dish and top with remaining feta cheese. Bake until bubbly, about 25 minutes. Remove from oven and let stand for about 10 minutes before serving.

Serves 8

SPECIALS
OF THE DAY

Even in the most unpretentious restaurant, a bit of drama attends the waiter's recitation of the Specials of the Day. These dishes always have a certain immediacy. They express the cook's sensitivity to the moment: to a triumphant hunt in the wild-mushroom fields, to a successful expedition where the salmon trout run. The day's specials reflect not only the climate but the weather. They are the rewards of taking advantage of the season's offerings.

In many of today's restaurants—especially but not exclusively, in

California—the menu changes monthly or weekly, often even daily. The cook is not restricted to poaching sole when the day's catch of delicate thin sand dabs is so magnificent, nor compelled to do carrots on the very day that asparagus is making its debut. It is in this spirit that we have named this chapter "Specials of the Day." But we know from experience that it takes more than spirit to get dinner on the table.

Even the most dedicated home cooks seldom find the time to roam the hills for wild berries or raise their own quail. However, one quick glance at the newspaper gives a good cross section of what's in season. Once you know what's available, what's possible, you can go down the list of these specials and decide what appeals to you that day. Based, for the most part, on fresh seasonal ingredients, these recipes are designed around what you can buy in the market and make at home, not what you might order in a professionally staffed restaurant. You will find these specials practical, often quite simple, and organized specifically for the home cook.

Often these recipes involve a judicious blending of herbs or an inspired juxtaposition of textures, rather than a lot of manual dexterity. The smoky with the buttery-sweet, the citrus with the savory: Each dish has an especially clean, untrammeled goodness. As examples of today's California cooking, they are often richly flavored but lightly sauced; complex in taste but simple to prepare. From grilled lamb and fish to a Poussin Pot Pie, these specials draw upon the best of America's cooking, past and present. If there is a disadvantage here, it is that these specials may lead to that awful pause in the dinner conversation while everyone agrees that this is probably the best food they've had since the last time you made dinner for them.

To plan a complete dinner around these recipes, you may want to consult the chapter "Suggested Menus and Wines."

Truffled Salmon in Champagne
Grilled Salmon with Four Butters
Molded Salmon Quenelles Napped in Lime Ginger
Parchment-Baked Halibut in Basil Butter

Grilled Red Snapper with Tomato Salsa Cruda
Petrale Sole Breaded in Pecans Served in Herb-Nut Butter
Pan-fried Sand Dabs with Ginger-Lemon Butter
Scallop Sauté Niçoise with Toasted Pecans
Shrimp with Vermouth and Sun-dried Tomatoes
California Jambalaya with Red Peppers and Saffron
Berkeley Bouillabaisse
Breast of Chicken Poached on Shredded Baby Carrots and
Leeks
Chicken Sautéed with Apples and Applejack
Chicken Breasts with Artichoke-Walnut Dressing
Whole Chicken Stuffed Under the Skin with
Sourdough Crumbs, Lemon, and Garlic
Drumsticks Stuffed with Pistachioed Mousseline
Poussin Pot Pie
Duck Stuffed with Fresh Figs and Louisiana Pecan Rice
Roast Duck Glazed with Green Peppercorn Mustard and
Nectarine Chutney
Grilled Squab with Lavender Honey and Black Pepper
Sautéed Medallions of Veal in Hot-Sweet Mustard
Veal Scallops Sauced with Asparagus Puree
Veal Ragout with Artichokes, Brandied Raisins, and
Crème Fraiche
Breast of Veal Stuffed with Wild Rice and
Garlicky Mustard Greens
Shredded Beef with Mushrooms Served on Crisp Romaine
Allspice- and Cinnamon-Scented Beef Ragout with
Dried Fruits and Almonds
Zinfandel Beef Stew with Celery Root and Parsnips
Lamb Scallopini with Hazelnuts
Sautéed Baby Lamb Chops with Shallot Puree
Spring Lamb Simmered on Herb Branches with
Chestnuts and Sugar Peas
Tender Lamb Tossed with California Chèvre,
Olives, and Tomatoes
Grilled Leg of Lamb with Hot-Sweet Mustard and Sherry
Vinegar
Loin of Pork and Dried Apples Sautéed in Walnut Oil and
Hard Cider

Truffled Salmon in Champagne

Since the seventeenth century, when the process of making champagne was perfected, very little champagne has been set aside for kitchen use. In fact, the home of the world's most famous wine, Champagne, is about the only region in all of France where the cuisine does not make use of its own wine in its cooking. In California, by contrast, the growing champagne industry is a tempting resource for the experimental cook. Although no cooking method has yet managed to preserve the bubbles, many recipes, such as ours, take advantage of champagne's ability to infuse food with a characteristic, faintly sweet "champagneness." Along with its subtle flavor, the champagne also imparts to this dish that special spirit of celebration of which it alone is capable. (Not that the truffles don't do their part!) Perhaps most exhilarating of all, any nice, inexpensive California sparkling wine will serve quite well in this recipe. However, if you would like to continue with the same champagne for the meal, pick out something you'd like to drink as well.

1½ cups California champagne	8 tablespoons butter
½ cup fish stock*	½ cup heavy cream
1 shallot, chopped	½-ounce can truffle
6 1-inch-thick salmon fillets	peelings, drained
or steaks	salt and pepper

In a large shallow pan, bring champagne and fish stock to a boil. Add shallot and reduce heat to a bare simmer. Place salmon in simmering liquid, cover, and cook over low heat for 8 minutes. Remove salmon and keep warm.

Strain cooking liquid into a small saucepan and boil over high heat until reduced* to about ½ cup. Stir in butter piece by piece, whisking continuously, until sauce has thickened. Add cream, truffle peelings, and salt and pepper to taste, and cook another minute.

Nap each serving of salmon with some of the sauce.

Serves 6

TRUFFLE PEELINGS NOTE: Like truffles, truffle peelings are available in infinitesimal-size cans, protected in the vaults of grocery stores and specialty shops. They are exactly what their name describes—peelings —and as such are much less expensive than the truffles themselves, though they communicate a similar aromatic intensity. If unavailable, you may try a bit of California golden caviar** as a lovely glistening substitute. Instead of stirring it into the sauce, simply top each serving with a little golden dollop. If all else fails, and you can afford it, regular ordinary fresh truffles will do.

Grilled Salmon with Four Butters

The only true American sauce, observed one eighteenth-century traveler to this country, is melted butter. Served in sauce boats or oversized cups, melted butter put the finishing touch on many cooked vegetables and even roast beef. On the frontier, where butter was scarce, the same idea prevailed in the form of venison grease and bear's oil, though these recipes, for obvious reasons, have been less enthusiastically preserved.

As a spread for bread, olive oil was once much more popular than butter, which was originally used as a medicine. "Marseilles butter" actually is oil, just as "Marseilles vanilla" is really garlic. Essentially, butter is an ancient method of preserving milk, a simple and necessary invention of herdsmen. Seasoned butters, or composed butters, are savory combinations of herbs or seasonings mixed with good basic fresh butter, cooked or uncooked. We offer four of them here, each with its distinct character, a generous array which adds a lavish touch to a simple preparation.

Baja Butter

4 tablespoons butter, room
temperature
1 small jalapeño pepper,*
seeded and deveined
½ teaspoon ground cumin

1 tablespoon imported
tomato paste**
1 tablespoon chopped fresh
coriander leaves
salt and pepper

Good Green Butter

4 tablespoons butter, room
temperature
1 tablespoon chopped fresh
parsley
1 tablespoon chopped fresh
watercress

1 tablespoon chopped fresh
chives
salt and pepper

Garlic-Nut Butter

4 tablespoons butter, room
temperature
2 cloves garlic, minced
2 tablespoons ground
hazelnuts

1 tablespoon chopped fresh
parsley
1 tablespoon Pernod
salt and pepper

Orange-Saffron Butter

4 tablespoons butter, room
temperature
¼ teaspoon saffron, dissolved
in 1 tablespoon fresh
orange juice

½ teaspoon grated orange
zest*
1 teaspoon chopped shallot
salt and pepper

6 1-inch-thick salmon fillets
or steaks

vegetable oil
salt and pepper

Make each butter by pureeing the ingredients in a blender or food processor. Store each butter in a separate crock. Butters may be prepared well in advance and stored, covered, in the refrigerator. They should be brought to room temperature before serving.

Heat grill or broiler until very hot. Blot salmon dry, brush with oil, and sprinkle each side with salt and pepper. Grill or broil for 5 minutes on each side.

Serve salmon surrounded by individual servings of the different butters or pass the crocks around the table.

Serves 6

Molded Salmon Quenelles Napped in Lime Ginger

This is one of the most easily accomplished of the recipes in this book, though it is based on a dish that once demanded enormous energy and patience. The difference is the replacement of the mortar and pestle by the food processor. This recipe is even easier because the quenelles are packed safely in molds for cooking instead of being dropped precariously into simmering stock.

We like to think of quenelles as dumplings, since that seems more homey and certainly more American (Larousse Gastronomique, in fact, defines them as dumplings). The word itself derives from the Anglo-Saxon knyll, meaning "to grind or pound." From this root, we get the old Pennsylvania Dutch dish, Schnitz and Knepp (apples and dumplings). It is also clear, etymologically at least, that a quenelle is a knaidle is a gnocchi.

Quenelles

1½ pounds salmon fillets, skinned
salt and pepper
2 teaspoons chopped fresh dill

1 egg yolk
1½ cups heavy cream

Sauce

4 tablespoons butter
1 shallot, chopped
2 slices fresh ginger, finely minced
3 tablespoons flour
1 cup fish or chicken stock*
juice and grated zest* of 1 lime, plus 1 lime, thinly sliced

1 cup heavy cream
1 teaspoon ground ginger
salt and pepper

Have all ingredients for quenelles well chilled. Cut salmon into 1-inch cubes. Place in the bowl of a food processor with salt and pepper, dill, and yolk. Process until smooth. While motor is running, slowly add the cream through the feed tube. Chill mixture about 30 minutes.

Preheat oven to 325°F and butter well twelve 4-ounce oven-proof molds or ramekins. Fill each mold three-quarters full with salmon mixture. Place in bain marie.* Cover entire bain marie with buttered parchment paper* or foil and bake for about 25 minutes. You may leave in bain marie until ready to unmold.

To make sauce: Melt butter in a saucepan and sauté shallot and ginger until soft. Stir in flour and cook for about 3 minutes over low heat (do not let flour color). Add stock, lime juice, grated lime zest, and cream and continue cooking over low heat, stirring with whisk, until thickened. Add ground ginger and salt and pepper to taste.

To serve, unmold quenelles, draining any liquid that may have accumulated into sauce. Nap with sauce and garnish with lime slices.

Serves 6

Parchment-Baked Halibut in Basil Butter

Baking anything in parchment helps retain juices and flavors. The parchment itself browns and puffs during cooking, making a dramatic impression on unsuspecting guests, who seldom confuse it with a bag lunch despite a slight superficial similarity.

Veal chops, rabbit, sand dabs, and Spanish mackerel have been known to benefit from this method, but not as much as the roving bands of thieves once associated with a dish called Bandits' Lamb. In that unusually titled recipe, the entire meal was prepared in and eaten from wrappings; it was palatable as well as portable, an important consideration for such galloping gourmets.

Another famous wrapped dish, Pompano en Papillote, originated in the great kitchens of Antoine's in New Orleans. Parchment cut in the shape of a heart encases the legendary pompano, pride of the Gulf Coast, a fish "as delicious as the less criminal forms of sin," according to Mark Twain. The words en Papillote or "in paper" originally referred to a confection wrapped in silver or gold paper containing a message or poem. The silver has its modern counterpart, perhaps, in aluminum foil, which will work equally well in this dish. In fact, we have noticed no difference at all as far as taste is concerned, though we feel the parchment makes a handsomer presentation. In either case, the method produces a basil-anointed halibut that is not only carefree but perfect every time.

6 1-inch-thick halibut fillets or steaks	1 teaspoon oregano
salt and pepper	2 cloves garlic
¼ cup white wine	6 12"-×-10" sheets of parchment*
4 tablespoons butter	2 zucchini, shredded
½ cup fresh basil leaves	vegetable oil

Preheat oven to 500°F.

Season both sides of fish with salt and pepper. Sprinkle with wine. Set aside.

In a food processor or blender make a paste of the butter, basil, oregano, and garlic.

Place each fish fillet on the lower half of each parchment sheet. Sprinkle fish with zucchini and dot with basil butter paste. Brush edges of the parchment with oil and fold over to enclose fish, pressing edges with finger (the oil will seal the edges together). Make double folds along all three edges and place on baking sheet or directly on oven rack. Bake for 10 minutes.

May be served directly from the parchment, on individual plates for a very dramatic, but sometimes messy, effect.

Serves 6

Grilled Red Snapper with Tomato Salsa Cruda

When the Industrial Revolution brought improved refrigeration, transportation, and preservation methods, food began to arrive at the table in much better condition than ever before. Sauce lost one of its major roles, that of disguising the taste of less-than-fresh meat, fish, and game. Heavy, overpowering sauces yielded to lighter fumets and essences, which accented rather than camouflaged the flavor of foods. Nothing could be more basic than this dish, which depends completely on the radiant freshness of snapper and uncooked salsa.

Similar to gazpacho, this cumin-scented sauce is a relative of the early California Salsa, which was also uncooked but much less spicy. Two sauces common in Texas and the Southwest are also not-too-distant relations: Sauce Serrano, hot with chile peppers, and Ranchero Sauce, redolent of cumin. These cooked, tomato-based sauces owe their origins to Spain and its influence on the cooking of the western United States. But a late-nineteenth-century American cookbook carries an interesting recipe for an uncooked tomato sauce; it is called "Professor Rachel Bodley's Tomato Catsup."

If the tomatoes are good, you can't go wrong with this recipe. As for the state of fish, we love the obvious but often-overlooked advice of Andre Simon: "Do not listen to the man or woman who has to sell the fish; look at the fish. . . ."

6 medium to large snapper fillets

salt and pepper
juice of 2 limes

Tomato Salsa Cruda

2 large tomatoes, peeled, seeded,* and coarsely chopped
1 onion, chopped
2 cloves garlic, minced

3–4 jalapeño peppers,* seeded, deveined, and cut into strips
½ cup chopped fresh coriander

pinch sugar

½ teaspoon ground coriander

½ teaspoon ground cumin

salt and pepper

Blot fish fillets dry. Sprinkle both sides with salt and pepper and rub with lime juice. Set aside to marinate for 30 minutes.

To make salsa: In a bowl mix all ingredients together, saving a bit of coriander for garnish. The salsa improves in flavor if made a few hours before using.

Preheat grill or broiler until very hot. Cook snapper fillets for about 3 minutes on each side. (Because of the lime juice marinade, the fish needs less cooking time.) Serve snapper topped with salsa and garnished with fresh coriander. If there is extra sauce, pass it separately.

Serves 6

Petrale Sole Breaded in Pecans Served in Herb-Nut Butter

Petrale is West Coast sole. It is much favored for its delicacy of texture and taste, especially when poached or lightly sautéed. With its mild, distinctive flavor, petrale closely resembles rex or English sole, though it can be much larger, up to five pounds. It is perfect for stuffing with seafood or spinach and is always available filleted.

In this recipe, the petrale emerges sun-gold and crisp from its coating of pecans and cayenne. Underneath, the sweet flesh is tender, flaky, scented with the buttery oregano sauce. Any North American flatfish, fillets of sole or flounder, will take beautifully to this preparation.

6 petrale sole fillets or thick
fillets of sole or flounder
1 egg beaten with 1
tablespoon milk
1 cup finely chopped pecans

salt and pepper
½ teaspoon cayenne
4 tablespoons butter
2 teaspoons vegetable oil

Herbed Nut Butter

6 tablespoons butter
2 tablespoons ground pecans
1 tablespoon lemon juice
salt and pepper

2 tablespoons chopped fresh
parsley
1 teaspoon oregano

Blot fillets dry. Dip each fillet in egg mixture and dredge in pecans mixed with salt, pepper, and cayenne. Let dry on rack about 5 minutes.

In a large skillet heat butter and oil. Sauté fillets for about 3 minutes on each side. Remove to a platter and keep warm.

To make herb butter: Heat butter in same skillet and add remaining ingredients. Cook just until hot, about 2 minutes. Pour over fish and serve.

Serves 6

Pan-fried Sand Dabs with Ginger-Lemon Butter

Just thinking about cornmeal-coated, deep-fried fish recalls Mississippi and all the other southern contenders for the title of catfish capital. Quick cooking not only preserves the sweet delicacy of any flaky, moist fish, but also ensures a corn-toasted dimension to the taste. Our recipe is a melding of such seemingly different influences as the Deep South and the Asian: It adds the snap of ginger to country-crisp cornmeal and crosses deep-frying with stir-frying. Sand dabs are a small, West Coast flounder; in other areas substitute any sole, flounder, or butterfish.

¼ cup cornmeal
½ cup flour
1 teaspoon ground ginger
1 teaspoon salt
2 pounds sand dabs, cleaned
1 cup milk

¼ cup vegetable oil
¼ cup butter
½-inch slice fresh ginger, finely minced (see Note)
juice of ½ lemon

Mix cornmeal, flour, ginger, and salt in a bowl. Dip sand dabs in milk and dredge in flour mixture. Let dry on rack for 10 minutes.

In a large skillet heat oil and brown fish (see Note) for 3 minutes on each side. Remove from skillet and keep warm.

Heat butter in skillet and add fresh ginger and lemon juice. Cook for about 2 minutes on low heat. Pour over sand dabs and serve immediately.

Serves 6

PAN-FRYING NOTE: For this or any recipe with breading or coating, the oil must be very hot, about 375°F, when cooking begins. If it is not hot enough, the coating will not crisp but will fall apart into the pan. When the oil starts to glaze, throw in a bit of batter to test it. Drying out the breaded fish on a rack, as we suggest, helps set the coating.

GINGER NOTE: Ginger that is rock hard and fresh does not have to be peeled.

Scallop Sauté Niçoise with Toasted Pecans

Scallops have always had a sort of charisma, attracting everyone from lovers of shellfish to lovers of sea shells. It must have been their eyesight that fascinated Euell Gibbons, who tells us, in Stalking the Blue-Eyed Scallop, that they have about fifty eyes. Even the names of scallops are intriguing, Canadian digby, zig-zag, and calico being a few of the three hundred species, all of which are edible. They're also fun to watch, since they have an unusual method of moving around, which can only be compared to hopping.

They lend their name to many recipes which contain no scallops at all; scalloped refers to dishes prepared and served in scallop shells. For centuries, they have been a symbol of Saint James, immortalized in the famous Coquilles St. Jacques. Their sweet, lush taste, often compared to lobster, is perfect for various lime-"cooked" seviches and, of course, for scallops with olives and pecans.

¼ cup flour	½ cup Niçoise olives,**
salt and pepper	pitted and halved
2 pounds scallops	1 cup white wine
4 tablespoons butter	½ cup heavy cream
1 tablespoon shallot, minced	¼ cup chopped fresh parsley
2 cloves garlic, minced	for garnish
1 large tomato, peeled,*	1 cup coarsely chopped
seeded, and chopped	toasted pecans* for garnish

Mix flour and salt and pepper in a bowl and dredge scallops lightly.

In a large skillet melt butter and sauté scallops over medium-high heat, about 4 minutes, tossing well. Remove to a plate and keep warm.

In the same skillet sauté shallot and garlic until slightly limp, adding more butter if necessary. Add tomato and olives and cook for another 2 minutes. Deglaze* pan with wine and cook until reduced* and slightly syrupy, about 8 minutes. Add cream and return scallops to skillet just to heat through. Sprinkle with chopped parsley and toasted pecans. Wonderful with green pasta.

Serves 8

Shrimp with Vermouth and Sun-dried Tomatoes

Mint is reportedly included in more recipes than any other aromatic herb. Perhaps this is due to its salubrious virtues, such as calming the stomach, killing fleas, warding off field mice, and last but surely not least, curing hangovers, though only if worn as a wreath on the brow. This single restorative property would be sufficient to explain the herb's appearance as afterdinner mints, popular even at the presidential table in the early days of the Republic. Martha Washington's cookbook contains a recipe for just such a confection, under the more delicate name of "Mint Cakes." Henry Clay found mint indispensable for his early-morning bourbon juleps, and outside Kentucky the herb was accompanied by rum, whiskey, or brandy at any (and every) hour of the day.

Mint's rather risqué beginnings can be traced to the nymph named Minthe, who enjoyed entwining herself among the limbs of other people's husbands. One enraged spouse reacted by stomping Minthe into the ground with such determination that she will stay there, as anyone knows who's ever planted mint, for all eternity. We introduce just a bit of this little vamp of an herb to intrigue the palate. But, as most people—including enraged mythological wives—would agree, a touch of mint can be quite provocative.

4 tablespoons olive oil
2 pounds large shrimp, peeled and deveined
1 shallot, chopped
1 clove garlic, minced
¼ cup sun-dried tomatoes,** cut into strips

½ cup dry vermouth
1 cup heavy cream
salt and pepper
½ cup chopped fresh mint for garnish

In a large skillet heat oil and quickly sauté shrimp, just until they turn pink. Do not overcook. Remove to a dish and keep warm.

Add shallot, garlic, and tomatoes, and sauté until wilted. Deglaze* pan with vermouth and cook until syrupy. Add cream and cook for another 5 minutes. Add salt and pepper to taste and return shrimp to pan. Reheat, sprinkle with chopped mint, and serve.

This dish is perfect served in a nest of fresh buttered noodles.

Serves 8

California Jambalaya with Red Peppers and Saffron

The word <u>jumble</u> has nothing to do with the Louisiana dish "jambalaya," except that it so accurately characterizes both its contents and its history. Basically, jambalaya is rice cooked with whatever the whim of the cook or the day's provender dictates. Perfectly legitimate jambalayas may harbor anything from a menagerie of seafood and sausages to a highly seasoned melange of chicken and vegetables. If, as one theory proposes, its name derives from the Spanish <u>jamon,</u> it may originally have contained only ham.

Jambalaya is often referred to as one of the great New Orleans–Creole creations. Some authorities insist, however, that it is more accurately described as a product of Cajun cookery. Also based in Louisiana's bayou country, the Cajun heritage derives from the French-Canadian fishermen and farmers exiled from Quebec in the mid-eighteenth century. Jambalaya's similarity to Paella Valenciana, especially in its flexibility of ingredients, suggests strong Spanish influences, also evident in this West Coast interpretation. Although we feel that just about any excuse to serve Dungeness crab will do, this is an especially fine one.

4 tablespoons olive oil
2 cloves garlic, minced
1 bunch leeks, white part only, thinly sliced
2 red bell peppers, seeded and cut into strips
2 jalapeño peppers,* seeded and deveined, cut into strips
2 tablespoons chopped fresh parsley
½ teaspoon saffron
¾ cup dry vermouth

¾ cup fish stock*
2 ears of corn, cleaned and cut into 2-inch-thick slices
2 dozen mussels, scrubbed
1 pound squid, cleaned and cut into rings
1 pound large shrimp, cleaned and shelled
1 large Dungeness crab, cooked, cut into 6 pieces
salt and pepper
½ cup toasted pine nuts* for garnish

In a large pot heat oil and sauté garlic, leeks, and peppers until wilted. Stir in parsley and saffron. Add vermouth and fish stock and bring to a gentle boil. Place corn and seafood in the pot, reduce to a simmer, cover, and cook for about 4 minutes. (Mussels should open at this time.) Taste for salt and pepper and correct seasonings.

Serve in soup plates over plain boiled rice, if you wish, and sprinkle with toasted pine nuts.

Serves 6

Berkeley Bouillabaisse

In 1750 the Boston Evening Post published a recipe for a fish stew made with wine, spices, and herbs. Up and down the Atlantic coast, more fish stew recipes followed, many of them published, a few forever secret. Some had fish, some shellfish, some both; flavorings were lemon, catsup, curry, apple cider, tomatoes, milk, pork, or just ground crackers. Even the names changed, though on that coast the word for fish stews was, more often than not, chowder. The word is supposedly derived from the French chaudière, a big pot in which fish—or any stew or thick soup—was cooked.

Two other French words, meaning "boil" and "stop" (i.e., to cook quickly), make up the name bouillabaisse, which became the glory of Louisiana's fish dishes. Based on redfish, blackfish, snapper, or, like all other fish stews, whatever came ashore that day, the southern version inspired paeans by the likes of William Makepeace Thackeray, who declared it better than any he'd ever had in Marseilles or Paris.

This recipe borrows the classic bouillabaisse custom of ladling the soup over toasted bread slices, though here they are spread with sorrel sauce.

Soup

¼ cup olive oil	large pinch saffron
2 leeks, white part only, sliced	large strip dried orange peel (with vegetable peeler remove strip from orange and let dry, uncovered, overnight before using)
1 onion, sliced	
1 large can tomatoes, or 2 pounds fresh coarsely chopped tomatoes	
6 cloves garlic, minced	8 cups fish stock*
1 teaspoon thyme	3 tablespoons chopped fresh parsley
1 teaspoon fennel seeds	

Fish

1 pound snapper, boned and cut into small pieces	½ pound shrimp, cleaned and shelled
1 pound halibut, boned and cut into small pieces	½ pound mussels, cleaned and debearded

Spicy Sorrel Sauce

3 cloves garlic, peeled	½ cup fresh bread crumbs
1–2 fresh jalapeño peppers,* deveined and seeded	1 egg yolk
1 cup sorrel leaves, stems removed	salt and pepper
	¾ cup olive oil

French bread, cut into ½-inch-thick slices

In a large stockpot heat olive oil and sauté leeks and onion for about 5 minutes, or until limp. Add tomatoes and garlic and sauté another 5 minutes. Stir in remaining ingredients and bring to a boil. Turn down to a simmer and cook, uncovered, about 30 minutes. Strain or puree soup and return to pot.

Bring soup back to a boil and add the fish. Simmer gently for about 5 minutes. Do not overcook.

In a food processor or blender puree all sauce ingredients except oil. While machine is running add oil slowly and process until mixture forms a mayonnaise-like consistency. Taste and correct seasonings.

To serve: Lightly toast slices of French bread. Spread toast with sorrel sauce and place in each soup plate. Ladle fish soup on top and pass any additional sauce.

Serves 6

Breast of Chicken Poached on Shredded Baby Carrots and Leeks

In a sense, the American chicken was born on November 14, 1849, at the first annual Boston Poultry Show. A man named Dr. John C. Bennet organized this unprecedented gathering of poultry to stir up interest in increased production and consumption of chickens. Chicken soon became a fad, the Boston Poultry Show returned by popular demand every year thereafter for a hundred years, and other cities across the country sponsored similar shows to display their own sophistication. Since then, chicken has certainly come to inhabit just about every pot in the country under the gustatory guises of Yankee Chicken Pie, Brunswick Stew, Chicken Corn Soup, and Southern Fried. For his efforts, Dr. Bennet has occasionally been called the "Father of the American Chicken," a title under which he was reportedly reluctant to be immortalized.

Our chicken recipe begins with butter-stewed fresh leeks and carrots bathed in white wine, dill, and mustard. Cooked atop this melange, the chicken breasts inherit all its considerable flavor and aroma. A final dash of dill makes it handsome as well.

4 tablespoons butter
1 bunch of baby carrots, peeled and shredded
1 bunch leeks, white part only, cleaned and julienned*
¼ cup white wine
¼ cup chicken stock*
2 tablespoons chopped fresh parsley

1 tablespoon chopped fresh dill
2 tablespoons hot-sweet mustard**
6 boned and skinned chicken breast halves
salt and pepper

In a large skillet or sauté pan melt butter and sauté carrots and leeks over medium heat, about 8 minutes, or until vegetables start to become limp. Add wine and stock and cook for another 2 minutes. Stir in parsley, dill, and mustard, cover, and cook for about 8 minutes, or until vegetables are soft. Place chicken breasts over vegetables, cover, and cook for 15 minutes over low heat. Add salt and pepper to taste.

To serve: Place a bed of carrots and leeks on each plate topped with a chicken breast half. Sprinkle with additional dill and/or parsley if desired.

Serves 6

Chicken Sautéed with Apples and Applejack

All them apples they used ter plant raound New Hampshire was jest fer cider. Eatin' apples come in style considdable later. The way them Old-Timers et their apples was in cider, and 'twas a good 'un.

Samule, the hired hand, in
A Sense of Humus by Bertha Damon

The loving labors of Johnny Appleseed (John Chapman), the nineteenth-century ecologist who planted apple seedlings from Pennsylvania through Indiana, have produced as much folklore as fruit. Of the seemingly limitless varieties that once covered the countryside, relatively few are widely marketed. North Grafton, Massachusetts, houses an apple museum growing many almost extinct varieties, such as Sterling, Yellow Newton, and Roxbury Russet.

In early New England, baked sweet potatoes and apples were a feast-day dish. Most farm kitchens put up an annual supply of apple butter and served it with every meal year-round. For some farmers, notably the French writer, statesman, and author of Letters from an American Farmer (1782), Michel de Crevecoeur, apple pie and milk was the staple main course meal every night throughout the long winter. In our countrified dish, cinnamon brings out the rural farm character of this warming meal.

2 tablespoons butter	5 pounds chicken pieces of
3 medium Golden Delicious	your choice
apples, peeled, cored, and	¾ cup heavy cream
cut into ¼-inch-thick	salt and pepper
slices	1 teaspoon cinnamon
4 tablespoons vegetable oil	¼ cup applejack

In a large skillet melt butter and sauté apples until they soften slightly, about 5 minutes. Remove and set aside.

Heat oil in same skillet and sauté the chicken pieces until golden. Reduce heat, cover, and cook over low flame for about 25 minutes. Remove to serving dish and keep warm.

Return apple slices to skillet, heat through, and arrange around chicken pieces. Add cream to skillet and deglaze,* scraping up cooking juices. Cook for about 5 minutes over medium-high heat until reduced* by half. Add salt and pepper, cinnamon, and applejack, and cook for another 3 minutes.

Pour sauce over chicken and serve.

Serves 6

Chicken Breasts with Artichoke-Walnut Dressing

This quietly spectacular dish uses boneless chicken like thin veal slices to enfold a delicious, oregano-flecked stuffing made with two California specialties-of-the-state, walnuts and artichokes. Both of these ancient foods are being rediscovered daily, as any of the latest restaurant menus will show. Whole roasted walnuts add substance to main course salads; and ground or chopped walnuts enrich sauces and soups. The high protein content and meaty qualities of walnuts make them attractive in many vegetable dishes.

Pairing walnuts and chicken is an Italian influence, as are many of the most ingenious renditions of artichokes. We have read of walnuts and artichokes served together as a dessert, but we prefer to eat them more toward the beginning or middle of meals. The interplay of their flavors is particularly harmonious in this stuffed chicken breast, which is quickly sautéed to crisp the outside slightly. A brief sojourn with the vermouth-infused pan juices enhances the individual flavors.

6 large skinned and boned chicken breast halves	3 tablespoons grated Parmesan cheese
12 fresh or frozen artichoke hearts, cooked* until tender	1 egg flour mixed with salt and pepper for dredging
½ cup toasted walnuts*	4 tablespoons butter
3 anchovy fillets	½ cup dry vermouth
½ teaspoon oregano	1 cup chicken stock*

Pound chicken breasts until thin and rectangular in shape.

For dressing: Finely chop 6 artichoke hearts, walnuts, and anchovies and place in a bowl. Mix in oregano, cheese, and egg until you have a fairly smooth forcemeat.

Spread about 1 tablespoon of dressing in center of each breast and fold edges over to make a neat package. Seal edges by pounding them lightly. Dredge the filled chicken breast in flour mixture and set aside.

In a large skillet melt butter and quickly brown chicken breasts, 3 minutes on each side. Remove breasts to a buttered baking dish.

Preheat oven to 350°F. Add vermouth and stock to skillet and cook over medium-high heat, deglazing* pan, about 8 minutes or until slightly thickened and syrupy. Pour over chicken in baking dish and bake, covered, for about 15 minutes. Remove cover and bake for another 5 minutes.

Serve garnished with remaining artichoke hearts.

Serves 6

Whole Chicken Stuffed Under the Skin with Sourdough Crumbs, Lemon, and Garlic

This stunning dish borrows some of its glory from the great French classic, Truffled Turkey. Stuffed between the flesh and skin with slices of Cognac-soaked truffles, the turkey is given a long marination to imbue it thoroughly with the precious flavors. The brilliant teacher and cook, Richard Olney, author of Simple French Food, certainly was affected by the truffled wonder in creating his famous stuffed chicken, Poulet Fendu Farci. He used ricotta blended with herbs and either zucchini, mushrooms, or spinach. In this recipe, the sourdough crumbs, mixed with garlic, grated cheese, and lemon zest, make a characteristically Californian stuffing.

The technique used here is not only a blessing for the flesh, keeping the breast basted and moist throughout, it also crisps the skin beautifully. It is uncomplicated to prepare, since the chicken skin pulls easily away from the flesh. Finally, because of the initial presplitting, the finished dish is simplicity to carve.

Chicken

1 3½-pound fryer
1 teaspoon salt
1 teaspoon paprika

2 tablespoons olive oil
1 tablespoon fresh lemon juice

Stuffing

¾ cup fresh bread crumbs made from sourdough bread
4 large cloves garlic, minced
3 tablespoons chopped fresh parsley
1 tablespoon grated lemon zest* (see Note)

2 tablespoons butter
3 tablespoons grated Parmesan cheese
salt and pepper
1 egg

Split the chicken along the back and lay it out flat, skin side up, in front of you. With the palm of your hand pound the breast, breaking the breast bone so that the chicken will lie even flatter and will be easier to stuff. With your fingers working between the flesh and skin, loosen the skin all over the chicken.

Mix salt, paprika, oil, and lemon juice in a bowl and rub into skin and cavity side of chicken. If you have time, allow the chicken to marinate for about 2 hours.

Preheat oven to 450°F. Mix all ingredients for stuffing together in a bowl until you have a stiff, smooth paste. Push the stuffing under the skin, a handful at a time, smoothing the skin on top. Continue until chicken is evenly stuffed all over.

Place chicken, still skin side up, in a roasting pan and bake for about 15 minutes. Reduce heat to 375° and roast another 45 minutes, basting with pan juices every 15 minutes.

Allow chicken to rest for about 10 minutes before carving.

This dish is divine hot, warm, or cold. It makes wonderful picnic fare.

Serves 4

ZEST NOTE: Take great care to use only the yellow part of the skin for this recipe because the pith, the white part, can turn the stuffing bitter during cooking.

Drumsticks Stuffed with Pistachioed Mousseline

"Virginia ham," according to one possibly biased Virginia cookbook, "is about as different from most other hams as chalk is from cheese." Often considered the king of country hams, Virginia's Smithfields get their distinctive taste from the peanuts (or corn, black-eyed peas, and/or potatoes) on which local pigs feed, and from the smoldering hickory wood (or pecan, red oak, or apple boughs) over which they are slowly smoked and aged. It is a primitive process that yields a taste particularly American in its appeal: robust, honest, and complex. Roasted, this ham is often the center of the Christmas buffet, though it also serves as a savory filling for the humble beaten biscuit or a surprising complement to spiced fruits.

But Smithfields are not the only country hams in the nation. Tennessee uses its own home-cured, mahogany-colored country ham in its famous dish, Ham 'n' Red-Eye Gravy. This substantial plate, with a gravy made from the meat drippings mixed with coffee, is always served with grits. In Iowa and other parts of the Midwest, German families smoke their hams over hickory fires to produce a truly authentic American-Westphalian country ham.

For this recipe, in which the stuffing flavors establish the refined yet country character of the dish, you can use whatever country ham is closest to home.

Stuffing

2 ounces Smithfield or country ham**	salt and pepper
6 ounces skinned and boned chicken breast	½ teaspoon ground nutmeg
	1 teaspoon marjoram
½ cup heavy cream	3 tablespoons coarsely chopped pistachios**
1 egg	

Drumsticks

6 chicken drumsticks	bouquet garni*
1 small onion, sliced	¾ cup heavy cream
1 carrot, sliced	salt and pepper
½ cup white wine	shelled pistachios for garnish
1 cup chicken stock*	

To make stuffing: In a food processor or blender make a puree of all stuffing ingredients except pistachios. Mix in pistachios by hand. Set aside.

To bone drumsticks, hold end of drumstick and, with small pointed knife, cut through tendons attaching flesh to bone. Scrape meat from bone, keeping knife as close to bone as possible. Cut end of bone from the skin, leaving meat and skin intact. The drumstick will appear to be turned inside out. Turn it right side in.

Fill drumstick cavities with stuffing, tuck in ends to enclose stuffing, and tie ends with kitchen string.

Spread onion and carrot slices in a saucepan large enough to hold drumsticks. Set them on top, pour in wine and stock, and add bouquet garni. Bring to a boil, lower heat, cover, and poach until chicken is tender, about 30 to 40 minutes. Remove chicken to platter, remove strings, and set chicken aside.

Strain cooking liquid and return to saucepan. Reduce* cooking liquid by half and add cream. Add salt and pepper to taste. Cook another 10 minutes until slightly thickened. Return drumsticks to sauce until heated through. Serve each drumstick bathed in sauce and garnished with pistachios.

Serves 6

Poussin Pot Pie

A relative newcomer to the game and poultry department, poussin is often called baby chicken. It is, in fact, a distinct variety, being fully mature at three weeks when it weighs less than a pound. It resembles Cornish game hen, but only in size, since its white meat is much more delicate and succulent.

The popularity of poussin is growing throughout the country, especially in California, where it is often substituted in recipes for squab and quail. Our potted preparation enhances the character of the meat, while six simple sheets of phyllo, draped on top, transform it into an elegant pie.

1 lemon, halved
2 poussins, cut into serving
    pieces
    flour
2 tablespoons butter
2 tablespoons vegetable oil

12 small white onions, peeled
4 carrots, peeled and cut into
    ¼-inch-thick sticks
6 ounces green beans, cut
    into 1-inch pieces

4 ounces small mushrooms,
quartered
4 small red new potatoes,
scrubbed and quartered
½ cup white Zinfandel
1 cup chicken stock*
½ cup heavy cream

2 tablespoons finely chopped
fresh dill
salt and pepper
6 sheets phyllo dough
(available in freezer or deli
section of supermarket)
½ cup butter, melted

Rub 1 lemon half over poussin pieces and dredge them in flour. In a large skillet heat butter and oil and brown poussins, remove, and reserve.

Add more oil to skillet if needed and sauté vegetables until well coated. Return poussins to skillet, cover, and cook for about 30 minutes over low heat.

Remove contents of skillet to oven-proof casserole. Deglaze* skillet with wine and stock. Bring to a boil and reduce* until syrupy. Add cream, dill, and juice of other half of lemon, cooking over high heat until thickened, about 10 minutes. Add salt and pepper to taste.

Preheat oven to 400°F and pour this sauce over chicken and vegetables in the casserole.

Brush each sheet of phyllo dough with melted butter and layer them into a stack of 6. Place on top of casserole and, with sharp scissors, cut the stack to fit, leaving a 1-inch overhang all around. Brush the top and edges of dough generously with butter and bake for 15 minutes, then reduce heat to 350° and bake for another 25 minutes. (If dough appears to be getting overly brown, cover with aluminum foil.)

Remove from oven and let cool for about 10 minutes before cutting and serving.

Serves 6

Duck Stuffed with Fresh Figs and
Louisiana Pecan Rice

Figs have been around a long time, judging from the attire attributed to Adam and Eve. What this couple did with the actual figs themselves, however, remains shrouded in mystery, at least in the biblical sense. But the religious affiliations of figs have persisted through the ages. The Franciscans first planted them along California's El Camino Real, and today these mission figs are one of several varieties, including Kadota, Calimyrna, and white, which now make California the United States' major commercial producer of figs. Other varieties come from Utah, Hawaii, and parts of the South.

At one time, fig syrup was used like honey as an all-purpose sweetener. Early American recipes include Steamed Fig Pudding with Ginger and Molasses, Pickled Figs, and Port-Soaked Fresh Figs. Jefferson preferred his straight (straight from Marseilles). Figs have inspired quite a bit of poetry, arousing the passions into such epithets as "darling of my heart, a dried fig" (from Alexis of Thurii). There is even the would-be truism, "Nothing is sweeter than figs" (Aristophanes). On the other hand, some people don't care a fig.

Figs have served as food for hogs, geese, and ducks, which were literally fattened with the fruit to improve the flavor of the meat. A similar idea underlies this savory dish, in which the duck absorbs the intense flavors of plump, juicy figs ensconced in the pecan-rice stuffing.

4 tablespoons butter	¾ cup Louisiana wild pecan
2 onions, chopped	rice**
duck giblets, cut into	2 cups duck or chicken
small pieces	stock*
10 ripe black figs, sliced	salt and pepper
lengthwise into 6 pieces	1 5-pound duck
(see Note)	cayenne

To make stuffing: In a large saucepan melt butter and sauté onions and giblets for 8 minutes. Add figs, cook for about 3 minutes, and stir in rice. When grains are well coated with butter, add stock and salt and pepper; bring to a boil. Reduce heat, cover, and simmer gently, about 25 minutes, or until all the liquid has been absorbed.

Preheat oven to 450°F. Dry the cavity of the duck and stuff it with rice-fig mixture. Truss* duck and place on a rack in a roasting pan. With ice pick or similar object prick duck skin all over. This allows the fat to drain and bastes the duck at the same time. Sprinkle with cayenne and roast for about 20 minutes. Lower heat to 375°, prick skin again, and roast another 50 minutes.

Place duck on a serving platter, remove trussing, and wait about 10 minutes before carving. Then instead of carving the bird with stuffing in place, we suggest removing stuffing, and then carving the bird. Make a bed of stuffing on serving platter or individual plates and place duck portions on top.

Serves 4

FIG NOTE: If you cannot obtain ripe figs, soak dried figs in 1 cup warm stock for 1 hour. Drain, reserving the stock for the recipe.

Roast Duck Glazed with Green Peppercorn Mustard and Nectarine Chutney

Canvasback, mallard, pintail, teal, ring-necked, goldeneye—these are just a few of the numerous varieties of wild duck that once crowded the nation's skies. They were prepared in many different ways, depending on the occasion. Roast duck formed part of the first Thanksgiving feast, along with turkey and goose. Martha Washington's duck recipes included "a little time, margerum...some clarret wine." In the mid-1800s, New York's grand restaurant, Delmonico's, began democratizing duck by serving it with hominy. By this time, wild duck was so common that a foreign visitor to New York advised "you Americans have made a mistake, your emblematic bird should have been a canvasback, not an eagle."

The domesticated duck with which most people are familiar, Long Island duckling, is descended from a species of Peking duck. Many California restaurants favor a duck bred from the Muscovy and Peking strains, which yield a large meaty breast. For many of us, some sort of supermarket duck will be the only available choice, so we have tailored our recipe to make a prize of it. Under its foil tent, the meat cooks to succulent perfection; and the skin crisps up beautifully during a final peppery glazing.

1 5-pound duck	⅓ cup good-quality mustard
salt and pepper	⅓ cup nectarine chutney**
1 cup duck or chicken stock*	
2 tablespoons green peppercorns,** rinsed and drained	

Preheat oven to 400°F.

Split duck in half and salt and pepper both sides. Prick skin all over with sharp tines of a fork or ice pick and place on a rack in a roasting pan. Roast for about 45 minutes, pricking skin again every 15 minutes. By then, most of the fat should have drained out of duck.

Pour off fat. Pour stock over duck and cover duck loosely with foil. Return to 300° oven. Cook for another 20 minutes, basting occasionally with pan juices.

To prepare glaze: Mash the peppercorns with a mortar and pestle, or with the back of a spoon, and mix in a bowl with the mustard and chutney.

Remove duck from oven and discard foil. Raise oven temperature to 400°, brush duck skin liberally with glaze, and roast another 10 to 15 minutes, or until skin is brown and crisp.

Serves 4

Grilled Squab with Lavender Honey and Black Pepper

Squab is defined as unfledged pigeon; that is, a pigeon which has no feathers or has never flown. So numerous were pigeons only one hundred years ago that James Fenimore Cooper, in The Pioneers, describes the heavens as "alive" with them: "You may look an hour before you can find a hole through which to get a peep at the sun." Indeed, they were often beaten from the sky with long poles and became common fare in public taverns as well as in private homes.

Traditionally, pigeons were baked into pies or served dried or pickled. The luscious squab bred for consumption today has dark, full-flavored, slightly gamey meat with nice texture, all of which comes through fully in this straightforward, grilled treatment.

6 squabs, split in half, or 3
  Cornish hens
3 tablespoons freshly ground
  pepper
1 tablespoon vegetable oil
⅓ cup lavender honey**

3 tablespoons good white
  wine vinegar
2 tablespoons lime juice
¼ cup olive oil
salt

Blot squabs dry. Make a mixture of 1 tablespoon pepper and 1 tablespoon vegetable oil and rub into skin of birds. Let rest for about 1
hour.

To make marinade: Mix remaining ingredients and spread over
squabs. Place squabs in a noncorrosive dish, cover, and refrigerate for
at least 24 hours, but no more than 48.

Remove from refrigerator and bring to room temperature. Meanwhile, preheat grill or broiler until very hot. Cook birds about 6 inches
from heat for 30 minutes, or until joints move easily. Turn birds
frequently while cooking, since the honey in the marinade may char if
exposed to heat for long periods of time.

Serves 6

Sautéed Medallions of Veal in Hot-Sweet Mustard

At one time, Mock Turtle Soup could be found as easily on an
American dinner menu as in the pages of Alice in Wonderland.
Even more surprising, it was veal that made the mockery. Even
so, veal was generally unknown outside certain ethnic communities because people were unfamiliar with its proper preparation. On midwestern farms and southern plantations, abundance
forced a change in attitude. As the population of young calves
increased, new veal recipes proliferated until veal attained its
current popular status and elegant connotations.

Always most prized were the thin, impeccable slices of tender-
loin, such as these in our recipe. They take on a wholly unexpected character in the presence of the recipe's intriguing and
tangy mustard.

12 ¼-inch-thick slices of veal, cut from the tenderloin	½ cup veal or chicken stock*
salt and pepper	¾ cup heavy cream
2 teaspoons sage	3 tablespoons hot-sweet mustard**
4 tablespoons butter	

Season veal with salt and pepper and sage. In a large skillet melt butter and sauté veal for about 3 minutes on each side. Remove to a platter and keep warm.

Deglaze* pan with veal or chicken stock, scraping up brown bits that cling to bottom of pan, and cook until reduced* to a syrupy stage. Mix in cream and mustard, cooking over medium heat until thickened, about 8 minutes. Return veal to pan and cook for about 2 minutes.

To serve: Place 2 tablespoons of sauce on a plate, top with 2 medallions of veal, and nap with additional sauce.

Serves 6

Veal Scallops Sauced with Asparagus Puree

People have always been quite passionate about asparagus, the lovely member of the lily family, which shows its colors from ivory white to purple to lush green. All over the world, asparagus festivals herald the beginning of its long-awaited season, while in France, the fortunate members of the Confraternity of the Asparagus can visit the Asparagus Museum in Argenteuil any time the mood strikes them. At least one French chef (Jean Troisgros) has decided the American asparagus is the best in the world, though the variety depends on the region. California has its thick jumbos, New England boasts slender, delicate shoots which are delicious even raw, and Pennsylvania and New Jersey grow a few patriotic species called Washingtons and Martha Washingtons.

The name "Asparagus in Ambush" may sound like a vegetarian Western, but it was once a very fashionable American preparation. It involved inserting asparagus spears into buttered rolls and then covering the entire construction with Hollandaise sauce. Escoffier's fondness for the vegetable led him to create an asparagus ice cream; our own presentation, though somewhat unusual, still confines asparagus to the predessert courses. Combined with a bit of cream, the asparagus becomes a luscious green sauce for the tender veal, which is then adorned with the barely cooked asparagus tips. It is easy though opulent.

1 pound asparagus, peeled	6 tablespoons butter
salted water	1 cup veal or chicken stock*
12 veal scallops, pounded	½ cup heavy cream
lightly (see Note)	4 tablespoons chopped fresh
½ cup flour	parsley for garnish
salt and pepper	

Boil asparagus in plenty of salted water until tender, about 3 to 8 minutes, depending on their thickness. Drain and cut off woody ends and reserve tips for garnish. Puree stems in a food processor or pass through a food mill. Set puree aside.

Dredge veal scallops in flour mixed with salt and pepper. In a large skillet melt butter and sauté veal for about 3 minutes on each side. Remove veal to platter and keep warm.

Add stock to skillet, bring to a boil, and deglaze* the brown particles in bottom of pan. Stock should thicken slightly. Blend in asparagus puree and cream, and heat.

Pour over reserved veal scallops and garnish with chopped parsley and asparagus tips.

Serves 6

VEAL NOTE: With the flat side of a mallet or the broad bottom of a heavy fry pan, pound scallops just enough to flatten them slightly, being careful not to tear them.

Veal Ragout with Artichokes, Brandied Raisins, and Crème Fraîche

In this country, veal recipes strongly reflect their ethnic and regional origins. California Italians found artichokes and tomatoes, olives and peppers the perfect accompaniments for their classic veal cutlets, rolls, and shanks, while midwestern Germans modified their schnitzels, devised New World sausages, and added nasturtium seeds to veal roasts. In Little Switzerland, Wisconsin, meat was braised with sour cream, served on noodles, and named not surprisingly, "Veal à la Suisse." Poles who traditionally simmered their veal with wine managed to see their favorite recipes through Prohibition almost uncompromised by making a single modification in spirit: They substituted homemade vodka mixed with some relevant herbs.

With its brandied raisins, crème fraiche, and artichokes, this multiethnic ragout is especially flavorful served atop the unusually textured and delicate melon seed pasta.

1 cup golden raisins	salt and pepper
½ cup brandy	2 tablespoons flour
3 pounds stewing veal, cut into 1-inch cubes	1 cup chicken or veal stock*
	¾ cup white wine
8 tablespoons butter	bouquet garni*
2 cups sliced mushrooms	1 cup crème fraiche*
1 cup quartered artichoke hearts*, fresh or frozen	

In a bowl soak raisins in brandy for 1 hour. Drain raisins, reserving brandy, and set both aside.

Pat veal dry. In a large skillet melt 4 tablespoons butter and brown veal cubes, several at a time if pan is not large enough to accommodate them without crowding.

In a small saucepan warm reserved brandy, ignite, and pour over veal. When flames die down, remove veal from pan and set aside.

Add 2 tablespoons butter to pan and sauté raisins, mushrooms, and artichokes for about 5 minutes, adding salt and pepper. Remove and reserve.

Melt 2 more tablespoons butter in pan and blend in the flour to make a roux. Cook over low heat, stirring, about 2 minutes.

Raise heat, add stock, wine, and bouquet garni, and stir constantly with a whisk until mixture comes to a boil. Return veal to pan. Simmer for about 1 hour, or until veal is tender.

Add reserved mushrooms, raisins, and artichoke hearts. Remove bouquet garni. Blend in crème fraiche and bring to a boil. Taste and correct seasonings.

Serve with noodles or rice. (We like this dish accompanied by melon seed pasta.**)

Serves 6

Breast of Veal Stuffed with Wild Rice and Garlicky Mustard Greens

The current insistence on fresh vegetables and herbs coincides with the increasing popularity of veal, such an excellent vehicle for the flavors with which it is cooked. Here we take advantage of that attribute by surrounding the meat with several contrasting textures and tastes. After it is stuffed with a well-garlicked forcemeat of wild rice and mustard greens, the meat bastes for hours in a rich, vermouth-flavored stock. But it is the sauce that really assures that nothing will be lost. It is made by pureeing the accumulated pan juices with the sauce-suffused, cooked vegetables. This is a meal for recapturing the spirit and contentment of an old-time Sunday dinner.

Stuffing

3 tablespoons butter
1 medium onion, chopped
3 large cloves garlic, minced
½ cup chopped fresh parsley
⅓ cup raw wild rice**
2 eggs
¼ cup Cognac or brandy

2 teaspoons salt
1 teaspoon freshly ground pepper
½ pound ground meat (beef, veal, lamb, or a mixture)
4 ounces mustard greens cut in chiffonade*

Veal Breast

salt and pepper
1 4–5-pound veal breast,
  with pocket for stuffing
  (ask butcher to make
  pocket)
2 tablespoons butter
2 tablespoons vegetable oil

2 cloves garlic, minced
1 bay leaf
1 cup veal or chicken stock*
1½ cups dry vermouth
1 medium onion, sliced
1 medium carrot, sliced

To make stuffing: Melt butter in a skillet and sauté onion and garlic until wilted. Combine with rest of stuffing ingredients in a large bowl. The best tools to use for mixing this thoroughly are your hands.

Salt and pepper the pocket of the veal breast. Fill with stuffing, but do not overfill. Seal opening of pocket by pressing edges together. Salt and pepper exterior of meat.

Preheat oven to 350°F. In a heat-proof casserole or roasting pan just large enough to hold veal heat butter and oil. Brown veal on all sides. Add remaining ingredients. Bring to a boil on top of the stove, cover, and place in oven for 2 hours. Remove cover and roast another 30 minutes, basting with pan juices occasionally.

Remove meat to platter and keep warm. Skim fat off pan juices and remove bay leaf. Cook juice until thickened, then puree in a blender or food processor. Slice breast and serve with sauce, reheated if necessary.

Serves 6

Shredded Beef with Mushrooms Served on Crisp Romaine

We've come a long way, maybe, since the ancients and their belief that mushrooms bestowed immortality on all who ate them. Now we believe that we can provide mushrooms with a certain semblance of immortality, if we dry and store them prop-

erly. We do this with a high degree of enlightened self-interest, however, since we intend eventually to enjoy the mushrooms in all their musty, well-preserved glory.

The most commonly available dried mushrooms are the sliced, meaty cepes often perfuming Italian dishes as porcini mushrooms. Cepes (or porcini) would be even more visible were they not kept in cork-stoppered jars on the top of delicatessen display cases that are always too high. Japanese shitake mushrooms are usually either sun-dried or heated for long hours over charcoal; this method is also employed for the wonderfully named Chinese wood ear and paddy straw fungus.

The big, broad-topped mushrooms in our recipe are true black beauties which, though not exactly immortal, have been known to win the undying gratitude of appreciative dinner guests. This recipe can also be used as an hors d'oeuvre, served on small, crisp lettuce leaves.

3 large dried black Oriental mushrooms** (available at Oriental markets)
   hot water
1½ pounds top or bottom round, semi-frozen and cut into thin shreds
3 tablespoons rice wine (available at Oriental markets)

1 teaspoon sugar
1 teaspoon cornstarch
1 teaspoon Chinese chile sauce (available at Oriental markets)
2 teaspoons soy sauce
¼ cup vegetable oil
½ pound fresh small mushrooms

12 large, crisp romaine lettuce
    leaves, ice cold

½ cup chopped green onion
    for garnish

Soak the dried mushrooms in a bowl of hot water to cover for about 45 minutes. Strain liquid and reserve about 3 tablespoons. Remove and discard stems and cut mushrooms into shreds.

Mix beef with rice wine, sugar, and cornstarch. Stir to coat beef well and let sit at room temperature for about 30 minutes.

In a small bowl mix chile sauce, soy sauce, and mushroom liquid. Set aside.

Heat a wok or skillet, add oil, and heat until rippled. Add beef and stir-fry for 45 seconds. Add both dried and fresh mushrooms and stir-fry for 45 seconds. Stir in chile sauce mixture and continue cooking for 30 seconds. Serve immediately on lettuce leaves and sprinkle with green onions. (The lettuce leaves must be icy cold. That is what makes this dish special.)

Serves 6

Allspice- and Cinnamon-Scented Beef Ragout with Dried Fruits and Almonds

Counterfeiting cinnamon was a crime that did pay, and quite well, just a few centuries back. Once the costliest of spices, cinnamon meant great wealth to the Dutch who grew it, under heavy guard, in Holland's famous eighteenth-century "cinnamon gardens." Even when only the wealthy could afford it, they used it lavishly to flavor their wines, sweeten their breath, and scent their sauces. When cinnamon finally became more generally available, it was soon the world's most widely used spice, as part of Indian curries, Chinese five-spice powder, and Middle Eastern tagines. It flavored Spanish cocoa and all manner of English cookery; in Pennsylvania Dutch kitchens, its powdery sweetness was dusted freely over the cookie batter and into the pot roast. This recipe clearly follows the fashion for combining nuts, fruits, and spices in savory dishes that came in with the spice trade and never went out.

Cinnamon "quills," the dried bark of the tree, are easily broken into pieces and ground up in a coffee grinder. Like freshly ground coffee beans, this method yields an intensified flavor and fragrance, as you will see as soon as you bring this multinational ragout to the simmer.

4 tablespoons vegetable oil	1½ cups beef or chicken stock*
salt and pepper	⅓ cup ground toasted
3 pounds top round, cut into	almonds,* plus ½ cup
1½-inch cubes	toasted almond slivers
1 onion, chopped	1 teaspoon cinnamon
¼ pound each dried apricots	1 teaspoon allspice
and pitted prunes, soaked	1 teaspoon ground cumin
for 1 hour in enough red	1 teaspoon ground coriander
wine to cover	

In a 4-quart saucepan heat oil. Salt and pepper beef cubes and sauté with onion.

Drain dried fruit, reserving wine. Set aside half the fruit. Pass other half of the fruit through a food mill or puree in a food processor. Add puree to meat along with reserved wine, stock, ground almonds, and spices and bring to a boil. Reduce heat and simmer, covered, for about 1 hour, or until meat is tender. Add reserved dried fruit and cook another 5 minutes. Serve sprinkled with toasted almond slivers.

Serves 6

Zinfandel Beef Stew with Celery Root and Parsnips

As a multiethnic nation deriving much from the melting pot, we can boast of few advantages that are as symbolic and substantial as stew. Louisiana Gumbo, Philadelphia Pepper Pot, the Irish Stew of New England, Brunswick Stews from the South, and Nok Qui Vi—a Hopi stew of the Southwest—all contribute to the tradition. Basically one-dish meals, stews have taken as their raw materials seafood, tripe, beef, lamb, squirrel, or whatever else was available at the moment. No less a figure than George Washington makes an appearance in this aspect of culinary development, since he purportedly ordered the chefs at Valley Forge to prepare a hearty meal, notwithstanding the absence of any ingredients save peppercorns and tripe. Since the ultimate creator in this case was a chef from Philadelphia, his home town was honored in the title of the resulting "Philadelphia Pepper Pot." Other recipes also commemorate their origins with fine accuracy, such as "East Chicago Beef Stew with Dill" and "South St. Louis Rabbit Stew."

In our recipe, the sweet nuttiness of parsnips and the stalwart celery root contribute their distinct natures to the flavorful, wine-marinated beef. The final dash of brandy adds something sensual and elegant to the meal as well as to the occasion.

2 tablespoons olive oil	3 onions, sliced
1 teaspoon oregano	salt and pepper
3 cups Zinfandel (see Note)	3 tablespoons flour
3 pounds beef chuck, cut into 1-inch cubes	¼ cup brandy bouquet garni*
4 tablespoons vegetable oil	2 cloves garlic, minced
1 medium celery root, peeled and julienned* (see Note)	water
3 medium parsnips, peeled and sliced	4 tablespoons chopped fresh parsley for garnish

In a bowl mix olive oil, oregano, and Zinfandel and marinate meat in this mixture for 3 hours, turning every so often.

In a large skillet heat vegetable oil and sauté celery root, parsnips, and onions over low heat for 20 minutes.

Remove meat from marinade, reserving liquid. With a slotted spoon remove vegetables from skillet and set aside. Raise heat and brown meat on all sides, adding salt and pepper. Sprinkle flour over meat and continue cooking for another 5 minutes. Return vegetables to pan, stir everything together, and pour in brandy and reserved marinade. Stir and scrape bottom of pan to loosen caramelized particles.

Preheat oven to 300°F and transfer contents of skillet to a heat-proof casserole. Add the bouquet garni, garlic, and enough water to cover. Bring to a boil, cover, and cook for 2 hours. During this time, skim fat from top and occasionally stir the bottom of casserole to make sure meat is not sticking. Remove from oven.

With a slotted spoon remove meat and vegetables from sauce and discard bouquet garni. Pass sauce through a food mill or puree in a food processor. Return meat and vegetables to casserole.

In a small saucepan bring sauce to a boil and cook until thickened. Pour sauce over meat in casserole and heat. Garnish with parsley and serve.

Serves 6

WINE NOTE: Many people are under the impression that wine which has passed its point of drinkable interest is still a candidate for cookery. We like to discourage that notion; it seems a shame to go through all the cooking and preparation of a wine-infused dish only to discover that it was indeed too late for that particular wine. If you don't want to drink it, you won't want to eat it.

CELERY ROOT NOTE: The gnarled, folded-up vegetable is not easy to clean unless you resign yourself at the outset to wasting some of it. A plain, ordinary swivel peeler is of little help. Use a small, sharp paring knife and cut off the tough protrusions. If you don't use the celery root immediately, keep it in acidulated water: a few teaspoons of vinegar or lemon juice to a quart of water.

Lamb Scallopini with Hazelnuts

Like garlic and red peppers, hazelnuts are often tied together in long strings and hung in kitchen doorways. Italian produce markets sometimes sell these attractive resta (strings) to be used for decorative purposes. Hazelnuts have always been even more popular for eating. According to an old summer solstice custom, when excessive rains posed a threat to the new nut crop, lovers of hazelnuts could stave off the unwanted precipitation by banging all of their kitchen utensils together. Many hazelnuts survived, whatever the reason, and their popularity has risen sharply, particularly in the past few years.

Merely toasting hazelnuts in the oven turns the kitchen invitingly fragrant. Here we chop the roasted nuts together with orange zest and sprinkle them on delicately sautéed, paper-thin scallops of lamb. They combine with the brandy-laced cooking juices to make a delicately tart, heady sauce.

½ cup coarsely chopped toasted hazelnuts*
1 tablespoon grated orange zest*

half a leg of lamb, boned
salt and pepper
¼ cup vegetable oil
⅓ cup brandy or Cognac

Mix nuts and orange zest and set aside.

Cut lamb into thin slices, less than ¼ inch thick. Blot dry and sprinkle with salt and pepper.

In a large skillet heat oil and sauté lamb quickly, a few slices at a time, about 20 seconds per side. As you set each batch aside, sprinkle with nut-orange mixture.

When all the lamb has been cooked, skim off the fat and deglaze* pan with brandy or Cognac. Spoon over lamb and serve immediately.

Serves 6

Sautéed Baby Lamb Chops with Shallot Puree

A traditional Cherokee recipe calls for a whole lamb to be stuffed with apples and nuts and then roasted carefully over an open fire, a preparation that reflects an appreciation of the festive and succulent possibilities of young lamb. Often associated with celebratory events, lamb is the center of attention at Southwest fiestas, where descendants of the Spanish who first brought sheep to this country enjoy borrego, or baby lamb. In Nevada, Colorado, and parts of the Rockies, Americans of Basque descent make sumptuous meals of mutton—they are about the only Americans who do. Visitors to the annual Italian San Gennaro festival in New York meander down Mulberry Street snacking on barbecued lamb called "chawarma." In Florida, a two-century-old Greek community, originally sponge fishermen, feasts on spring lamb stuffed with rice and pecans. Lebanese Americans around Pittsburgh enjoy lamb shish kebab and kibbe. Even Hollywood had its version of the lamb feast, propagated by none other than Alfred Hitchcock, who regularly ordered his personal plane sent forth to round up fresh spring lamb from New York's finest butcher shops. And in Pittsfield, Massachusetts, the first agricultural fair held in this country, in 1811, centered around an exhibit of sheep. Lamb was underappreciated, however, in Mrs. Rorer's 1886 cookbook, where it was described as a meat which, like veal, "is unwholesome if not thoroughly cooked."

Our recipe captures the splendor of lamb, cooked quickly with a delicate touch of sage and mellowed with a vinegar-splashed shallot sauce.

12 1-inch-thick baby lamb chops, fat removed
salt and pepper
1 tablespoon dried sage
2 tablespoons vegetable oil
2 tablespoons butter

3 large shallots, finely minced
1 small carrot, finely chopped (see Note)
¼ cup raspberry vinegar**
¼ cup white wine

½ cup chicken stock*
½ cup heavy cream

6 fresh sage leaves or sprigs
of parsley for garnish

Season chops with salt and pepper and sage. In a large skillet heat oil and butter and sauté chops for about 5 minutes on each side. Remove chops to platter and keep warm.

In same skillet sauté shallots and carrots until wilted, about 5 minutes.

Deglaze* pan with vinegar and wine and cook until syrupy. Pour in stock and cream and cook over medium-high heat until reduced* to about ¾ cup liquid. Puree cream-shallot mixture and strain through food mill or strainer. Reheat sauce if necessary.

Place 2 chops on each plate and top with shallot puree. Garnish with a sage leaf or a sprig of parsley.

Serves 6

COLOR NOTE: We use carrots to add a hint of color to the puree. You can, if you wish, use tomatoes for an even ruddier complexion.

Spring Lamb Simmered on Herb Branches with Chestnuts and Sugar Peas

Chestnuts were once so abundant that they were considered a winter staple, eaten instead of far more expensive potatoes. Chestnuts are the basis of a Native American bread, a type of Italian American polenta, and a thick veal stew of rural America.

Roasted or boiled, chestnuts are common in the stuffings, cakes, and puddings that always make November smell as good as it does. In this recipe, they are simmered with lamb and served with sugar peas, resulting in a dish that is both delicate and substantial.

4 tablespoons olive oil

3 pounds lamb, cut from leg, cubed

1 bunch green onions, cleaned and root ends cut off

2 branches each oregano, thyme, and marjoram (see Note)

1 cup chicken or beef stock*

2 cups peeled cooked chestnuts (or vacuum packed)

1 pound sugar peas or snow peas, stems and strings removed

salt and pepper

In a Dutch oven heat oil and brown lamb lightly. Remove and reserve. Sauté green onions in same pan until slightly limp. Place herb branches on top of onions and pour in stock. Bring to a simmer and place lamb and chestnuts on top of herbs. Cover and simmer for 45 minutes. (Check every so often to make sure that liquid has not completely evaporated from pot. If it has, add more stock or water.) Add peas and cook, covered, another 5 minutes. Add salt and pepper to taste. Remove and discard herb branches.

Serve the lamb garnished with the green onions, peas, and chestnuts.

Serves 6

BRANCH NOTE: Though grocery stores are making herb branches more available than ever before, you may have to substitute 2 teaspoons each of the corresponding dried herbs. If so, stir them into the sautéed green onions, pour in the stock, and proceed with the recipe.

Tender Lamb Tossed with California Chèvre, Olives, and Tomatoes

American olives currently exist under four main identities: the Spanish-style pimento-stuffed green; the medium green Sicilian, cracked and crisp; the black-purple Greek, Kalamata type; and the Lindsay, the well-known black "California" pitted olive.

Since the state produces ninety-nine percent of the nation's commercial crop, virtually all, in fact, are California olives. But the crop itself owes its very existence to the efforts of one woman from Illinois.

In the early 1890s, Freda Ehmann was overcome with curiosity about what it might be like to live in a California olive orchard. Fortunately for Freda she had a son with several such orchards in the Oroville area and a daughter with a back porch in Oakland. Freda also had quite a bit of nerve, a characteristic which eventually won her the complete directions for lye-curing olives from a University of California, Berkeley, agriculturalist. When the Oroville harvest came in, she gathered up her son's olives on her daughter's back porch and, with the professor's recipe, pickled the first batch of mild cured olives. That product would become known as the California or American olive.

For a while, interest in the olive centered on its physical measurements, a very American criterion, which began with the three predictable categories of small, medium, and large. But the demands of commerce soon dictated such refinements as colossal, supercolossal, and special supercolossal. At present, from Olivet, New Jersey, to Olivia, Texas, taste-conscious consumers define their olives more meaningfully as smooth or crinkly, bland to almost bitter.

In every weight, shape, or form, olives over the centuries have been credited with such boons as alleviating pain, curing drunkenness, and preventing lightning. Spanish legend assures the wife who hangs an olive branch in the house that her husband will be forever faithful and that she will be undisputed master. Perhaps this tantalizing possibility is responsible for the incorporation of olives into many California dishes, such as Olive Bread (made with chopped black olives) or garlic-suffused Cream of Olive Soup. We've wrapped up pimento-stuffed green olives and California chèvre cheese with tender bits of lamb for an unusual packaged feast.

3 pounds boneless lamb, cut
from leg, cubed
½–¾ cup olive oil
3 cloves garlic, minced
3 tablespoons fresh lemon
juice
1 cup chopped pimento-
stuffed olives**
½ cup dry sherry

2 teaspoons oregano
salt and pepper
6 10"-×-12" sheets of
parchment* or foil
1 large tomato, seeded and
coarsely chopped
6 ounces chèvre cheese,**
crumbled
3 tablespoons butter

Preheat oven to 400°F.

In a large bowl mix lamb with ½ cup oil, garlic, lemon juice, olives, sherry, oregano, salt and pepper.

Brush parchment or foil with olive oil. Remove a portion of meat mixture and arrange in the center of each sheet. Sprinkle each portion with tomato and cheese and top with ½ tablespoon butter. Fold parchment or foil over this mixture and crimp edges tightly to seal. Bake the "bags" for 45 minutes.

Remove to individual serving plates.

Serves 6

Grilled Leg of Lamb with Hot-Sweet Mustard and Sherry Vinegar

Grilled food is closest to nature, closest to uncooked. For its success it depends on neither decoration nor disguise. It is, literally, out in the open. No wonder it appealed to the early Americans, who distrusted elaborate "made dishes," like fancy ragouts and fricassees. In fact, an 1838 American cookbook condemned these dishes as "too rich, and too highly seasoned to be wholesome." Then, as now, American cooking was viewed, at least by Americans, as straightforward, simple, nutritious. In a word, honest.

Perhaps these values underlie the current resurgence of interest in grilling as a cooking method. Equally popular is mesquite charcoal as a cooking medium, and for some good reasons. Mesquite contains no chemicals nor does it require chemical starters. Made only from the dense wood of the Mexican mesquite, this charcoal is the end result of long and personal tending. The jungle areas where the fifty-year-old trees flourish are the province of the Yaqui Indians of north-central Mexico, who fell their prize forty-foot-high beauties judiciously and with ecological concern. To turn the wood into charcoal, they construct a pyramid-shaped structure from the mesquite trunks. This is covered with adobe clay and then ignited. For three weeks it smolders continuously, after which the clay covering is removed. The charcoal is then ready for transport to a growing number of suppliers, restaurants, and backyard barbecuers—at least to those who have not yet switched to a new fad, like grapevines.

Our recipe uses the intense heat of a broiler or charcoal (mesquite or otherwise) grill to seal in the ripened flavors of its pungent sherried marinade. Requiring little last-minute preparation, the method retains the natural juiciness of the lamb in a balance of tastes at once hearty and subtle.

1 5-pound leg of lamb, boned and butterflied	2 tablespoons olive oil
4 cloves garlic, slivered	2 tablespoons sherry vinegar**
½ cup chopped fresh mint leaves	salt and pepper
4 tablespoons hot-sweet mustard**	

Using a small, sharp knife, cut slits in the meat and insert garlic slivers and ¼ cup mint leaves. Mix the remaining ¼ cup mint in a bowl with mustard, oil, vinegar, and salt and pepper and rub all over the lamb. Refrigerate overnight in a covered stainless-steel or glass pan.

Two hours before cooking, bring the lamb to room temperature. In a grill with cover, grill the lamb, uncovered, over red-hot coals or mesquite, about 5 inches above the coals. With cover on and vents open, grill about 20 minutes, turning lamb about 4 times. Using a meat thermometer, cook to an internal temperature of 128°F. Let meat rest off heat for about 15 minutes before slicing.

To broil in a conventional oven, put lamb on an oiled rack 6 inches from the heat source. Broil about 20 minutes, turning lamb about 4 times. Remove from oven and let rest about 15 minutes before slicing.

Serves 8 to 10

RECYCLING NOTE: Leftover lamb can be cut into strips, tossed with a zesty Mustard Vinaigrette (see page 119 in "Appetizer Salads") with tarragon added, and served on a chiffonade* of butter lettuce. Chop up some pistachios** to crown each serving. Don't forget crusty French bread, warmed, and a generous pot of fresh sweet butter. This is an extraordinarily tasteful salad because the ingredients have already had time to become suffused with flavors, which are then delightfully heightened for their second appearance.

Loin of Pork and Dried Apples Sautéed in Walnut Oil and Hard Cider

The three sows and one boar arriving in the Jamestown of 1608 got right to work, multiplying into sixty pigs in the first year. By the 1700s pork had become an important export of Virginia and Maryland and a diarist wrote of New England, "As to their pork, they challenge the world." The Dutch and Germans loved it, the latter making it into scrapple, sausages, and those rich meat puddings which led to the proverbial German wish for "short sermons and long puddings."

Pork was also important in the West and South, where meat often was synonymous with pork. Kentucky became known as "the land of pork and whiskey," while eastern Florida was "the land of hog and hominy." "Old Ned" was a Tennessee pet name for that state's much-savored bacon. A Georgia commentator remarked that the whole country might be called the "Republic of Porkdom." And yet there were holdouts. The Carib Indians, for example, were convinced that eating pork would result in little squinty eyes.

Cookbook writers like Eliza Leslie counseled that pork should not be eaten without applesauce. Likewise, in California, a colorful accompaniment for pork with the intriguing name, Painted Ladies, consisted of small, poached apples, their "cheeks" painted bright with melted currant jelly.

Our recipe coordinates these influences with a little anointing from hard cider. This American version of apple brandy, which was already an important New Jersey industry three centuries ago, is, nevertheless, not always readily available today in all parts of the country. If that is the case, substitute half apple cider and half brandy. That will do it.

Marinade

3 large garlic cloves	3 tablespoons hard cider
½ teaspoon each thyme, sage, parsley	salt and pepper
	bay leaf
2 tablespoons walnut oil	

Pork

1 3–4-pound boneless pork loin, butterflied	2 tablespoons ground walnuts
20 slices dried apple soaked in 1 cup hard cider	2 tablespoons butter, softened
½ cup beef stock*	

To make marinade: Mash garlic in a bowl with herbs, then add remaining marinade ingredients. Rub marinade all over meat and leave for several hours or overnight in refrigerator.

When ready, preheat oven to 375°F and place meat in an oiled heat-proof casserole, fat side down. Cook for about 1½ hours, basting several times with pan juices until a meat thermometer registers 150°. Remove from oven. Turn roast fat side up. Score fat in several places and place roast under broiler for 10 minutes.

Meanwhile, drain apples, reserving cider, if there is any left. Skim fat from pan juices, add ½ cup stock and any remaining cider from apples. If apples have absorbed all cider, add ¼ cup additional hard cider to pan juices. Cook liquids in a saucepan over high heat, scraping up browned bits in bottom of pan, until reduced* and thickened slightly. Add walnuts and whisk in 2 tablespoons butter.

Stir a few tablespoons of this sauce into the apples, and surround the roast with them. Spoon a little sauce over the meat. Serve the rest separately.

Serves 6 to 8

VEGETABLES

We had now fair sunshine weather and so pleasant a sweet aire as did much refresh us, and there came a smell off the shore like the smell of a garden . . . .

from Winthrop's Journal: History of New England, describing the coast of Massachusetts, Spring 1630

The Age of Vegetables is upon us. The American garden has become a place of respect, if not sanctity, as people discover the possibilities and pleasures of vegetables. Whether they are pre-

239

sented as a side dish or a main course, vegetables do much of the work themselves. Many are so fragrant, they act as their own herbs. They provide texture, flavor, and color. A vegetable, pureed with cream, is quite different when stir-fried with slivers of toasted almonds. And vegetables can be cooked quickly, often for the better.

Vegetable appreciation has changed over the centuries. When the first Europeans characterized this land as the New World garden, they gladly devoured its resources. But when it came to planting food, few vegetables were cultivated except for corn, beans, and root vegetables. These became preeminent because they were satisfying and hearty, especially when meat and dairy products were in short supply. Most other vegetables remained an optional food, perhaps because they didn't fit the nation's meat-and-potato self-image. Except in the middle and upper classes, vegetables were of little interest until the beginning of this century.

Once there was a demand for vegetables, however, there were vegetables available. New nutritional information helped generate some enthusiasm. Certain foods like broccoli, artichokes, and eggplant became more prevalent after the immigration of certain nationalities who used them in their traditional cooking. Even such exotica as endives and avocados began to appear in response to the growing affluence and sophisticated palates of urban society.

But fresh vegetables suffered a significant setback in the 1950s. Middle-class suburbia celebrated the miracles of technology, including frozen and canned vegetables. As one cookbook of the era put it: "Our cooking ideas and ideals have their roots in many lands and cultures, but our new way of achieving gourmet food can only happen here—in the land of the mix, the jar, the frozen-food package, and the ubiquitous can opener . . . [which is] fast becoming a magic wand."

The sleight of hand performed by the ubiquitous wand turned out to be slight indeed. As part of the revolutionary sixties, consumers questioned the virtues of processed foods, causing a resurgence of fresh produce. And when fresh vegetables returned, they did so with a vengeance. Enthusiasm and even fanaticism have replaced the previous stance of indifference. Perhaps this acceptance of vegetables represents an informed concern about healthy bodies; or perhaps we just know a good thing when we taste it.

As early as a century ago, a visiting English journalist noted that, in California, "the change from winter to summer is discerned with difficulty in the market-place as far as the supply of most fruits and vegetables is concerned." The statement is even more accurate today. Called the "nation's garden," California produces and supplies this country's entire commerical crop of tomatoes, artichokes, and olives, and almost all asparagus, broccoli, celery, carrots, and lettuce—not to mention most of our fruit.

In this chapter, we include forty-seven recipes for vegetables. Some of them are meant to accompany a main course; others are more substantial dishes and could as justifiably fit into the "Littlemeals" chapter. If you are interested in a specific vegetable, consult the Index for a complete list of the recipes in which that vegetable is included.

———

Artichoke, Mushroom, and Potato Stew
Carrot Cream in Artichoke Bottoms
Stir-fried Asparagus and Mushrooms in Black Bean Sauce
Sautéed Beets in Lemon Butter
Broccoli Spears with Walnuts and Raspberry Vinegar
Broccoli Timbales with Herbed Cheese Sauce
Walnut Brussels Sprouts
Braised Cabbage and Apples in Riesling Wine
Orange-Ginger Carrots
Carrot Shreds in Bourbon and Brown Sugar
Carrots in Fresh Dill Cream
Cauliflower and Broccoli Rouille
Cumin Cauliflower with Red Pepper
Gratin of Celery Root and Basil

Chard and Chile Chunks
Grilled Baby Corn with Chive Butter
Fresh Corn Flapjacks with Basil
Cucumber Crescents with Goat Cheese
Eggplant Parmesan Custard with Fresh Tomato Sauce
Ratatouille in Sourdough Garlic Crust
Fennel with Chardonnay and Parmigiano-Reggiano
Braised Fennel with Garlic
Green Beans in Shallot-Mustard Sauce
Lemon Caraway Green Beans
Mushrooms in Tomato-Mint Butter
Chopped Mushrooms with Ginger, Mustard, and Cashews
Braised Onion Medley with Pine Nuts and Raisins
Leek and Carrot Hash
Silky Leeks and Smoked Salmon
Parsnips in Chard-Walnut Crust
Fresh Peas with Mint Shreds and Butter Lettuce
Potato-Spinach Pudding
Potatoes with Lemon, Garlic, and Parsley
Springtime Sauté of Radishes and Leeks
Red Pepper and Onion Marmalade with Celery
Wild Rice and Sorrel Flan
Spaghetti Squash Alfredo
Spinach-Ricotta Pancakes
Spinach in Garlic Cream
Pan-fried Sunchokes and Mushrooms with Red Peppers
Sweet Potato Fritters
Pan-fried Cherry Tomatoes in Garlic Butter
BLT Puree
Turnips Glazed in Jalapeño Jelly
Mock Zucchini "Pasta"
Zucchini in Lime and Thyme
Zucchini Wedges Sautéed in Balsamic Vinegar and Pine Nuts

Artichoke

"Hartichoak Pie," in <u>Martha Washington's Booke of Cookery</u>, may have been one of the first artichoke recipes made in this country. It was also probably one of the last, at least for a century or so. Before becoming seduced by its taste, people are often suspicious of the artichoke, especially when served whole. Its architecture seems odd, demanding that the polite host provide a refuse bucket to each guest, although as Laurel Robertson of <u>Laurel's Kitchen</u> muses, "it's fascinating to see how differently people cope with them if you don't." Almost anyone who has not undergone formal artichoke training has a personal story about chewing the undissolvable leaves interminably until, as one friend confessed, "I finally just hid them in my pocket."

Artichokes have another fascinating aspect which is prompting interesting research. After eating the vegetable, some people find that ordinary water tastes sweet. Investigators found that two substances in the artichoke caused this reaction by "fooling" the taste buds into perceiving sweetness, a discovery that could lead to the development of a natural sweetener to replace sugar.

But artichokes never stay as sweet as they are. In fact they get sweeter. The newly picked vegetable may contain only ten calories, but this can actually rise to fifty-three calories as it sits around. This happens because its carbohydrate content, in the form of inulin, gradually converts to sugar as it is stored. At any rate, we have tried to capture all the charms of artichokes here, playing them against textures like mushrooms and potatoes, or sparking them with touches of marjoram and shallots.

Artichoke, Mushroom, and Potato Stew

4 tablespoons butter
2 shallots, chopped
1 clove garlic, minced
1 pound new potatoes,
    scrubbed and quartered
½ pound uncooked fresh or
    frozen artichoke hearts,
    quartered
¾ pound medium
    mushrooms, quartered

salt and pepper
1 teaspoon ground coriander
¼ teaspoon cayenne
½ cup white wine
½ cup chicken stock*
2 tablespoons lemon juice
¼ cup chopped fresh dill or
    parsley for garnish

In a large skillet melt butter and sauté shallots and garlic until wilted. Add potatoes, artichokes, mushrooms, and seasonings and cook over medium heat, stirring, for about 10 minutes. Add wine and stock, raise heat, and bring to a boil. Cover and simmer for 5 minutes. Add lemon juice and simmer, uncovered, another 5 minutes.

Sprinkle with dill or parsley and serve.

Serves 6

Carrot Cream in Artichoke Bottoms

½ pound carrots, cleaned and
    sliced
1 shallot, peeled
    salted water
3 tablespoons butter,
    softened

¼ cup heavy cream
½ teaspoon marjoram
    salt and pepper
6 fresh or frozen artichoke
    bottoms, cooked

Cook carrots and shallot in boiling salted water until tender, about 10 minutes.

In a food processor or blender make a smooth puree of the carrots, shallot, butter, cream, marjoram, salt and pepper. Place in a pastry bag fitted with star tip and pipe mixture into artichoke bottoms.

This dish may also be served warm. To heat, arrange on a heat-proof serving dish, cover with foil, and place in preheated 350°F oven for 10 minutes.

Serves 6

Asparagus

One of the most distinctive characteristics of asparagus is that Thomas Jefferson is almost certainly not the first person to have planted it in this country. Actually another man of politics has been linked with the first planting of asparagus in New England, an eighteenth-century Dutch consul named Diederich Leertower.

According to the prevailing wisdom, "sparrow grass," as it was commonly mispronounced in those days, grew much better if planted with the shavings of a ram's horn. This must have been common knowledge among birds, since they are mainly responsible for the migration of asparagus around the world.

The earliest asparagus recipe in this country may well be the daredevil directions in Martha Washington's Booke of Cookery: "Hold the roots in your hands," it instructs, "and dip in the green ends whilst the water boyls." Aside from, or possibly because of, this recipe, asparagus was cooked but rarely for a long time after that. About one hundred years ago recipes for preparing the "tops" began to appear in such diverse compendiums as Mrs. Rorer's cookbook and Oscar of the Waldorf's published repertoire. Early this century, Fannie Farmer provided instructions for asparagus on toast or with "crusts," sauced or in salads (with catsup); but she includes the warning that a bunch of asparagus may cost up to a dollar.

By now such experts as James Beard and Andre Simon have contributed the last word on the proper treatment of asparagus. Beard: "Place asparagus in a skillet. Pour in enough cold water to cover and add salt. Bring to a boil." Simon: "Never put asparagus in cold water and bring the water to the boil."

We may have avoided the issue in this recipe, but we do go back to Beard for another thought on the subject. However you cook asparagus, "do not plan to serve it sparingly," he says.

Asparagus creates another concern of a particularly Californian nature: what to drink with it. Because of its sulphur content, asparagus imparts a sweet taste to wine. Since chances are, fortunately, slim that you will be able to locate asparagus wine, once considered a fashionable "ladies' drink," we recommend a nice dry white, like a California Gewürztraminer.

Stir-fried Asparagus and Mushrooms in Black Bean Sauce

2 tablespoons fermented black beans (available in Oriental markets)
2 tablespoons dry sherry
1 clove garlic, minced
1 teaspoon chopped fresh ginger
4 tablespoons vegetable or peanut oil

1 pound asparagus, peeled and diagonally cut into 1-inch pieces (see Note)
½ pound mushrooms, cleaned and quartered
½ cup chicken stock*
1 tablespoon soy sauce mixed with 1 teaspoon cornstarch
4 green onions, chopped

Rinse black beans under cold water in a strainer for a few seconds. Drain well and in a bowl combine with sherry, garlic, and ginger. Set aside.

246

In a wok or skillet heat oil until very hot. Add asparagus and mushrooms and cook over medium-high heat for about 2 minutes. Pour in stock and continue to cook for 2 minutes longer. Add soy mixture and cook until liquid thickens slightly. Add black bean mixture and green onions and cook 1 minute more.

Serves 6

ALTERNATE VEGETABLE NOTE: Instead of asparagus you can also use green beans or broccoli.

Beets

In this country, beets have had a busy and diversified life-style. As Harvard Beets, they were much esteemed by all except those who favored their natural rival, Yale Beets. Actually the recipes are identical, except that the Yales cook in orange juice, the Harvards in lemon and vinegar. Despite these academic affiliations, beets are equally at home in another New England dish with the unpretentious name "Red Flannel Hash," which are beets made with bacon and potatoes. The deep burgundy vegetable has also been useful for coloring everything from the icing of cakes to the batter for a favorite colonial dish, Pink-colored Pancakes.

In the South and Midwest, the red root was all but neglected in favor of the delicious tops, which were often cooked with herbs and other greens as a tasty vegetable.

Some markets sell beets already boiled in their skins, a custom borrowed from English greengrocers. But in this country we usually cook our own in favorite old ways. Here, we hope, is a favorite new one.

Sautéed Beets in Lemon Butter

4 tablespoons butter
6 beets, peeled and grated
   salt and pepper
4 tablespoons fresh lemon
   juice

1½ tablespoons superfine
   sugar*
   grated zest* of ½ lemon
4 tablespoons chopped fresh
   parsley for garnish

In a medium skillet melt butter and sauté beets with salt and pepper over a high heat for about 3 minutes.

Meanwhile, in a small cup mix lemon juice, sugar, and zest until sugar dissolves. Pour over beets, cover, and cook for 3 minutes. Uncover, stir, and cook for another 3 minutes, or until some of the liquid has evaporated.

Serve sprinkled with parsley.

Serves 6

Broccoli

When broccoli first came to this country, it was referred to as "Brockala." But its fame under any name was limited. The fact that John Randolph of Williamsburg included it in his 1775 Treatise and that Jefferson cultivated broccoli at Monticello didn't help. Another century was to pass before broccoli received any serious consideration in an American cookbook, and then it was almost too serious. Cooks were warned to tie the vegetable up in cheesecloth to keep it from falling apart, and then to plunge it into boiling water with a chunk of bread to absorb its strong odors, which otherwise might intrude upon the sweet fragrance of the kitchen.

A member of the cabbage family, this dark green flowering vegetable is no longer a rarity. In fact, because it is grown in all parts of the country, fresh broccoli is available year-round. Even so, it seldom shows all its true colors, which range from deep purple to cauliflower white. Here a simple sauté with raspberry vinegar followed by a more elaborate cheese custard dish display the range of its enchantments.

Broccoli Spears with Walnuts and Raspberry Vinegar

salted water
1 large bunch broccoli, separated into spears, stems peeled
3 tablespoons walnut oil
1 tablespoon butter

1 cup coarsely chopped walnuts
2 tablespoons raspberry vinegar**
salt and pepper

In a large pot of boiling salted water, blanch* broccoli for 2 minutes. Drain and set aside.

In a skillet heat oil and butter and sauté walnuts until slightly browned, about 3 minutes. Add broccoli, sprinkle with vinegar, and cook just until heated through. Add salt and pepper to taste.

Serves 6

Broccoli Timbales with Herbed Cheese Sauce

Timbales

2 cups coarsely chopped
   cooked broccoli (see Note)
4 eggs
   salt and pepper
½ teaspoon thyme

4 tablespoons grated
   Parmesan cheese
1 cup heavy cream

   hot water
   butter

Sauce

1½ cups heavy cream
4 tablespoons chopped fresh
   herbs such as dill, parsley,
   basil, etc.

4 ounces goat cheese,**
   crumbled
   salt and pepper

Preheat oven to 375°F.

In a bowl mix broccoli with remaining timbale ingredients and pour into 6 individual buttered ramekins or custard cups. Place in a pan of hot water and cover tops with buttered parchment* or foil. Bake for about 25 minutes or until custard is set.

To make sauce: Heat cream until it is reduced* to ¾ cup. Add remaining ingredients and heat until cheese melts.

Turn out timbales and pour some sauce over each one.

Serves 6

ALTERNATE VEGETABLE NOTE: Instead of broccoli you can use spinach, mushrooms, zucchini, or a combination of cooked vegetables.

Brussels Sprouts

"Rose cabbage" is the word for Brussels sprouts in German (Rosenkohl), a name recalling their petallike appearance. Brussels sprouts with chestnuts, or even without chestnuts, are among the standard holiday vegetables that come to mind at Thanksgiving. People who could do nothing else to help with the preparations could always manage to cut the little x's in the bottoms of the Brussels sprouts. From that plateau, they progressed quickly to the cutting of little x's in the bottoms of the chestnuts.

Reason suggests that Brussels sprouts come from Belgium, but no one has been able to make that connection definitively. In this country, they can be traced directly to Monticello, where Jefferson first planted them in 1812. California and New York are now the nation's major producers.

Jack cheese and toasted walnuts make this a festive vegetable dish, enlivened with the appealing bite of cayenne pepper.

Walnut Brussels Sprouts

2 pounds very small, firm Brussels sprouts	2 ounces Monterey Jack cheese, shredded
water	salt and pepper
4 tablespoons butter	½ teaspoon cayenne
½ cup toasted walnuts*	¼ cup chopped fresh chives
¾ cup heavy cream	for garnish

Remove loose outer leaves from Brussels sprouts and, with sharp knife, cut an X in the base of each. Cook, uncovered, in boiling water for 5 minutes. Drain and set aside.

In a medium skillet melt butter and sauté walnuts and Brussels sprouts over medium heat for about 5 minutes. Pour in cream, heat until bubbles form around edge, and add cheese, salt and pepper, and cayenne. Cook over medium heat for 5 minutes.

Sprinkle with chives and serve.

Serves 6

Cabbage

Cabbage, n. A familiar kitchen-garden vegetable about as large and wise as a man's head.

Ambrose Bierce, The Devil's Dictionary

The unassuming modesty of the common, everyday cabbage belies the fact that it is one of the most upwardly mobile of vegetables. From the Latin word caput, meaning "head," the cabbage has taken its name quite seriously, developing its head in many ways. Conical or pointy-headed varieties, like leafy collards and kale, may have been the earliest form of cabbage. Later, there evolved rounder and more hard-headed types, such as the curly milan, the crinkly savoy, and an assortment of reds. Some cabbage plants formed small budding heads at the junction of the leaf and stem, thus becoming Brussels sprouts. Those with delusions of grandeur concentrated on developing their flowers and became the most advanced versions of the vegetable, broccoli and cauliflower.

In this country, cabbage has always been esteemed in the South. It often accompanied ham dishes, a combination praised in a nineteenth-century southern cookbook as "the daily and favorite dish of nine-tenths of the country people." The Pennsylvania Germans prepared both fresh cabbage and sauerkraut; the Dutch included "koolslaa" as part of almost every meal.

Here, a cup of California Riesling and a few herbs and flavorings bring out some of the cabbage's finer culinary virtues.

Braised Cabbage and Apples in Riesling Wine

4 tablespoons butter
1 head cabbage, shredded
1 onion, chopped
3 Golden Delicious or pippin
apples, cored and cubed
salt and pepper

1½ teaspoons crushed fennel
seed
1 cup California Riesling
½ cup chopped fresh parsley
for garnish

In a medium skillet melt butter and sauté cabbage, onion, apples, salt and pepper, and fennel seed over high heat until vegetables begin to sweat. Add Riesling, bring to a boil, cover, and simmer for 15 minutes. Uncover, raise heat, and cook another 3 minutes.

Sprinkle with chopped parsley and serve.

Serves 6

Carrots

"Underground honey" is an old Irish phrase for carrots, an obvious reference to their sweetness. Except for beets, carrots have the highest sugar content of all vegetables. Their sugars are easily caramelized and carrots are often browned right along with the roast. Carrot breads have a strong German heritage and carrot cookies were a favorite Christmas gift in New England. But Texas is the site of the biggest carrot renaissance of recent times, for it was there, at the Guadalupe County Fair, that the carrot cake won first prize in 1960.

As a vegetable or part of a salad, carrots are popular in California, where Holtville in the Imperial Valley is convinced it produces enough carrots to call itself the "Carrot Capital of the World." In the following recipes dill, bourbon, or fresh orange juice bring forth some of the hidden glories of "underground honey."

Orange-Ginger Carrots

1 pound carrots, peeled and
cut into ⅛-inch-thick
slices
4 cups salted water
1 teaspoon ground ginger
4 tablespoons butter
1 teaspoon grated fresh
ginger
1 teaspoon brown sugar

2 tablespoons good-quality
orange marmalade
2 tablespoons fresh orange
juice
1 tablespoon fresh lemon
juice
salt and pepper
¼ cup chopped fresh chives or
green onions for garnish

In a large saucepan cook carrots in boiling salted water with ground ginger for 5 minutes. Drain and set aside.

In a large skillet melt butter and add fresh ginger, brown sugar, marmalade, and juices. Cook over low heat until mixture becomes slightly thick and syrupy, about 6 minutes. Add carrots, toss well to coat, and cook over medium heat for 3 minutes. Season with salt and pepper to taste and sprinkle with chopped chives.

Serves 6

Carrot Shreds in Bourbon and Brown Sugar

1 pound carrots, peeled and
shredded
salted water
3 tablespoons butter

2 tablespoons brown sugar
3 tablespoons bourbon
salt and pepper

Blanch* carrots in a large pot of boiling salted water for 1 minute. Drain well and set aside.

In a large skillet melt butter and add sugar and bourbon; cook over medium heat until sugar dissolves. Add carrots, toss well in butter mixture, and cook until heated through. Add salt and pepper to taste.

Serves 6

Carrots in Fresh Dill Cream

½ cup chicken stock*
1 pound carrots, peeled and
   cut into ¼-inch-thick
   matchsticks

¾ cup heavy cream
2 tablespoons chopped fresh
   dill
   salt and pepper

In a medium saucepan bring chicken stock to a boil and add the carrots. Simmer for 4 minutes and remove carrots with slotted spoon. Boil chicken stock until it is reduced* by half. Add cream and dill and cook for another 5 minutes, until slightly thickened. Return carrots to cream and heat through. Add salt and pepper to taste.

Serves 6

Cauliflower

The darling of Madame du Barry, mistress to King Louis XV, cauliflower was the aristocrat of vegetables in the eighteenth-century French court. The Dutch brought their love of cauliflower to the New World and, according to legend and to James Beard, we owe all our cauliflower to just one Dutch family who planted its seeds near Setauket, New York. Today the Pennsylvania Dutch still include cauliflower as part of their "chow-chow," a relish made at the end of summer. Rumanians make a kind of moussaka of cauliflower, substituting it for eggplant. Vegetarians are especially fond of it because it is the only vegetable that provides substantial amounts of folic acid, as well as calcium in a form assimilable by nonmilk-drinkers. The frugal cook simmers cauliflower's tender leaves, which are almost identical to the cabbage's. Cauliflower, with its creamy puffed head, is the flowery member of the cabbage family cultivated for its flowers, or white "curds," rather than its leaves.

California has recently become one of this country's important cauliflower suppliers. With garlic-suffused rouille or with toasted cumin seeds and coriander, these recipes emphasize cauliflower's California identity.

Cauliflower and Broccoli Rouille

1 head cauliflower, cut into
　flowerets

1 bunch broccoli, stems cut
　into ¼-inch-thick sticks
　and flowers cut into
　flowerets

Rouille

3 cloves garlic, peeled

1 2-ounce jar chopped
　pimento, well-drained

½ cup fresh bread crumbs
1 egg yolk
½ teaspoon oregano

½ teaspoon dried red pepper
flakes
1 cup olive oil

Steam or cook cauliflower and broccoli until barely tender, about 4 minutes. Refresh under cold water in colander and drain thoroughly.

To make rouille: Puree all rouille ingredients in a blender or food processor.

Spread half the rouille on the bottom of a serving dish. Arrange cauliflower and broccoli flowerets in alternating concentric circles with broccoli stems mounded in the center. Pour remaining rouille over vegetables. May be served warm or at room temperature.

Serves 6 to 8

Cumin Cauliflower with Red Pepper

1 large head cauliflower,
trimmed and cut into
flowerets
salted water
3 tablespoons butter
1 large red bell pepper,
seeded, deveined, and cut
into strips

1 clove garlic, minced
1½ teaspoons crushed toasted
cumin seed
½ cup heavy cream
salt and pepper
½ cup chopped fresh
coriander for garnish

Cook cauliflower in a large pot of boiling salted water for 3 minutes. Drain and set aside.

Heat butter in a skillet and sauté red pepper over medium heat, stirring, for about 3 minutes. Sprinkle with garlic and cumin, cook for 1 minute more, and add the cream, salt and pepper. Add the cauliflower and cook, stirring, about 2 minutes, or until cauliflower is hot.

Sprinkle with coriander leaves and serve.

Serves 6

Celery Root

Celery root has several pseudonyms: turnip root celery, celeriac, celery knob, all somewhat misleading. This convoluted, usually dusty-looking vegetable is not the root of celery, nor does it produce long green stalks, but it does look somewhat like a gnarled turnip. In all probability, its name comes from one Stephen Switzer, who first planted it in the 1720s in England, describing it as a "foreign kitchen vegetable."

It has never been widely popular in this country, though Americans of eastern European and German descent cook it with wild mushrooms or bake it into their chicken dishes. A brief blanching brings out its excellent qualities for salads and for this cheese-dusted, golden-brown gratin.

Gratin of Celery Root and Basil

1 large celery root (about 1½ pounds), peeled and shredded
water
½ cup heavy cream
salt and pepper
½ teaspoon thyme
1½ cups fresh bread crumbs (use half whole-wheat for an interesting touch)

½ cup coarsely chopped fresh basil leaves
1 clove garlic, minced
½ cup grated Parmesan cheese
4 tablespoons butter

Cook celery root in a large pot of boiling water for 3 minutes. Drain well.

Preheat oven to 375°F and butter 9- or 10-inch baking dish.

Mix celery root with cream, salt and pepper, and thyme in a bowl. Place in prepared baking dish.

In another bowl combine bread crumbs, salt and pepper, basil, garlic, and cheese. Sprinkle mixture over celery root. Dot with butter, place in oven, and bake for about 20 minutes, or until topping is golden.

Serves 6

ALTERNATE VEGETABLE NOTE: Green beans or carrots can be used instead of celery root.

Chard

If there is any justice in the world, the ecology movement should soon be making a hero of chard. Not only is it as easy as a weed to grow, it is actually two vegetables in one. The stalk can be separated from the leaves and cooked like asparagus, cardoons, or celery, while the leaves are often substituted in spinach or cabbage dishes. Of course, both parts have earned their own specific recipes, especially from the French, who have cultivated two distinct subvarieties, one for the stalks and one for the stems. The stalks offer a choice of colors, white or red, the latter sometimes called "rhubarb chard." Though chard is sometimes considered a less genteel form of spinach, it also contains far less oxalic acid than spinach, a substance that adversely affects the body's use of calcium. An ancient ancestor of the sugar beet, chard is also known as leaf chard, sea kale beet, and Swiss chard, though it is not particularly associated with Switzerland.

With its slivered jalapeños and sour cream, this dish makes a lively first course or an appropriate addition to a Mexican dinner. When preparing chard, the best accompaniment is undoubtedly a good pair of scissors. And don't forget to save the stalks for another day.

Chard and Chile Chunks

butter
3 tablespoons olive oil
1 large bunch chard, leaves
    only, coarsely chopped
1 clove garlic, minced
1 small onion, chopped
2 jalapeño peppers,* seeded,
    deveined, and slivered

4 eggs
½ cup sour cream
½ cup grated Monterey Jack
    cheese
salt and pepper

Preheat oven to 350°F and butter a 9-inch-square baking pan.

In a large skillet heat oil and sauté chard, garlic, onion, and jalapeños until wilted, about 5 minutes.

Combine remaining ingredients in a large bowl and add chard mixture. Mix well. Pour into baking pan and bake for 25 minutes. Allow to rest 10 minutes and cut into squares.

Serves 6 to 8

Corn

"When the oak trees' leaves are as big as mice ears"—that was the time to sow corn, according to Indian instructions to the Plymouth colonists. For the Virginia colonists also, corn was life itself. It was their bread, their porridge, their flour, their animal feed. Eventually corn was also the center of an important social event in farming areas: the corn-husking party. In autumn, families met in one another's barns, settled themselves amidst the corn, and husked away. They chatted, told stories, and sang songs, always with an eye to spotting the rare red ear of corn.

This entitled the finder to an extra moment with the whiskey jug or to a kiss from the person of his or her choice. The husking feast that followed included Burgoo Stew in Kentucky, Brunswick Stew in the South, and dancing everywhere.

Sweet corn, more delicate than the maize or field corn of the colonists, could be eaten from the cob. It was first "discovered" in 1779 along the Susquehanna River, where the Iroquois had long been cultivating it. Corn became popular enough to be called a "standing dish" at the American table by the mid-nineteenth century. Cooking instructions from that era belie a certain awe for the exotic vegetable. A recipe called "Mrs. Harland's Corn on the Cob" advised cooking it for thirty minutes, while Mrs. Rorer's recipe has a separate section entitled "To Eat." There she advises: "Score every row of grains with a sharp knife . . . and with the teeth press out the center of the grain leaving the hull on the cob."

By now corn is available almost year-round. Its many varieties and hybrids include Spring Gold, Golden Bantam, Country Gentleman, Shoe Peg, Silver Queen, and Seneca Beauty. They are especially delectable in this recipe, grilled and smeared with chive butter.

Our flapjacks recall the taste of traditional corn oysters (so called for their resemblance to the shape of oysters). These flapjacks, however, are thin and custardy, bursting with sweet fresh kernels of corn.

Grilled Baby Corn with Chive Butter

6 ears young corn (preferably picked the same day), cleaned

3 tablespoons vegetable oil

6 tablespoons butter, room temperature

4 tablespoons chopped fresh chives

salt and pepper

Brush corn with oil and place on preheated grill, 2 inches from source of heat. Cook just until kernels start to color, turning frequently, about 6 minutes.

While corn is cooking, mix butter with chives in a small bowl until well combined. Spread chive butter on hot corn and sprinkle with salt and pepper.

Serves 6

Fresh Corn Flapjacks with Basil

4 ears fresh corn, uncooked, to make 2 cups corn kernels
1½ cups flour
2 tablespoons sugar
1½ teaspoons baking powder
salt and pepper

¼ cup chopped fresh basil leaves
2 eggs
½ cup milk
1 tablespoon butter, melted

With a sharp knife, cut corn from cobs, scraping cobs to release juices.

Sift dry ingredients together into a bowl and combine with basil, eggs, milk, and butter. Stir only until moistened. Add corn and corn juices.

Ladle ¼ cup of batter onto hot, well-greased griddle or skillet and cook for about 3 minutes on each side.

Serves 6

Cucumbers

American cookbooks of the not-so-distant past usually contained a large number of recipes for cooked cucumbers. They were recommended as a substitute in many zucchini or summer squash recipes. Mrs. Rorer and Fannie Farmer offered several possibilities for cucumbers stewed, boiled, stuffed with veal "Force-meat," fried in a batter, and made into sauces. Possibly the authors were trying to meet the needs generated by the once-popular three-week cucumber diet, which attracted people with its promise of beautiful skin and hair, and sometimes nails.

At any rate, the Shakers wrote in the 1800s: "It does not seem to be generally known that the cucumber is one of the most valuable vegetables we raise." The Pennsylvania Dutch cooked their cucumbers with a bit of cream, an idea whose time has come back, this time along with goat cheese and tarragon.

Cucumber Crescents with Goat Cheese

2 large English cucumbers,
  peeled, cut in half
  lengthwise and seeded
  salted water
3 tablespoons butter
1 shallot, chopped

1 cup heavy cream
3 ounces goat cheese**
1 teaspoon fresh tarragon, or
  ½ teaspoon dried tarragon
  freshly ground pepper

Cut cucumber halves into ¼-inch-thick slices and blanch* in boiling salted water for 1 minute. Drain well and set aside.

In a large skillet or sauté pan melt butter and sauté shallot until wilted. Add cucumber crescents and cook over medium heat for about

5 minutes. Add cream, bring to a boil, then simmer for about 5 minutes, or until cream thickens. Add remaining ingredients and cook for another 3 minutes.

Serves 6

Eggplant

People have been cooking eggplants for several thousand years so it is no wonder we have inherited considerable wisdom about the vegetable. We know, for example, that eggplant must be salted, according to Larousse Gastronomique, because salting gets rid of its bitterness, as Elizabeth David explains in French Provincial Cooking. Tom Stobart's Cook's Encyclopedia tells us that eggplant rarely needs salting because, as Jane Grigson's Vegetable Book makes clear, salting has no effect on the flavor. James Beard called the salting step nothing more than an "old wives' tale" but does inform us that the smaller the eggplant the better, a question that Grigson also addresses—she proclaims that size is irrelevant.

Older American cookbooks also reveal some of the ancient enigma of the eggplant. It seemed to Eliza Leslie, in the mid-eighteenth century, that eggplant was a natural for breakfast. A bit later in the century, Mrs. Rorer gives us the formidably named "Fried Eggplant Number One," concluding with the dictum "Tomato catsup should be served with it."

Fortunately, our recipes here include some nice fresh tomatoes; so you can, if you wish, hold the catsup.

Eggplant Parmesan Custard with Fresh Tomato Sauce

Fresh Tomato Sauce

2 tablespoons olive oil
2 cloves garlic, minced
2 pounds fresh ripe tomatoes, seeded and coarsely chopped, or 1 28-ounce can imported Italian tomatoes, chopped

1 bay leaf
½ teaspoon oregano
salt and pepper
1 sprig parsley

Custard

2 pounds small eggplant
½ cup vegetable oil
2 cloves garlic, peeled
4 eggs
1 cup heavy cream

½ cup grated Parmesan cheese
1 teaspoon fresh thyme, or ½ teaspoon dried thyme
salt and pepper
2 tablespoons butter

Heat olive oil in a skillet and sauté garlic over medium heat for 2 minutes. Add remaining ingredients and simmer for about 25 minutes, or until sauce thickens slightly. Remove bay leaf.

Preheat oven to 375°F and butter a 1½-quart soufflé dish.

Peel eggplant and cut into ½-inch-thick slices. In a large skillet heat oil and sauté eggplant on both sides until golden. Drain on paper toweling to remove excess oil. Place eggplant and remaining custard ingredients in a food processor and puree until smooth.

Fill soufflé dish with puree. Place a buttered piece of parchment* or foil on top, butter side down, and bake for about 50 minutes.

Put fresh tomato sauce through a food mill, heat through, and add 2 tablespoons butter, bit by bit, until well blended.

Allow eggplant custard to rest out of oven for about 15 minutes. Unmold on serving platter and spoon sauce over custard.

Serves 6

Ratatouille in Sourdough Garlic Crust

Ratatouille

4 tablespoons olive oil
1 clove garlic, minced
1 onion, thinly sliced
1 small eggplant, cut into
   1-inch chunks
½ pound zucchini, thinly
   sliced
½ pound mushrooms, cleaned
   and thinly sliced

2 large ripe tomatoes, seeded
   and sliced
1 teaspoon oregano
   salt and pepper
¼ cup chopped fresh basil
   leaves

Crust

2 cups bread crumbs made
   from sourdough bread
¼ cup grated Parmesan cheese
2 cloves garlic, finely minced
   salt and pepper

2 tablespoons chopped fresh
   parsley
2 tablespoons chopped fresh
   basil leaves
½ cup butter, melted

In a large skillet heat olive oil and sauté garlic and onion until wilted. Add eggplant, cover with zucchini, and cook until softened slightly. Add mushrooms, cover with tomatoes, oregano, salt and pepper, and basil. Cover and simmer for about 10 minutes.

Preheat oven to 375°F and transfer vegetables without too much stirring to a heat-proof 10-inch dish. Try to keep ingredients in layers.

Mix all crust ingredients except butter in a bowl and sprinkle over ratatouille. Pour melted butter over crust and bake for 20 minutes.

Serves 6

Fennel

"...the fennel is beyond any vegetable, delicious," wrote Thomas Appleton in 1824 to someone who paid attention to that sort of enthusiasm. "It greatly resembles . . . celery, perfectly white, and there is no vegetable equals it in flavour." With that, Mr. Appleton packed two separate varieties of fennel and sent them to Thomas Jefferson, who planted them in his gardens. Few other Americans would know much about the crisp celery-like vegetable for another hundred years, when Italian restaurants and groceries made people curious about its licoricelike charm. So well did fennel adapt to California's climate, that it has become a virtual weed, its tall feathery branches waving from the off-ramps of freeways and from the middle of gardens in which it was never planted.

Florence fennel is the variety prized for its fat, crunchy stalks, which look like bulbs. They are good raw or cooked, make an excellent accompaniment to seafood, and can be served as a dessert with chèvre or creamy rich cheeses. Fennel may be substituted easily in any celery or cardoon recipe and usually benefits from a dash of Pernod. Fennel often flavors pickled capers, olives, and cucumbers. Some domesticated rabbits are given it in their daily meals because it imparts a distinctive savoriness to their flesh. Though hardly rabbit food, fennel has an ancient reputation as a diet aid as well as a restorer of eyesight.

Whatever its ultimate destiny, fennel should be well cleaned and trimmed of all stringiness. We include two recipes; in one the vegetable is dusted with Parmigiano-Reggiano, in the other it is gently stewed with bits of garlic.

Fennel with Chardonnay and Parmigiano-Reggiano

2 pounds fennel (see Note)
2 tablespoons olive oil
    salt and pepper
½ cup Chardonnay or dry
    white wine

¼ cup water
    butter
½ cup grated Parmigiano-
    Reggiano

Preheat oven to 375°F.

Trim and quarter fennel bulbs. Cut into thin slices and place in a 10-inch baking dish.

Drizzle with oil, add salt and pepper, and pour in wine and water. Cover with buttered parchment* or foil and bake for 25 minutes. Stir well, uncover, and continue cooking until almost all the liquid has evaporated, about 30 minutes. Sprinkle with cheese and serve.

Serves 6

ALTERNATE VEGETABLE NOTE: Celery can be used instead of fennel.

Braised Fennel with Garlic

4 tablespoons olive oil
3 cloves garlic, chopped
6 small or 3 large fennel
  bulbs, trimmed and
  quartered (see Note)

salt and pepper
¾ cup chicken stock*
4 tablespoons chopped fresh
  parsley for garnish

In a large skillet heat oil and cook garlic, fennel, and salt and pepper over medium heat for 10 minutes. Add the stock, cover the skillet, and lower heat. Cook for about 15 minutes or until fennel is tender.

Sprinkle with parsley and serve.

Serves 6

ALTERNATE VEGETABLE NOTE: Celery can be used instead of fennel bulbs.

Green Beans

When it comes to beans, regional preferences can sound like codes of culinary law. For example, a Pennsylvania Dutch cookbook dictates: "Green beans need vinegar. If vinegar isn't added by the cook, the vinegar cruet will be on the table." By contrast, southerners have been just as adamant about what green beans needed: bacon. And they needed to stew all day in bacon until they emerged, smoky in flavor, almost gray in color, and delectable in taste. Another traditional recipe, used by the Shakers but current in tone, calls for cooking the beans al dente with nasturtium pods and leaves.

In the following recipes the beans are cooked quickly to retain their pleasant bite and then tossed with lemon and caraway or in a simple hot-sweet mustard sauce.

Green Beans in Shallot-Mustard Sauce

1½ pounds green beans,
    topped and tailed, cut into
    2-inch pieces (see Note)
    salted water
2 tablespoons butter
2 tablespoons chopped
    shallots

½ cup chicken stock*
2 tablespoons hot-sweet
    mustard**
    salt and pepper

Cook beans in boiling salted water to cover, about 3 to 5 minutes, until crisp-tender. Drain and set aside.

Heat butter in a medium saucepan and sauté shallots until wilted. Add remaining ingredients and simmer for about 5 minutes. Add beans and cook until heated through.

Serves 6

ALTERNATE VEGETABLE NOTE: Asparagus, broccoli, or snow peas can each be used instead of green beans.

Lemon-Caraway Green Beans

1 pound green beans, topped
    and tailed
1 tablespoon caraway seed
1 teaspoon grated lemon zest
2 tablespoons fresh lemon
    juice

4 tablespoons butter, room
    temperature
    salt and pepper

Steam green beans in a pot for 3 minutes.

Meanwhile, crush caraway seed in mortar and pestle or with back of spoon. Add seeds, lemon zest, and juice to butter, combining well.

Remove green beans to serving dish and toss with caraway-butter mixture. Add salt and pepper to taste.

Serves 6

Mushrooms

In a sense, cultivated mushrooms were first discovered in this country during the 1970s. During that decade, the annual per capita consumption of the common "supermarket" mushroom rose from about half a pound to 2.2 pounds. Some people began to use mushrooms as low-calorie "potatoes," since both vegetables share the ability to absorb or reflect their surrounding flavors. Because mushrooms are eminently edible raw, they were sliced into salads or arranged on the trays of crudités that were all too ubiquitous in the seventies.

The common cultivated mushroom is a relatively new food. It evolved largely from the efforts of Lewis Downing, who first successfully propagated it in 1926. Because Pennsylvania's limestone caves provided such an ideal growing environment, that state became the first major center of the commercial mushroom industry. A Mushroom Museum established at Kennett Square, Pennsylvania, made that town the mycological mecca of the nation.

Because cultivated mushrooms are of such recent vintage, there really are no traditional American recipes specifically for them. But wild mushrooms, or field mushrooms, are treated respectfully in such directives as how to dress a "Dish of Mushrumps" and Fannie Farmer's "Mushrooms Under Glass." For that elaborate presentation, each guest was served an individual glass bell which, when lifted, released all the trapped aromas of the cooked mushrooms underneath. The following two buttery mushroom recipes are as wonderful to breathe in as they are to eat up, with or without the bells.

Mushrooms in Tomato-Mint Butter

4 tablespoons butter
2 cloves garlic, minced
1½ pounds small mushrooms,
   cleaned
1 large ripe tomato, seeded
   and chopped

2 tablespoons chopped fresh
   mint leaves
salt and pepper

In a skillet melt butter and sauté garlic and mushrooms over a medium-high heat for about 5 minutes, tossing to coat with butter. Add
remaining ingredients and cook another 5 minutes.

Serves 6

Chopped Mushrooms with Ginger,
Mustard, and Cashews

¼ cup butter
2 cloves garlic, minced
2 tablespoons grated ginger
1 shallot, minced
2 teaspoons good-quality
   mustard
6 tablespoons finely chopped
   cashews
½ cup white wine
1 teaspoon chopped fresh
   parsley

salt and pepper
pinch nutmeg
juice of half a lemon
1½ pounds mushrooms,
   cleaned and coarsely
   choppped
1 tablespoon bread crumbs
1 small onion, thinly sliced

In a large saucepan melt butter and sauté garlic, ginger, and shallot.
Do not brown. Add all other ingredients except 3 tablespoons of the

cashews, bread crumbs, mushrooms, and onion. Stir until sauce begins to bubble, about 2 minutes. Add mushrooms to the sauce and cook 3 or 4 minutes. Remove to noncorrosive ovenproof dish. When ready to serve, preheat oven to 450°F. Sprinkle on cashews and bread crumbs and arrange sliced onions on top. Bake for 8 to 10 minutes or until sauce begins to bubble.

Serves 6

Onions

"All cooks agree in this opinion, no savory dish without an onion." That was the poetic advice of the 1808 edition of American Domestic Cookery. Cooks today are even less likely to disagree. Onion appreciation is a flourishing activity, especially in California, where some markets vie with each other for the honor of displaying the latest, most fashionable onion. Depending on its personality, an onion can be everything from a sweet, raw crudité to the sturdy foundation for a flavorsome stock. Onions offer crispness when fried, sweetness when caramelized, festiveness when studded with cloves and baked alongside an important-size roast. And when necessary, they can always be dried for storage over long winters. Early health-food faddists claimed that onions, dribbled with honey and eaten prior to breakfast, were a boon to the body.

We have included four different types of onions in the following three recipes. Shallots are small clustered onions with both delicacy and bite. The Walla Walla or Granex add sweetness. Leeks contribute their unique and pleasing texture. Red onions are one of the most decorative of the species.

Braised Onion Medley with Pine Nuts and Raisins

2 tablespoons butter
3 tablespoons olive oil
1 large red onion, thinly
  sliced
2 large sweet yellow
  onions** (Granex or Walla
  Walla), peeled and thinly
  sliced
3 leeks, white part only,
  cleaned and thinly sliced

2 shallots, chopped
1 clove garlic, minced
½ teaspoon oregano
½ teaspoon thyme
  salt and pepper
½ cup golden raisins
½ cup chicken stock*
½ cup toasted pine nuts*

In a large skillet heat butter and oil. Sauté onions, leeks, shallots, and garlic over a medium-low heat until wilted, about 10 minutes. Add oregano, thyme, salt and pepper, raisins, and stock; bring to a boil, cover, and simmer for 20 minutes. Add pine nuts and cook uncovered another 5 minutes.

May be served hot, cold, or at room temperature. Great accompaniment for grilled food and wonderful to stuff in your hamburger bun along with your burger.

Serves 6

Leek and Carrot Hash

½ pound good-quality bacon,
  diced
2 bunches leeks, cleaned,
  trimmed, and thinly sliced

1 pound carrots, cleaned and
  diced
  salt and pepper
1 teaspoon dried sage

In a large skillet brown bacon until most of the fat is rendered. Remove and drain on paper toweling.

Add to skillet leeks and carrots and cook, stirring frequently, until leeks turn golden. Cover and cook over low heat for about 5 minutes or until tender. Add salt and pepper, sage, and reserved bacon; stir well and cook over high heat, uncovered, until browned, about 10 minutes.

Serves 6

Silky Leeks and Smoked Salmon

4 tablespoons butter	¼ pound smoked salmon,**
6 large leeks, white part	cut into ½-inch strips
only, sliced	¼ cup chopped fresh parsley
¼ cup heavy cream	salt and pepper

In a medium skillet melt butter and sauté leeks over low heat until translucent, about 10 to 15 minutes, stirring occasionally. Pour in cream and cook until thickened or reduced* by half. Add smoked salmon and parsley and stir to combine. Add salt and pepper to taste.

Transfer mixture to a shallow heat-proof dish and place in preheated broiler for about 3 minutes, or until top is golden.

Serves 4 to 6

Parsnips

Parsnips appeared in what is considered the first American cookbook, published in 1796 by Amelia Simmons. Her recipe for Fricassee of Parsnips declares that "Parsnips are a valuable root, cultivated best in rich old grounds." These words contrast sharply to those of M. F. K. Fisher who, two centuries later, says fondly of her childhood garden "the soil was impossible for roots like parsnips, thank God. . . ."

It is true that this anemic-looking vegetable, with its bony white body, reminds one of the middle of winter. But its flavor can be as rich as yams and sweet enough for desserts such as the faddish Parsnips Pie. When parsnips are stored, their sugar concentrates and the vegetable actually gets sweeter and more delicious as winter draws on. Vladimir Estragon had nothing but fine words for parsnips, buttered or otherwise: "Cut open a parsnip, breathe in," he directed, "and it's like walking through a rainsoaked hayfield." Better yet, cook them with some chard and walnuts.

Parsnips in Chard-Walnut Crust

8 tablespoons butter
1½ pounds parsnips, peeled and coarsely shredded
   water
   salt and pepper
1 teaspoon rosemary
4 ounces chard, stems removed and leaves cut into chiffonade*

1 cup coarsely chopped walnuts
2 ounces Jarlsberg cheese, grated
¼ cup heavy cream

Preheat oven to 375°F and grease a 9- or 10-inch baking dish with 2 tablespoons butter.

Cook parsnips in a large pot of boiling water for 5 minutes. Drain and in a bowl toss with 4 tablespoons butter, salt and pepper, and rosemary. Pour parsnip mixture into baking dish. Over this sprinkle chard, walnuts, and cheese. Dot with remaining 2 tablespoons butter and drizzle with cream. Bake for 25 minutes. Check at the end of 15 minutes to make sure chard is not charring. If it is, cover lightly with foil and continue baking.

Serves 6

ALTERNATE VEGETABLE NOTE: Carrots or sunchokes can be used instead of parsnips.

Peas

In the days when New Jersey was mostly a garden, the train that carried its bounty to the urban marketplace was called the "Pea Line," a tribute to fresh garden peas as the very symbols of spring. Fresh peas were always appreciated: Captain John Smith first praised "Virginia pease" in his notes from 1608, and even earlier, explorers on New England's Cuttyhunk Island mentioned the planting of peas. Christopher Columbus himself was impressed enough to remark on their presence on Isabella Island, in 1493.

Early American cookbooks include several different kinds of peas, mostly dried, in recipes for everything from succotash to bread. Today, in areas where small growers are dabbling with different varieties, tiny and exquisite petits pois may be obtainable or the small, wrinkled "English" pea. The smoothly beautiful American peas, found anywhere in season, will give lovely results in this recipe.

Fresh Peas with Mint Shreds and Butter Lettuce

2 tablespoons butter
2 heads butter lettuce,
   coarsely shredded
   salt and pepper
1 pound fresh peas, shelled

2 tablespoons chopped fresh
   parsley
¼ cup heavy cream
¼ cup coarsely chopped fresh
   mint leaves for garnish

In a medium saucepan heat butter and add lettuce, salt and pepper, peas, and parsley. Cook covered over medium heat for about 5 minutes. Uncover, add cream, stir well, and cook for another 3 minutes.
   Sprinkle with chopped mint and serve.

Serves 6

Potatoes

In 1707, the formal dinner for the newly installed president of Harvard College included potatoes on the menu. This may have been the high point in the American potato's career for quite some time to come. Later that same century, in demonstration of the sacrifices he was prepared to make in the name of freedom, John Adams announced: "Let us eat potatoes...rather than submit." Around that same time, the famous French gastronome, Brillat-Savarin, stated his feelings unequivocally when someone attempted to serve him potatoes: "None for me."

In all fairness, it should be said that potatoes of the Revolutionary era were not all created equal. They improved considerably once under cultivation by the Dutch, Germans, and Scotch-Irish. Potatoes soon began to appear in mouth-watering dishes from breakfast through dinnertime and from one extreme to the other. Settlers from England loved them with roast beef; and the Forty-niners, on their way through Utah, bought them by the thousands from Mormons. Eliza Leslie had collected an impressive number of "American recipes" for potatoes when she assembled her nineteenth-century cookbook.

Today, the prized Idaho baked potato and a seemingly endless catalog of other varieties have led to an annual consumption in this country of 120 pounds per person. One of our recipes is a lovely light pudding made with spinach, the other is simply an excuse for unbridled enjoyment of buttered potatoes, smothered in garlic and parsley.

Potato-Spinach Pudding

2 large baking potatoes, cooked, put through a ricer or mashed
6 ounces fresh or frozen spinach, cooked, well drained, and chopped
salt and pepper
pinch ground nutmeg
2 cloves garlic, crushed
½ cup chopped fresh chives
¼ cup butter, melted
1 egg
1 egg yolk
½ cup heavy cream

Preheat oven to 350°F and grease well a 6-cup soufflé dish.

In a large bowl combine potatoes, spinach, salt and pepper, nutmeg, garlic, chives, and butter.

In a small bowl mix well egg, yolk, and cream and add to potato mixture, stirring until well blended. Place mixture in soufflé dish and bake for 45 minutes. (If top is getting too brown, cover with a piece of foil.)

Serve directly from baking dish because this pudding does not unmold successfully.

Serves 6

Potatoes with Lemon, Garlic, and Parsley

12 new red potatoes, cooked in skins and cooled	½ cup chopped fresh parsley
grated zest* and juice of 1 lemon	2 tablespoons capers, drained
	3 tablespoons olive oil
3 cloves garlic, minced	2 tablespoons butter
	salt and pepper

Cut potatoes into ½-inch slices.

Mix lemon zest, garlic, parsley, and capers together in a bowl.

In a large skillet heat oil and butter. Add potatoes and cook until golden. Add parsley mixture, sprinkle with lemon juice, and cook, tossing well until potatoes are coated with parsley mixture. Add salt and pepper to taste.

Serves 6 to 8

Radishes

There is more to the radish than meets the eye. Depending on the variety, it may be black, white, pink, or even two-toned. And radishes have pretty names: Cherry Bell, Sparkler, French Breakfast, White Icicle. They can be the little, bite-size red ones or the hefty white "footballs" from Alaska. In Oaxaca, Mexico, giant radishes are carved into fantastic animal or human representations for the December 23 celebration called the "Night of the Radishes." Any size radish qualified for honors during England's Elizabethan Radish Feast, held on May 11.

Radish seed oil has been used for cooking, though radishes themselves were seldom cooked, except by the Japanese. And yet when sautéed over high heat, as in this recipe, radishes have a pleasing nutty taste. They can be substituted for turnips in many dishes. Radish greens are good in salads or cooked like spinach. In fact, according to Mrs. Rorer's late-nineteenth-century cookbook, the center leaves should be eaten because "they contain a substance that helps the digestion of the radish itself." Both she and Fannie Farmer (who calls radishes by the unflattering nickname "Blot") include directions on how to carve them up to look like tulips or roses or anything but radishes. Even without such fanciful sculpting, these sautéed "reds" are a pleasant and pretty surprise.

Springtime Sauté of Radishes and Leeks

4 tablespoons butter
1 bunch leeks, white part only, cleaned and sliced
2 bunches red radishes, washed, trimmed, and thinly sliced

2 tablespoons chopped fresh parsley
salt and pepper

In a large skillet melt butter and sauté leeks and radishes over medium heat for 10 minutes, stirring occasionally. Add parsley and continue cooking for 4 minutes. Season with salt and pepper.

Serves 6

Red Peppers

Sweet red peppers are making a comeback in this country. The proof is in the Pipérades Basquaise and Italian Peperonatas, French rouilles and Tunisian Chakchoukas, all dishes which showcase the glories of red peppers. And yet this interest is very recent. In fact, American cookbooks contained virtually no recipes for cooked peppers until this century, although there were, as any schoolchild knows, pecks of Pickled Peppers to pick from. There was even a salad: a decapitated red pepper filled with grapefruit pulp, celery, walnuts, and mayonnaise. When the 1906 edition of Fannie Farmer's Boston Cooking-School Cook Book appeared, it boasted several recipes for cooking red peppers, the most exotic of which called for a stuffing of sweetbreads and mushrooms.

All peppers, sweet to hot, red or otherwise, are a New World food. Some of the confusion over peppers is the legacy of none other than Christopher Columbus. Because his destination had been Asia, the source of peppercorns, the spice, he therefore ascribed the spicy hot taste in his food to "pepper." The word pepper has come to be commonly used for both the peppercorns and the vegetable, but they are botanically unrelated. At any rate, here is an unconfusing recipe for enjoying both the visual and gastronomic beauty of this new/old vegetable.

Red Pepper and Onion Marmalade with Celery

5 tablespoons olive oil
3 large onions, thinly sliced
3 red bell peppers, seeded,
  deveined, and thinly sliced
4 celery stalks, strings
  removed and thinly sliced
salt and pepper

1 teaspoon marjoram
1 teaspoon dried rosemary, or
  2 teaspoons chopped fresh
  rosemary leaves
¼ cup chopped fresh parsley
½–1 cup chicken stock*

In a large skillet heat oil and sauté onions, peppers, and celery over medium-high heat, about 3 minutes, or until vegetables just begin to wilt. Lower heat, add salt, pepper and herbs and cook, uncovered, for about 20 minutes, or until vegetables are very soft and thickened. Add enough stock to moisten well and cook for another 15 minutes. You may have to add some more stock during last 15 minutes if vegetables seem to be getting too dry.

    This dish is wonderful hot, cold, or room temperature. Served in a crock, it makes a rather tasty appetizer to be spread on some good bread.

Serves 6

Sorrel

For a weed, sorrel has attained a surprising measure of prominence. Rumor has it that the original Irish shamrock may well have been one of the cloverlike varieties of sorrel. And sorrel may actually have saved the lives of countless fish lovers: Since its high oxalic acid content can soften and even dissolve fish bones, sorrel makes an excellent choice for stuffing fish, especially the many-boned shad. "Hallelujah," a sorrel which becomes edible around Easter, also suggests restorative, if not downright mystical, powers.

Actually, sorrel has been undergoing a recent resurrection, evident by its frequent appearance in grocery shops, at herb counters, and in food magazine features. Perhaps the increased interest in fish, for which sorrel sauces are so complementary, accounts for some of it. Also the refreshing, lemonlike taste of its tender leaves makes sorrel distinctive in any array of anonymous salad greens. Americans of northern European background favor its souring effect in breads, and as a vegetable in itself. The Jewish favorite, Shav, is a cold sorrel soup. Sorrel Bounce is a rum and sorrel drink. The Alaskan Indians eat sorrel fermented with other greens such as watercress.

Sorrel has one interesting labor-saving effect: When cooked, it automatically dissolves into a puree. Its wild associations are extended here in a toothsome combination with wild rice.

Wild Rice and Sorrel Flan

2 tablespoons butter	1 cup half and half
2 cups sorrel leaves, stemmed and cut into chiffonade*	salt and pepper
	1 teaspoon oregano
2 cups cooked wild rice**	½ cup grated Monterey Jack
4 eggs	cheese

Preheat oven to 375°F and butter a 10-inch flan pan or quiche dish.

In a small skillet melt butter and sauté sorrel until wilted, about 4 minutes. In a large bowl combine contents of skillet with wild rice.

In a separate bowl stir together eggs, half and half, salt and pepper, oregano, and cheese and add to wild rice, mixing well.

Pour mixture into baking dish and bake for about 25 to 30 minutes, or until top is slightly golden. Serve in wedges.

Serves 6 to 8

Spaghetti Squash

Anything which is also known as "squash novelle" has the right-sounding name for culinary popularity. But Vegetable Spaghetti, Noodle Squash, and Squaghetti refer to this same, oddly constructed, ochre-colored squash. Whatever name you look it up under, you find very little information, and even fewer recipes. Julia Child was responsible for bringing spaghetti squash to national prominence by preparing it on her television show. When she split open the big golden gourd, her viewers marveled at the unfolding threads of ersatz vermicelli. Once people learned that inside that hard exterior was a virtual bowl of spaghetti, the search for spaghetti squash recipes was on.

A Spanish recipe known as Cabello de angel (angel hair) calls for cooking the threads in sugar until they become a thick jam. But most people enjoy this newcomer squash in the kinds of sauces associated with pasta, like this creamy Alfredo.

Spaghetti Squash Alfredo

1 large spaghetti squash	¾ cup heavy cream
water	½ cup grated Parmesan cheese
4 tablespoons butter	salt and pepper

In a large pot of boiling water, cook spaghetti squash, covered, for about 30 minutes or until it can be pierced with the tip of a knife.

When cool enough to handle, cut in half lengthwise. Remove seeds and, with a fork, scrape out insides. The flesh will come out looking like strands of spaghetti.

In a bowl toss squash with remaining ingredients and serve immediately or reheat gently if necessary.

Serves 4 to 6

Spinach

As anyone from the Popeye generation can attest, spinach was once presumed so essential a source of minerals and iron that force-feeding it to unwilling children was considered laudable. It has since been discovered that the vegetable's high oxalic acid content actually prevents the body from utilizing nutrients and calcium. Spinach has always been associated with the concern for better health; at the turn of the century, dietitians strongly urged its consumption, and congressmen seconded their motion by sending seeds home to their constituents. It was also one of the first vegetables to be canned and thus widely distributed. At the same time, cookbooks instructed that, for safety, fresh spinach be washed "in many waters," and boiled for at least half an hour.

New Zealand spinach represents still another mistake in the spinach identity. Discovered in 1770 by Sir Joseph Banks, a scientist on one of Captain Cook's voyages, New Zealand spinach is not spinach at all but a variety of ice plant. It grows in climates too warm for real spinach and, while it can be used in a similar manner, it lacks the delicacy and flavor of its namesake.

The "Spinach Capital of the World" is Zavala County, Texas, which, along with Oklahoma, supplies a good bit of spinach. But California actually produces half the country's crop. Wherever it's from, here are some California ways of serving it.

Spinach-Ricotta Pancakes

1 pound whole-milk ricotta cheese	½ pound spinach, washed, cooked, and chopped
4 eggs	½ cup grated dry Jack cheese

½ cup bread crumbs
¼ cup chopped fresh parsley
1 teaspoon oregano

salt and pepper
vegetable oil for frying

Mix all ingredients except oil until well blended. Allow to rest 30 minutes before using.

In a large skillet heat ½ inch of oil until very hot. Drop batter by heaping tablespoons into hot oil and cook for about 5 minutes on first side and about 3 minutes on second.

Blot pancakes on paper toweling and serve.

Serves 6

Spinach in Garlic Cream

2 tablespoons butter
3 cloves garlic, minced
3 pounds spinach, washed
   and chopped

6 ounces cream cheese, cut in
   pieces
pinch nutmeg
salt and pepper

In a large skillet melt butter and sauté garlic for 2 minutes. Add spinach, stir well, and cook over medium-high heat for about 3 minutes. Lower heat and add remaining ingredients. Cook, stirring, until cream cheese has melted and becomes smooth.

Serves 6

Sunchokes

Reputed to be the only New World vegetable originating in North America, sunchokes were first found in the Indian gardens

287

at Cape Cod in 1605 by Samuel Champlain. Some also credit him with giving them the name "Jerusalem artichokes," though they are actually the roots of sunflowers. These nutty, starchless tubers formed an important part of the Native American diet and were quickly adopted by the colonists for pickling and for soups. Amelia Simmons's <u>American Cookery</u> (1796) fully discussed their care and handling, yet they remain relatively unknown. Even their name is shrouded in mystery. One explanation for "Jerusalem" suggests that this is a mispronunciation of the Italian word for sunflower, <u>girasol.</u>

At any rate, its musty flavors mingle beautifully with the chunked mushrooms in this handsome presentation, laced with bright ribbons of red peppers.

Pan-fried Sunchokes and Mushrooms with Red Peppers

4 tablespoons butter
2 leeks, white part only, thinly sliced
2 red bell peppers, seeded and cut into ¼-inch-wide strips
1 pound sunchokes, peeled and sliced (see Note)

½ pound mushrooms, washed and quartered
½ cup chicken stock*
½ cup heavy cream
salt and pepper
3 tablespoons chopped fresh parsley for garnish

In a large skillet melt butter and sauté leeks over medium heat until tender, about 8 minutes. Add red peppers and cook for another 3 minutes. Add sunchokes and mushrooms, and cook, stirring, 5 minutes more. Pour in chicken stock and cook over medium-high heat until most of the liquid has evaporated. Cover and cook 3 minutes. Uncover, add cream, lower heat, and cook until cream becomes thick, about 3 minutes more. Season with salt and pepper to taste, and sprinkle with parsley.

Serves 6

SUNCHOKE NOTE: Select only very firm, rock-hard chokes and use a very sharp, small paring knife to trim.

Sweet Potatoes

Some people use yams and sweet potatoes interchangeably, but they are, botanically speaking, not even related. Yams are tropical or subtropical shrubs with a sweeter taste and juicier consistency than sweet potatoes. In some areas of the South, there is a class distinction between the two, with the yam winning the higher position. Still, sweet potatoes are much more nutritious and have a texture and chestnut flavor that make them generally more interesting. Certainly they were more interesting to George Washington Carver, who found one hundred new uses for the sweet potato, though few of them would qualify for good eating.

For an interesting twist, try using sweet potatoes in recipes for white potatoes. Or try these appetizing, ginger-sprinkled fritters.

Sweet Potato Fritters

4 large sweet potatoes	1 tablespoon lemon juice
water	2 cups flour
2 tablespoons soy sauce	2 cups beer
2 tablespoons honey	1 teaspoon ground ginger
1 tablespoon dry sherry	fat for deep-frying

Cook sweet potatoes in boiling water for 10 minutes. Drain and, when cool enough to handle, peel and slice into ¼-inch-thick rounds.

In a large shallow bowl, mix soy sauce, honey, sherry, and lemon juice. Marinate potato slices in this mixture for 1 hour.

To make batter, mix the flour, beer, and ginger in a bowl. Heat fat to about 375°F. Dip potato slices in batter and fry until golden brown.

Serves 6

ALTERNATE VEGETABLE NOTE: Turnips can be used instead of sweet potatoes.

Cherry Tomatoes

The design of the cherry tomato rivals the most brilliant feats of modern packaging. At the buffet table, cherry tomatoes make the perfect crudités—dippable, neat, each one no bigger than a mouthful. Easily washable, not too fragile, wholly self-contained, they are flavorful raw or cooked. They can be tossed easily in the salad or the sauté pan. Their recent popularity alone makes them appear like modern hybrids, developed for convenience as well as taste. And yet researchers have proposed that this small variety can probably be traced directly to the original sixteenth-century golden tomatoes of Peru.

As common as they are today, cherry tomatoes are always somewhat special, bubbling out of those little grocery store baskets that make them seem as rare as raspberries. Friends never fail to ask us for this recipe in which the tomatoes are lightly cooked and come to table dripping with garlic butter and crusted bits of Parmesan.

Pan-fried Cherry Tomatoes in Garlic Butter

2 tablespoons butter
2 tablespoons olive oil
2 cloves garlic, halved
3 cups cherry tomatoes
½ cup fresh bread crumbs

3 tablespoons chopped fresh
parsley
2 tablespoons grated
Parmesan cheese
salt and pepper

In a large skillet heat butter and oil. Add garlic and cook just until it becomes brown around edges, then discard. In same skillet sauté cherry tomatoes for about 5 minutes, tossing every so often.

In a bowl combine remaining ingredients, add to skillet, stirring gently to combine with tomatoes. Cook 2 minutes longer and add salt and pepper to taste.

Serves 6

Tomato

"A cooked tomato is like a cooked oyster, ruined...." or thus spake Andre Simon in his Encyclopedia. But he consoles us that, since the other ingredients in the cooking pot take in all the tomato's taste and nutrients, all is not lost. To cook or not to cook has always been the question with tomatoes. Some early cookbooks advise long hours on the flame, possibly to get rid of the suspected toxins and mysterious powers once attributed to the tomato. The first chef to prepare a dish of raw tomatoes does not, however, deserve the highest place of honor in tomato mythology. That accolade belongs to Colonel Robert Gibbon Johnson who, in 1830, publicly ate a raw tomato on the steps of the Salem, New Jersey, courthouse in order to disprove all the nasty rumors about its poisonous potential. Judging from subsequent tomato sales, news of Johnson's derring-do may have been convincing. The records of Boston's Quincy Hall market reflected a dramatic rise in sales. So did the tomato departments at the major vegetable markets from Philadelphia and Washington, D.C., to Cincinnati. Around the same time, Frances Trollope (Domestic Manners) called tomatoes "the great luxury of the American table."

Tomatoes were destined to have another day in court, this time the Supreme Court, which declared that although the tomato was, botanically, a fruit, it is a vegetable for all legal and commercial purposes. Author Jane Grigson has another word for the commercially produced vegetables: She calls them "tomatoes of the underprivileged kind." Nevertheless, if you don't grow your own, you can only select the best-looking specimens available and hope for the best. When they're good, they're absolutely wonderful raw, i.e., "unruined."

Tomatoes are best unrefrigerated, stored in a cool place, upside down. An empty egg carton is a good place to keep them. This recipe, with its comfortable lunch-counter name, is a pretty, savory way to serve a tomato dish in which the vegetable is still, essentially, uncooked.

BLT Puree

3 heads Boston lettuce, cored	8 strips of bacon, crisply
water	cooked, broken into small
½ cup heavy cream	pieces
2 tablespoons butter	6 medium tomatoes, tops
salt and pepper	removed and hollowed out

Cook lettuce in boiling water to cover for about 3 minutes. Drain well and allow to cool.

Puree lettuce with cream and butter until very smooth. Add salt and pepper, and bacon bits. Spoon onto tomatoes and serve.

Serves 6

Turnips

Turnips were originally called "neeps," from the Latin napus, the same origin as the French navet. The prefix "turn" was added to "neep" to signify their spherical shape. Turnips are also called "rutabagas" and "swedes," but this is a result of confusion among these similar-looking root vegetables. In general, rutabagas and swedes are not as smooth as turnips and often have several circles of ridges at the base of the leaves.

Turnips are important in several delicious dishes. The Pennsylvania Dutch so appreciate their delicate flavor that they grate them raw into their own variety of coleslaw. Early New Englanders mashed them with potatoes and ate them with mutton. People of Scottish background are familiar with "Haggis and Bashed Neeps," and another more spirited combination called "Neeps with Nips." The French stew, Navarin, is based on lamb and spring turnips.

Turnips may have reached the height of their powers when they inspired the great Escoffier to create his famous Stuffed Turnips. Pickled turnips have been used as imitation anchovies. In California, young white spring turnips are much favored, raw as well as cooked. Some of the vegetable's more unexpected delights are developed in this somewhat unusual treatment, in which the turnips are glazed with jalapeño jelly and speckled with chopped coriander.

Turnips Glazed in Jalapeño Jelly

1½ pounds turnips, peeled and
    cut into ovals, balls, or
    bite-size pieces
4 cups water with 1 teaspoon
    salt added

4 teaspoons butter
    salt and pepper
½ cup jalapeño jelly**
½ cup coarsely chopped fresh
    coriander leaves for garnish

Cook turnips in boiling salted water for 5 minutes. Drain and set aside.

In a large skillet melt butter and sauté turnips for 5 minutes. Add salt and pepper and jelly and cook until turnips are glazed, about 3 minutes.

Sprinkle with coriander and serve.

Serves 6

ALTERNATE VEGETABLE NOTE: Rutabaga can be used instead of turnips.

Zucchini

In July, many amateur zucchini growers are tempted to hide behind the couch when the doorbell rings. This is often the only way to avoid the generosity of neighboring zucchini growers, whose crop has also proliferated widely and too well.

This zucchini potlatch may have deep roots on this continent, since squash in general was always an important food to the Native Americans. The word squash is Narragansett Indian and means "something eaten green." Once adopted by America's settlers, squash became an object of fascination because of its dramatic range of sizes. In typical American fashion, contests were held for the largest specimens, taste being irrelevant. One such New England competition was thus described: "The only squash on earth that ever grew bigger than the 55-pound marrow squash that Bill Gray had brought from his Yarmouth acres was the one that Bill Gray had left at home, to keep for himself."

Most zucchini recipes, including these, will work with any of the summer squashes, including the club-shaped yellow crooknecks; the ruffled pattypans or cymlings; the pear-shaped, furrowed chayote; the yellow straightnecks; tapering, green-striped cocozzelles; and green-yellow Casertas.

Mock Zucchini "Pasta"

4 tablespoons olive oil
2 cloves garlic, minced
1½ pounds zucchini, scrubbed and finely shredded (the julienne disc of your food processor does a great job)
½ cup heavy cream
salt and pepper
2 tablespoons butter
4 tablespoons chopped fresh parsley
4 tablespoons grated Parmesan cheese

In a large skillet heat oil and sauté garlic until wilted. Add zucchini, toss to coat with oil, cover, and cook 30 seconds over medium heat. Add cream, salt and pepper, and cook, uncovered, for another minute. Add butter and parsley and mix well.

Top with grated cheese and serve.

Serves 6

Zucchini in Lime and Thyme

4 tablespoons butter
1½ pounds zucchini, scrubbed and thinly sliced
salt and pepper
3 tablespoons lime juice
1 teaspoon thyme for garnish

In a large skillet melt butter. Add zucchini, salt and pepper, and cook covered, over medium heat for 5 minutes. Uncover, raise heat, and cook for another 3 to 5 minutes, or until most of the liquid evaporates. Sprinkle with lime juice and thyme and serve.

Serves 6

Zucchini Wedges Sautéed in Balsamic Vinegar and Pine Nuts

6 medium-size firm zucchini,
scrubbed and quartered
lengthwise
water
4 tablespoons butter
1 clove garlic, minced

½ cup pine nuts
2 tablespoons balsamic
vinegar**
pinch sugar
salt and pepper
½ teaspoon oregano

Cook zucchini wedges in a large pot of boiling water for 1 minute. Drain and set aside.

In a large skillet melt butter and sauté garlic and pine nuts until garlic wilts and pine nuts color slightly. Add vinegar and sugar, stir, and cook over high heat for about 30 seconds, or until bubbles form around edges. Add zucchini, salt and pepper, and oregano. Cook over medium heat, tossing to coat with vinegar–pine nut mixture, about 5 minutes.

Serve hot or at room temperature.

Serves 6

ALTERNATE VEGETABLE NOTE: Cucumber can be used instead of zucchini.

THE BREAD
BASKET

Bread has suddenly become exciting. People have discovered that bread can actually be considered food, an important and whole-some part of the meal. This popularity may be due to the liberation of bread from the undesirable associations of its recent past. It was difficult to develop much affection for white bread that had all the character of cotton swabs, or for wheat bread that looked faintly promising but tasted whiter than white. In the past decade, people reacted against these nutritionless loaves and sought flours and breads that didn't have all the goodness processed out of them.

Food processors and mixers with dough hooks may have contributed to the boom in home-baked bread, but others found their motivation not in technology but in nostalgia. Those who left the locus of real Jewish rye or hefty pumpernickels had only themselves to turn to. They could trek through a succession of disappointing bakeries or they could bake bread at home. They did a little of each. They could also beseech visiting easterners to bring a dozen bagels which, even though they would arrive stale, would be better than the local ones with the raisins. Southerners, with a tradition of hoecakes, corn dodgers, and johnnycakes, have inherited a passion for and an expertise with spoon breads, corn muffins, and corn breads. Regional rediscoveries have uncovered such traditions as New England's "rye 'n' injun" bread and the mysteriously named "third bread" (a third each of rye, corn, and wheat). By digging up old family recipes and searching out regional ingredients, Americans are again enjoying the robust rye breads of the Pennsylvania Germans; the rice flour breads of South Carolina and Georgia; substantial whole-grain breads from the wheat-milling centers of the Midwest.

Traditionally, one preference was common to all regions: Americans have always liked their bread hot. In fact, though it is hard to claim originality in the age-old realm of bread, it might be proposed that this country initiated the eating of hot toast. Not toast; hot toast. The colonists had their toasting forks and wrought-iron toasting mechanisms. But no one bothered with the old toast racks of England, where hot slices were stacked until they got cold enough to eat.

Toasted or not, there is no denying the warmth that bread making can create. "It is pleasant," says M.F.K. Fisher, "one of those almost hypnotic businesses, like a dance from some ancient ceremony." Perhaps the most important reason for the current popularity of bread lies in the fact that bread is, in the words of Laurel Robertson's The Laurel's Kitchen Bread Book, the "convenience food par excellence."

That is doubly true of the breads in this section, many of which are as convenient for the cook as for the eater. It may seem odd that we have omitted the native California sourdoughs, but to be made properly, they need the more detailed instruction provided by specialized bread-baking books. The choices here run from yeast breads to scones, from crusty garlic wheat loaves to chile biscuits and wild rice muffins. For the most part, you can make them with ingredients you already have in the house.

FOOD PROCESSOR BREAD NOTE: Although the following recipes contain instructions for making bread by hand, all our yeast breads may be made successfully in the food processor fitted with a steel blade. In the processor bowl blend dry ingredients together. With machine running, add liquids, processing until a dough is formed. The processor motor generates a lot of heat, enough, in fact, to kill the yeast, so we recommend using the proofing* liquid no higher than 100°F (lukewarm). Partial kneading may be done in the processor, but we have found that some manual kneading gives the bread a better texture. Muffins and biscuits should be made as directed in the recipes. The food processor is too powerful to yield light results. (Beaten Biscuit Bites with Chives are an exception, designed specifically for the food processor.)

Country Caraway Bread
Whole-Wheat Garlic French Bread
Dried Mushroom and Dill Bread
Blush Bread
Basil Baguettes
Brown Sugar and Spice Brioche
Sun-dried Tomato Focaccia
Willie's Spoon Bread
Beaten Biscuit Bites with Chives
Chile-Cornmeal Biscuits
Peaches and Cream Scones
Herbed Olive Muffins
Black Muffins
Brown Sugar Muffins
Wild Rice and Cheddar Muffins
Fluffins

Country Caraway Bread

3 cups all-purpose flour
½ cup rye flour
½ cup whole-wheat flour
1 tablespoon caraway seed
  plus additional seeds for
  topping
1 teaspoon salt

3 tablespoons sugar
1 package dry yeast proofed*
  in 1½ cups warm water
  with 1 tablespoon honey
1 egg, room temperature
  milk for glaze

In a large bowl combine dry ingredients. Add yeast mixture and egg and stir well.

Turn out onto a floured surface (mixture will be sticky) and knead for about 2 minutes. Place in a 9"-×-5" greased loaf pan, cover with greased plastic wrap, and let rise in a warm place for about 45 minutes. Meanwhile, preheat oven to 425°F.

Bake about 30 minutes, remove loaf from pan, brush with milk, and sprinkle with caraway and return to oven to finish baking for another 20 minutes. Allow to cool on rack before slicing.

Makes 1 loaf

Whole-Wheat Garlic French Bread

4½ cups all-purpose flour
2½ cups whole-wheat flour
3 teaspoons salt
2 packages dry yeast
  proofed* in 3¼ cups warm
  water with 2 tablespoons
  sugar

2 cloves garlic, chopped
2 tablespoons cornmeal
  water

In a large bowl combine dry ingredients. Pour in yeast mixture and mix well until you have a soft dough.

Turn out on a floured surface, knead until smooth and elastic, about 5 minutes. Add additional flour as needed. Place dough in a greased bowl and cover with plastic wrap. Let rise in a warm spot until doubled —about 1 hour.

Punch dough down and turn out onto a floured surface. Knead for about 1 minute. Divide dough in half. Roll out half at a time to a 15"-×-10" rectangle. Sprinkle with half the garlic and roll up tightly on long side, like a jelly roll. Repeat with other half.

Place dough seam side down on a cookie sheet that has been sprinkled with cornmeal. Place in a warm spot and allow to rise 30 minutes. Meanwhile, preheat oven to 400°F.

With a sharp knife or razor make diagonal cuts on top of loaves. Brush with water and bake for about 35 minutes. Breads should give a hollow sound when tapped. Allow to cool on racks before slicing.

Makes 2 loaves

Dried Mushroom and Dill Bread

1½ ounces porcini (dried) mushrooms** soaked in hot water to cover for 30 minutes
2 teaspoons sugar
1 package dry yeast
2 tablespoons butter
1 shallot, chopped
3 cups all-purpose flour

2 teaspoons salt
3 tablespoons chopped fresh dill, or 1 tablespoon dried dill
2 tablespoons cornmeal
milk for glaze
2 tablespoons dill seed (optional)

Drain mushrooms and reserve water, which will be dark brown. If reserved mushroom water appears sandy, strain through double thickness of paper towel or cheesecloth and place in a measuring cup. Add enough warm water to make 1 cup of liquid. Proof* yeast with 1 teaspoon sugar in warm mushroom liquid.

Coarsely chop mushrooms. In a skillet heat butter and sauté mushrooms with shallots for about 5 minutes. Set aside.

In a large bowl combine flour, 1 teaspoon sugar, salt, and dill. Add yeast mixture, mix well, and turn out onto a floured surface. Knead until smooth and elastic, about 10 minutes.

Place dough in a greased bowl, cover with plastic wrap, and set in a warm spot to rise until doubled, about 60 minutes.

Punch dough down and roll out to a 10"-×-15" rectangle on a floured surface. Sprinkle with mushroom mixture and roll up tightly at long side, like a jelly roll. Pinch all edges to seal.

Place on a baking sheet sprinkled with cornmeal and let rise for about 45 minutes. Meanwhile, preheat oven to 400°F.

With a sharp knife make diagonal slashes on top of dough.

Bake for 15 minutes, brush with milk, and sprinkle with dill seed. Return to oven and bake for another 15 to 20 minutes. Allow to cool on rack before slicing.

Makes 1 loaf

Blush Bread

2 red peppers, roasted,* peeled, and seeded	1½ packages dry yeast
2 tablespoons imported tomato paste**	3½ cups flour
	½ cup polenta (or finely ground cornmeal)
1 tablespoon sugar	1 teaspoon salt
1 teaspoon sweet paprika	½ cup chopped green onions
¾ cup warm water	2 tablespoons olive oil

In a food processor or blender make a puree of the peppers, tomato paste, sugar, paprika, and water. Proof* yeast in this mixture.

In a large bowl combine flour, polenta, salt, and green onions. Add yeast mixture and oil and mix well. Turn out onto a floured surface and knead about 10 minutes, adding more flour if necessary, until dough is smooth and elastic.

302

Place in a greased bowl, cover with plastic wrap, and let rise 1 hour in a warm spot until doubled.

Punch dough down and knead for about 1 minute. Shape into a round and place in a greased 8- or 9-inch springform pan. Cover again with greased plastic wrap and allow to rise in a warm spot 1 hour or until dough rises just above top of pan. Meanwhile, preheat oven to 375°F.

With a sharp knife or razor make 4 criss-cross slashes across top of bread. Bake for about 25 minutes. Remove from pan and continue baking for another 15 to 20 minutes. Allow to cool on rack before slicing.

Makes 1 loaf

Basil Baguettes

3 cups all-purpose flour
1 tablespoon salt
1 cup finely chopped fresh
    basil leaves
2 packages dry yeast
    proofed* in 1 cup warm
    water with 1 teaspoon
    sugar

3 tablespoons olive oil
cornmeal
water
sesame seeds (optional)

In a large bowl combine flour, salt, and basil. Pour in yeast mixture and olive oil and stir until mixture holds together.

On a floured surface knead dough until smooth and elastic. Place dough in a greased bowl, cover with plastic wrap, and let rise in a warm spot until doubled, about 1 hour.

Punch dough down and divide into three pieces. Form into long, thin baguettes and place on a baking sheet sprinkled with cornmeal. With a sharp knife or razor, slash the tops diagonally. Brush with water and sprinkle with sesame seeds. Place in a cold oven and set temperature at 350°F. Bake for about 40 to 50 minutes, or until deep golden brown.

Makes 3 baguettes

Brown Sugar and Spice Brioche

2 cups all-purpose flour
2 tablespoons brown sugar
½ teaspoon each ground nutmeg, cinnamon, and mace
1 teaspoon salt
1 package dry yeast proofed* in ¼ cup warm water with 1 tablespoon honey

2 eggs
6 tablespoons butter, very soft
egg wash made by mixing 1 egg with 1 tablespoon water

In a large bowl of mixer place all dry ingredients and stir well. Pour in yeast mixture and eggs and beat until well combined. Add butter and beat again until all traces of butter have disappeared into the dough (dough will be sticky).

Turn out onto a floured surface and knead well, adding more flour if necessary, until dough becomes smooth and shiny. Place in a greased bowl, cover with plastic wrap, and let rise in a warm spot until doubled, about 1½ hours.

Punch dough down and refrigerate, covered, overnight.

Grease a 6-cup brioche mold or loaf pan and place dough in it. Cover and let rise again until doubled, about 1 hour. Meanwhile, preheat oven to 425°F.

Brush dough with egg wash and bake for 10 minutes. Then reduce heat to 350° and continue to bake for another 35 minutes, or until browned.

Makes 1 brioche

Sun-dried Tomato Focaccia

2½ cups all-purpose flour
½ cup whole-wheat flour
1 teaspoon salt
1 package yeast proofed* in
   ¾ cup warm water
6 tablespoons olive oil (use
   some from tomato jar)

6 sun-dried tomatoes,** coarsely chopped
2 cloves garlic, finely minced
4 tablespoons chopped basil

Combine flours and salt in a bowl. Add yeast mixture and 4 tablespoons olive oil, mix well, and knead dough into a ball. Place in an oiled bowl, cover with plastic wrap, and let rise in a warm spot until doubled, about 1 hour.

Punch dough down and knead in sun-dried tomatoes until they are well distributed throughout dough. Form into a ball again, place into oiled bowl, cover, and let rise about 1 hour until doubled.

Preheat oven to 425°F.

Roll out dough onto well-floured surface into a disc 12 to 14 inches in diameter—about ¼-inch thick. Make slight dents on surface with fingertips. Sprinkle with garlic and basil and press into dough. Brush with remaining 2 tablespoons olive oil. Bake on pizza stone, tiles, or

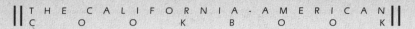
cookie sheet for 15 to 20 minutes or until golden brown. Serve hot, warm, or at room temperature.

Makes 1 focaccia

Willie's Spoon Bread

1 cup white cornmeal	1 cup buttermilk
1 teaspoon salt	¼ teaspoon baking soda
1 cup boiling water	3 eggs
¼ cup butter	

Preheat oven to 375°F and butter well a medium soufflé dish or casserole.

Pour cornmeal and salt into a pot or bowl of boiling water with butter. Slowly stir in buttermilk and baking soda. Beat in eggs.

Pour mixture into casserole and bake for 30 minutes. Serve with butter.

Serves 4 to 6

Beaten Biscuit Bites with Chives

¼ cup chopped fresh chives	4 tablespoons butter
1¾ cups all-purpose flour	4 tablespoons lard
¼ cup whole-wheat flour	½ cup ice water
1 teaspoon salt	

Preheat oven to 375°F.

In a food processor bowl place chives, flours, and salt. Process until chives are finely minced and well mixed with the other dry ingredients.

Add butter and lard by tablespoons and process with on-off turns until mixture is crumbly. With machine running pour in water and process until mixture forms a ball. Continue to process for 2 additional minutes.

Roll dough out onto a floured surface to ¼-inch thickness. Cut with 1½-inch round cutter. Re-roll scraps gently and cut again, then place biscuits on an ungreased cookie sheet. Prick tops with fork. Bake for 25–30 minutes, or until golden.

Makes about 36 bites

Chile-Cornmeal Biscuits

1½ cups all-purpose flour	½ cup cold butter, plus 2
½ cup cornmeal	tablespoons butter, melted
1 tablespoon sugar	½ cup buttermilk
½ teaspoon ground cumin	2 jalapeño peppers,* finely
1 tablespoon baking powder	minced
1 teaspoon baking soda	¼ cup chopped fresh
pinch salt	coriander leaves

Preheat oven to 450°F and grease a cookie sheet.

In a large bowl combine dry ingredients. Cut in pieces of cold butter until mixture is crumbly. Add remaining ingredients, except melted butter, and stir until mixture comes together to form a dough.

On a floured surface, knead 1 minute; roll out dough to ½-inch thickness. Cut biscuits with 2½-inch round cutter. Re-roll scraps gently and cut again. Place on the cookie sheet, brush with melted butter, and bake for 12 to 15 minutes, until golden.

Makes approximately 12 biscuits

Peaches and Cream Scones

2 cups all-purpose flour
2 tablespoons sugar
2 teaspoons baking powder
1 teaspoon baking soda
½ teaspoon salt

½ cup finely chopped dried
  peaches
3 tablespoons butter
1 egg beaten with ⅓ cup
  sour cream

Preheat oven to 400°F and grease a cookie sheet.

In a medium bowl combine flour, sugar, baking powder, baking soda, salt, and peaches. Cut in butter until mixture becomes crumbly. Stir in egg mixture just until dough holds together.

Place dough on a lightly floured surface and knead very briefly, about 1 minute. Pull off pieces the size of golf balls and with knuckles flatten them to ½-inch thickness.

Prick tops with a fork and place scones on the cookie sheet. Bake for 10 to 15 minutes, or until lightly browned.

Makes 8 to 10 scones

Herbed Olive Muffins

2 cups all-purpose flour
½ teaspoon salt
½ teaspoon oregano
1 teaspoon minced garlic
2 teaspoons baking powder
1 cup black California
  olives,** pitted and finely
  chopped

1 egg
1½ tablespoons olive oil
1 cup milk

Preheat oven to 400°F and grease 12 muffin tins.

In a bowl, combine flour, salt, oregano, garlic, baking powder, and olives.

In a separate bowl beat egg with oil and milk. Pour egg mixture into dry ingredients, stirring just enough to moisten. Batter will be slightly lumpy.

Fill muffin tins two thirds full and bake for 20 to 25 minutes.

Makes 12 muffins

Black Muffins

2 cups whole-wheat flour	1 tablespoon sugar
½ teaspoon salt	2 teaspoons baking powder
¼ teaspoon each cinnamon, mace, allspice, ground ginger, ground nutmeg	2¼ cups milk
	¼ cup vegetable oil
1 tablespoon unsweetened cocoa powder	1 egg

Preheat oven to 400°F and grease 12 muffin tins.

In a bowl combine dry ingredients.

In a separate bowl mix milk, oil, and egg until well combined. Pour milk mixture into dry ingredients and stir just until moistened. Batter will be slightly lumpy.

Pour batter into muffin tins and bake for 20 minutes.

Makes 12 muffins

Brown Sugar Muffins

½ cup butter
1 cup brown sugar
1 egg
2 cups all-purpose flour
1 teaspoon baking powder

1 teaspoon baking soda
pinch salt
1 cup milk
1 teaspoon vanilla
½ cup chopped pecans

Preheat oven to 400°F and grease 12 large or 24 small muffin tins.

In a large bowl, beat butter and sugar until creamy. Add egg and mix well.

In a separate bowl combine flour, baking powder, baking soda, and salt and add to butter mixture alternately with milk. Stir in vanilla and nuts.

Pour batter into muffin tins and bake for 15 to 20 minutes.

Makes 12 to 24 muffins

Wild Rice and Cheddar Muffins

1 cup cooked wild rice**
1⅓ cups all-purpose flour
2 teaspoons baking powder
1 teaspoon salt
1 tablespoon sugar
¼ cup chopped green onions

½ cup grated sharp cheddar
cheese
2 eggs
6 tablespoons vegetable oil
1 cup milk

Preheat oven to 425°F and grease 12 muffin tins.

In a large bowl combine rice, flour, baking powder, salt, sugar, green onions, and cheese.

In a separate bowl beat eggs with oil and milk. Pour egg mixture into rice mixture and stir just until blended.

Spoon batter into muffin tins and bake for about 15 minutes, or until golden brown.

Makes 12 muffins

Fluffins

1¾ cups unbleached white flour	pinch salt
2 tablespoons sugar	1 cup milk
2¼ teaspoons baking powder	1 egg, separated
	3 ounces butter, melted

Place an empty 12-mold muffin tin in the oven and preheat to 375°F.

Into a food processor measure flour, sugar, baking powder, and salt. Mix by processing on and off 3 or 4 times.

In a separate bowl mix milk, egg yolk, and melted butter. Pour through processor feed tube and process until mixed. Beat egg white until stiff and fold into the other ingredients.

Remove muffin tin from oven and grease lightly. Spoon batter into molds, filling about half full. Batter will be sticky. Bake about 25 to 30 minutes, until lightly browned.

Makes 12 muffins

FRESH FINALES

Dessert is on the table from the start, both as ornament and aperitif. A whole "election cake," perhaps, with three wedge-shaped pieces already cut—two to be eaten and one to refuse.... For good measure there may be a handsome pie, uncut as yet because "we may not get to it."

Bertha Damon, *A Sense of Humus*

Beginning with the first successful harvest, making dessert in this country became a favorite and often necessary pastime. Once under cultivation, the earth yielded its treasures in abundance. Fruit trees bowed under their own bounty. There was cream and butter and wheat. And then there was always winter. Many desserts, preserves, compotes, relishes, and dried fruits were a form of storage between harvests. The confections they became were honest dishes, evolving naturally from the work and process of living, forming a wholeness. As Evan Jones says in his wonderful work, American Food, these basic good things still conjure up "kitchens in farmhouses or in frame dwellings with porches opening to elm-shaded streets." Somewhere in back, behind the kitchen, a pie safe kept the day's productions secure, though usually not for long.

Even when the larder was all but depleted and the period called "the six weeks want" ensued, some persevering soul came through with the surprisingly passable Vinegar Pie. An imbalance of supplies must have had something to do with such unlikely inspirations as Tomato Meringue Pie, Pork Cake, Spinach Dessert Pudding, and Chocolate Potato Cake. Even on the frontier, the determination for a sweet to end the meal prevailed. Spotted Pup is an example of this wagon-train cuisine, though its exact ingredients remain, thankfully, lost in the dust.

American desserts were always homey. Their names had innocence in them: Blueberry Buckles, Slumps and Grunts, Shoofly Pie, Funny Cake, Maple Frango. Stack Cakes from the Smoky Mountains were layers of molasses cake with applesauce for mortar. White Mountain Cake was a big, white, fluffy affair proudly constructed by Colorado cooks who, using a series of graduated baking pans for the layers, simulated the surrounding mountainous topography, complete with snowfall. Cookies especially were whimsically named: Joe Froggers, Jumbles and Crinkles, Wasps' Nests, Tangle Breeches, and Jolly Boys.

In one form or another, dessert became the centerpiece of community events, as women contributed their Apple Brown Bettys and Indian Puddings to church bake sales, camp meetings, and political rallies. In Connecticut, politicos toasted their victories or defeats with big slices of brandy-blessed Hartford Election Cake which, like Independence Cake and Federal Cake, was also sold to raise campaign money. Dessert became so omnipresent by the early 1800s that an English visitor noted in his diary that his meals were followed by what could only be called "a wilderness of sweets." It was not unknown for wealthy hosts to have their guests, after dinner, escorted to a separate dining room where the table was set with ostentatious arrays of lavish desserts.

Sometimes dessert gave rise to informal social institutions, from brownie-making parties and taffy-pulling contests to intercollegiate fudge competitions. Some form of competition must have led to the Feuding Cake which had two other, perhaps more explanatory names: Whiskey Cake and Moonshine Cake. In contrast, people who made Scripture Cakes or Bible Cakes had to be familiar with the Good Book since the cooking instructions included specific biblical references. A series of children's stories by Rebecca Sophia Clarke led to a rage for Dolly Dimples Vinegar Candy. Some confections could be downright aggressive, such as the bonbons called Secrets and Wintergreen Hearts, into which the cook could bake little verses or personal messages. Doughnuts were always sacrosanct. The gift of doughnuts generated so much enthusiasm among the World War I military that appreciative soldiers acquired the nickname "Doughboys." And in Rockport, Maine, a plaque hangs on the house of Captain Hanson Crockett Gregory, who is credited with inventing the doughnut in 1847. Though only a child at the time, young Hanson still had the presence of mind to poke the holes out of his mother's round cakes before she fried them. This behavior may have merited no more than a good slap on the wrist as far as Hanson's mother was concerned, but doughnut lovers have cast it in bronze.

Many desserts had specific functions, often evident from their names. Preaching Pies were an Amish specialty given to children during church services to keep them quiet. In Pennsylvania Dutch country, the raisin-studded rosina pie has become one of the customary foods brought to wakes and burials, which accounts for its more common nickname, "Funeral Pie." But no one seems to know what the little cakes called Nun's Sighs were supposed to accomplish.

Some desserts were created to honor great occasions or visits by important personages. The most famous of these is probably Baked Alaska, a commemoration of the purchase of Alaska. This meringue-covered ice-cream concoction, whose flame-resistant qualities may be its greatest asset, was the 1867 brainchild of Chef Rahhofer of New York's Delmonico's restaurant, though similar constructions had existed for years. In 1824 Lafayette Cakes were everywhere in celebration of the return of the Revolutionary War hero. Maryland's Kossuth Cake honored the 1851 visit of the great Hungarian patriot, General Lajos Kossuth. New Orleans cooks are proud of an appropriately theatrical production called the "Sarah Bernhardt Cake."

But these famous-name cakes were usually made by professional chefs at luxury restaurants or in wealthy households. Designed to dazzle visually, their architectural attributes were often more important than their taste. They may have been beautiful, but professional creations are not the stuff that nostalgia is made of. Louisa May Alcott did not name her home for the stately Charlotte Russe or Croquembouche—she named it Apple Slump. Edgar A. Guest— and who could be more nostalgic than Edgar A. Guest—undoubtedly composed many an appreciative couplet for his all-time favorite, "apple pie and cheese." And when Emily Dickinson baked her Black Cake as a gift for friends, she made it exceptionally evocative by folding some of her verses into the batter.

The truth seems to be that, in this country, as dessert goes, so goes the nation. The legacy is in all of our kitchens: Apple Pandowdies and Blackberry Flummeries, Snickerdoodles and Petticoat Tails. As you will see in the desserts in this section, we have tried to keep a continuity with these traditions while developing new recipes that are as right and consistent with our lives now as past desserts were for their own times.

Blackberry Sour Cream Pie
Santa Rosa Plum Tart
Lime Meringue Pie with Pecan Crust
Orange-Chocolate Tart
Wild Blueberry and Cheese Open-Pie
Oregon Cherry-Berry Turnovers

Cranberry Black Bottom Pie
Mocha Mousse Mud Pie
The Cake of Four Chocolates
White Chocolate Pear Brownies
Buried Treasure Truffles
Ginger-Peachy Roulade
Persimmon Walnut Log
Apricot-Almond Pound Cake
Mint Julep Pound Cake
California Poppy Seed Coffee Cake
New-Fashioned Strawberry Shortcake
Sausalito Sophisticated Saucepan Torte
Pear and Cranberry Whole-Wheat Cobbler
Apricot Swirl Cheesecake
Oatmeal and Brown Sugar Wafers
Black and Whites
Persimmon Peanut Bars
Pistachio Meringue-Aroons
Sourdough Bread Pudding
Steamed Apple-Simmon Pudding
Burnt Cream over Huckleberries
Pumpkin Custard
Tangerine-Coconut Flan
Banana Split Soufflé
Nectarines in Caramel Cream
Baked Apples Alaska
Fall Fruits Gratin
Raspberries with Coffee Sabayon (Zabaglione)
Babcock Peaches Poached in Champagne with Blueberries
Compote of Dried and Fresh Fruits with Honey-Lime Sauce
Fresh Figs and Kiwis in Chardonnay with Crème Fraiche
Red and Green Grapes in Maple-Walnut Cream
Comice Pears Stuffed with Goat Cheese and Rolled in Walnuts
Dried Figs Stuffed with Walnuts and Dipped in Chocolate
White Chocolate–Hazelnut Mousse with Raspberry Sauce
Rhubarb-Strawberry Sherbet
Apple Ice Cream à la Mode
Maple–Pine Nut Ice Cream

Blackberry Sour Cream Pie

For Americans of eastern European descent, sour cream is a traditional and favorite food; it can be part of any course in the meal, from borscht to goulash to sour cream raisin pie. The Scotch-Irish of the eighteenth-century southern backcountry and western Pennsylvania produced quite a similar product called Bonny Clabber, and as early as 1796, Amelia Simmons in American Cookery was using sour cream as a basic ingredient in cookie recipes.

The sour cream in this recipe is paired with blackberries, once maligned as a bothersome weed, but now produced deliberately in great profusion. Served with cream, blackberries made a delicious nineteenth-century dessert called Blackberry Flummery. The simple addition of one tablespoon of cornstarch transformed a flummery into a less melodic dish called Blackberry Mush. Here the voluptuous whole berries burst their sweet juices into a slightly tart, creamy custard. Underneath it all, a sour cream shell adds to the festivities.

Crust

½ cup sweet butter	2 tablespoons sour cream
1¼ cups flour	½ teaspoon salt

Filling

4 egg yolks	¼ teaspoon salt
½ cup sugar	¾ cup sour cream
¼ cup flour	3–4 cups blackberries, washed

To make the crust: In a bowl cut butter into flour until crumbly. Add sour cream and salt until dough holds together. Form ball of dough into flat disc and chill about 1 hour.

Preheat oven to 375°F. Remove dough from refrigerator, roll out, and fit into a 9-inch pie pan. Bake about 20 minutes, or until light golden in color. Check after 10 minutes to make sure center is not puffing up. If it is, prick with a fork. Keep oven on after removing crust.

To prepare filling: In a bowl mix all filling ingredients except berries until smooth. Spread half the sour cream mixture in crust, fill with berries, and then drizzle remaining sour cream mixture over berries.

Bake pie for about 40 minutes, or until the filling is set and lightly browned. Serve warm or at room temperature.

Serves 8

Santa Rosa Plum Tart

Diaphanous Queen Claude sounds like a provocative creature, though she's only one of what Pliny called "the enormous crowd of plums." In the plum crowd, unusual names abound: the Chickasaw plum, Coe's Violet, mirabelle, the Pershore egg, quetsch. Some varieties are prized for eating out of hand, others for the superior jams and tarts that they can become, and still others as the most picturesque of ornamental trees.

With the possible exception of Antarctica, plums grow everywhere in the world. One variety, probably the beach plum, was part of the first Thanksgiving dinner in 1621. California produces ninety percent of this country's plums, which include forty separate varieties. Santa Rosa Plums, a major part of California's commerical crop, are derived from the Japanese plum, a fruit so important in its native country that the wet season during which it ripens is called the time of the "plum rains." When Luther Burbank brought the Japanese plum to this country, he named it after the northern California town in which he lived. Made into a tart with some ground California almonds, the Santa Rosa Plum makes a great regional specialty available to plum lovers everywhere.

Pâte Sucrée

1½ cups flour
pinch salt
4 tablespoons sugar
8 tablespoons cold sweet
butter

½ teaspoon vanilla
1 egg yolk
2 tablespoons ice water

Filling

½ teaspoon cinnamon
½ cup ground almonds
4–5 cups Santa Rosa plums,
pitted and quartered

½ cup sugar
2 teaspoons grated lemon
zest*

½ cup currant jelly

To make pâte sucrée: In a bowl or food processor mix flour, salt, and sugar. Cut in butter until mixture is crumbly. In a separate bowl combine vanilla, yolk, and water. Add to flour mixture and process or mix until dough holds together. Form into a disc, wrap, and refrigerate at least 1 hour before using.

Preheat oven to 350°F. Roll out pastry and fit into a 9- or 10-inch removable-bottom tart pan.

To make filling: Mix cinnamon and nuts in a cup and sprinkle over bottom of unbaked crust, pressing them in gently with fingertips.

Mix plums with sugar and lemon zest in a bowl. Place fruit in concentric circles on top of nut mixture to make a petallike design. Bake for 1 hour, or until fruit is bubbly in the center.

While tart is warm, brush with currant glaze made by boiling currant jelly for 1 minute. Serve with a dollop of crème fraiche* or unsweetened whipped cream, if you like.

Serves 8

Lime Meringue Pie with Pecan Crust

A nineteenth-century English visitor to this country noted in his travel journal that pie seemed to be "as important a factor in American civilization as the pot-au-feu" in France. At about the same time, Mark Twain was traveling abroad, reminiscing that one of the things he missed most was "all sorts of American pastry."

One of the most famous all-American pies is the classic lemon meringue, created at Boston's Parker House, which opened its doors in 1855. In this variation, the lime and ground toasted pecans completely transform the traditional taste and texture. And because this deliciously different pie looks so familiar, it is always a surprise.

Crust

1¼ cups flour
½ cup finely ground toasted pecans*
pinch salt
2 tablespoons powdered sugar

¼ pound sweet butter
1 egg yolk
3 tablespoons water
2 teaspoons lime juice

Filling

4 egg yolks
⅔ cup sugar
½ cup fresh lime juice (3–4 limes), plus 1 tablespoon grated lime zest*

8 tablespoons sweet butter
1 or 2 drops green food coloring (optional)

Meringue

4 egg whites
5 tablespoons powdered sugar

3 tablespoons finely ground toasted pecans*

To make crust: Mix dry ingredients in a bowl until blended. Cut in pieces of butter until crumbly; add yolk, water, and lime juice. Mix until dough holds together. Flatten into a disc, wrap, and refrigerate for 1 hour.

Preheat oven to 400°F. Roll out pastry and fit into a 9-inch pie pan. Line with parchment* and fill with weights. Bake for 12 minutes. Remove paper and weights and bake at 375° for 15 minutes, or until golden brown. Remove from oven and let cool.

To make filling: In top of a double boiler or in a heavy saucepan whisk egg yolks and sugar until slightly thickened. Stir in lime juice and place pan over low heat or simmering water. Cook, stirring, until mixture feels warm to the touch. Add the butter 2 tablespoons at a time, stirring, until mixture is the consistency of thick mayonnaise. Remove from heat, stir in zest and food coloring and let cool. (It will thicken as it cools.) Pour filling into pie shell and refrigerate until cold.

To make meringue: Preheat oven to 400°F. In a bowl beat egg whites until soft peaks form. Beat in sugar until whites become stiff and glossy. Fold in ground pecans. Pile the meringue on top of the lime filling with a spoon or pastry bag, making sure that the meringue has contact with the crust all around the tart. Bake for about 6 minutes, or until meringue is light golden brown.

Before serving, allow pie to cool thoroughly in refrigerator or at room temperature, about 2 hours, or filling may run.

Serves 8

Orange-Chocolate Tart

The intimate relationship between oranges and advertising began in Chicago in 1893. There during the Columbian Exposition, the state of California constructed a huge tower of oranges and planted groves of live trees all over the grounds. Early promotional campaigns linking oranges inexorably with vitamin C were so successful that many Americans were soon making morning orange juice a daily ritual. Florida and California now produce over twenty-five billion oranges a year, more than the combined total number of the next three orange-producing countries, Spain, Italy, and Mexico.

Oranges had been popular in the past, but for other reasons. Vitamin C content was almost certainly not Benjamin Franklin's concern when he just as devoutly mixed up his specialty, Orange Shrub, a drink in which the juices were augmented with generous quantities of rum. Oranges were dessert favorites of the eighteenth-century Seminoles, who ate them sliced and marinated in honey. In the South, the Orange Pie has been a traditional dessert for one hundred years, as have Ambrosia and a Louisiana froth called "Orange Cream." Under the lush orange cream in this colorful and irresistible tart, a thin veneer of chocolate awaits the unsuspecting taste buds and orange segments half-dipped in chocolate decorate its rim.

Tart Shell

1½ cups flour
pinch salt
2 tablespoons grated orange zest*

8 tablespoons sweet butter
2 tablespoons vegetable shortening
1 egg

Filling

8 ounces bittersweet chocolate, melted
4 egg yolks
½ cup sugar
juice and grated zest of 1 large orange, plus 1 small orange, peeled and sectioned

4 tablespoons sweet butter
1 cup heavy cream, whipped

To make tart shell: In a medium bowl combine flour, salt, and zest. Cut in butter and shortening until mixture resembles coarse meal. Add egg and stir until dough holds together. Wrap dough in plastic and chill for at least 30 minutes. Then press or roll dough into a 10-inch ungreased tart pan with a removable bottom. Place in freezer for 30 minutes or refrigerator for 2 hours. Bake in preheated 450°F oven for 15 minutes, or until light brown. Remove from oven and let cool on rack.

To make filling: With a pastry brush, coat bottom of tart shell with melted chocolate, reserving about ¼ cup for dipping orange sections. Let chocolate harden while preparing orange filling.

In a heavy saucepan combine yolks and sugar over low heat. Add orange juice and zest. Stir, adding butter piece by piece. Cook until thick, stirring constantly. Let cool, then fold in whipped cream.

Fill tart shell with orange cream mixture. Place tart in refrigerator for about 1 hour to firm up filling. Dip half of each orange section in reserved melted chocolate, let dry on rack, and arrange decoratively on top of filling.

Serves 8 to 10

Wild Blueberry and Cheese Open-Pie

New England Blueberry Grunt, Blueberry Slump, and Blueberry Buckle—the names of these traditional American desserts are as enchanting as they are uncomplicated. Native to New England, wild blueberries were sun-dried by the Indians and much appreciated by the colonists, who missed their currants and raisins. Boiled in puddings or baked into pies, wild blueberries never need more than a bit of nutmeg to enhance their wonderful, slightly tart flavor. (One late nineteenth-century cookbook advises that blueberry pies reach optimum flavor only if six chopped up green grapes are thrown into the filling.)

There is one danger in wild blueberries, however: You may never again be able to enjoy the ones at the corner grocer's. You can really use either wild or cultivated in this Open-Pie in which the juicy, fresh berries make a nice counterpoint to the fluffy, rich filling.

Crust

1 recipe pâte brisée*

Cheese Filling

4 large eggs
¼ teaspoon salt
½ cup heavy cream
grated rind of small lemon
4 ounces cream cheese

4 ounces whole-milk ricotta
cheese
4 tablespoons sugar
pinch nutmeg

Blueberry Topping

4 cups fresh blueberries,
cleaned
¼ cup sugar

grated rind and juice of
half a lemon
½ teaspoon cinnamon

To make pie crust: Preheat oven to 400°F and roll dough to fit into a 10-inch ungreased pie plate. Prick dough with fork and line with parchment* or foil and weights (rice, beans, or aluminum shot). Bake for 12 minutes, remove paper and weights, and bake for another 10 minutes. Allow to cool slightly while preparing filling. Keep oven on, reducing heat to 375°F.

To make filling: Mix all ingredients in a food processor or blender until smooth. Pour into partially baked pie shell and bake for 20 to 25 minutes, or until filling is set. Let cool while preparing topping.

In a heavy saucepan, combine 1½ cups blueberries, sugar, lemon rind and juice, and cinnamon. Cook over low heat, stirring until sugar dissolves. Raise heat and bring to a boil. Boil rapidly for about 8 minutes, or until mixture thickens to a jamlike consistency. Cool slightly. Add remaining blueberries and mix gently. Spoon over cooled pie.

Let pie cool completely at room temperature or in refrigerator before serving.

Serves 8 to 10

Oregon Cherry-Berry Turnovers

Cherry Bounce was a brandy drink of early New Englanders, who also mixed cherries with rum to make a liqueur. In the Midwest, where cherries were just as popular, more sober recipes prevailed: Tarts and pies made delicious use of the sour cherries abundant in that area. Sweet cherries flourished in the West and, in 1875, an Oregon grower named Bing developed and named for himself the most widely known of the "sweets."

We think it is kind to pit the cherries for these lovely flaky turnovers; but we know of someone who bakes unpitted cherries into pastry and has guests count up their share of pits when they're finished. This also solves the problem of what to do after dessert.

Pastry

1 cup sweet butter, cut into small pieces
½ cup sweet margarine, cut into small pieces
2 cups cake flour

2 cups all-purpose flour
½ cup sour cream
¼ cup sugar
1 teaspoon lemon juice
1 egg

Filling

½ pound fresh cherries, washed and pitted
1½ cups blueberries, cleaned
¼–½ cup sugar

3 tablespoons lemon juice
2 tablespoons all-purpose flour

1 egg beaten with 1 tablespoon water

To make pastry: Combine all ingredients in a bowl and mix until blended. Divide dough in half, wrap each portion in plastic wrap, and refrigerate overnight.

To make filling: Chop cherries coarsely in a bowl and mix with blueberries. Combine with remaining ingredients and let sit at room temperature for 1 hour.

To assemble: Preheat oven to 375°F and grease a cookie sheet. On a lightly floured board roll out one piece of dough at a time into a 16-inch square. Cut into 4-inch squares. Brush edges with egg wash. Place a heaping teaspoonful of filling on each square and fold opposite corners over filling to form a triangle. Seal edges with tines of fork and place on cookie sheet. Brush tops with egg wash and bake for 20 to 25 minutes, or until golden brown.

Makes 32 turnovers

Cranberry Black Bottom Pie

Although the cranberry comes from the finest of families—its relatives include both rhododendron and heather—it is most often found in bogs. The plump berries were a fortunate find for New England colonists, who discovered them growing wild in what would otherwise have been wasteland. Cranberries kept well too, assuring their pickers a winter's worth of puddings, sauces, breads, and cakes. When shipped to Europe, they were simply covered with water; they lasted for months, assuring a profitable trade, with no losses due to deterioration. Under refrigeration, this water-packed method preserves cranberries for up to eight months.

To harvest cranberries, the boggy fields are flooded until they fill with floating red berries. It is a study in scarlet. Cape Cod and Bandon, Oregon, home of the annual Cranberry Festival, remain the major suppliers of this American fruit.

Upon discovering cranberries, a European visitor, William Cobbett, once called them "the finest fruit for tarts that ever grew." Their distinctively refreshing bite, tempered with cinnamon and orange, is the essence of this unusually delectable pie, cooked on a cloud of chocolate. No description of its few and simple ingredients can suggest the pleasant subtleties of the finished dessert. This is one of those rare dishes that is much more than the sum of its parts.

Crust

4 ounces bittersweet
   chocolate
2 tablespoons orange juice
4 eggs, separated

¼ cup sugar
¼ teaspoon cinnamon
   pinch salt

Filling

¾ cup water
½ cup sugar
½ teaspoon cinnamon
1 tablespoon grated orange
   zest*

8 ounces cranberries
1 cup heavy cream whipped
   with 2 tablespoons Grand
   Marnier and 2 tablespoons
   powdered sugar

shaved chocolate (optional)

To make crust: Melt chocolate with orange juice in a small heavy saucepan or double boiler over low heat. Stir until smooth and let cool.

Preheat oven to 350°F and butter well a 10-inch pie plate.

Beat yolks with sugar in a bowl until very thick and pale in color. Add cinnamon and melted chocolate, beating slowly until blended. Beat whites with salt until stiff. Add whites one third at a time to chocolate mixture, folding gently with rubber spatula.

Pour mixture into the pie plate, level with spatula, and bake for about 25 minutes. Allow to cool. As crust cools it will sink in the center, forming a shell.

To make filling: In a saucepan bring water to a boil with sugar, cinnamon, and orange zest. Add cranberries while boiling. Lower heat and let simmer for about 15 minutes, until thick, stirring occasionally. Let cool and refrigerate.

Fill cooled pie shell with cranberry mixture. Spread with whipped cream and sprinkle with shaved chocolate, if desired.

Serves 8

Mocha Mousse Mud Pie

"Six-shooter coffee" was the name given the most renowned drink of the Old West. It was made by boiling coffee in vats for at least half an hour, or until it became strong enough to float a gun in. This attribute may not have enhanced its flavor, but it did emphasize the masculine, frontier identity of coffee. Because of, or in spite of this image, coffee became everybody's favorite beverage, from cowboys to city merchants. No matter where coffee appeared, however, Americans have always drunk it to excess. At formal dinners, in the 1700s, coffee was served continuously throughout the meal. Even the most fashionable hosts, emulating the European style of serving coffee only at the meal's conclusion, scandalized foreign guests by accompanying it with pots of milk and sugar.

Cities like Boston and New York had coffeehouses dating from as early as 1670, and they functioned as centers for business and social interaction. Most of them served only two items, coffee and chocolate, the two most favored beverages of the New World. This coffeehouse spirit pervades our special frozen dessert with its ice-creamy center, crumbly chocolate crust, and coffee-brown veneer. It sounds earthy; it tastes ethereal.

Crust

4 tablespoons sweet butter
1 tablespoon instant coffee

8 ounces chocolate wafer
crumbs

Mousse

3 eggs, separated
¼ cup plus 2 tablespoons
sugar

2 tablespoons unsweetened
cocoa dissolved in ¼ cup
strong brewed coffee
1 cup heavy cream

Topping

6 ounces bittersweet
chocolate
2 tablespoons sweet butter

½ cup heavy cream
2 tablespoons coffee liqueur
1 teaspoon corn syrup

To make crust: Melt butter in a saucepan and stir in instant coffee until dissolved. Mix with wafer crumbs and press mixture into a 10-inch pie plate. Let chill in refrigerator for at least 1 hour.

To make mousse: In a bowl beat yolks with ¼ cup sugar for about 10 minutes, until pale in color and very thick. Beat in cocoa-coffee mixture and set aside.

In a chilled bowl beat cream until it mounds softly. Do not beat until stiff.

In a separate bowl beat whites until they start to hold a shape. Gradually beat in remaining 2 tablespoons sugar until soft-peak stage.

In a large bowl fold with a spatula all 3 mixtures together at once, just until blended. Pour into chilled crust and place in freezer until frozen.

To make topping: Melt chocolate and butter in a double boiler, or in a saucepan over low heat. Stir in cream and coffee liqueur and cook, stirring, until smooth. Add corn syrup and cook for about 5 minutes, until thick. Let cool slightly and pour over pie.

Return pie to freezer until ready to serve.

Serves 8 to 10

The Cake of Four Chocolates

From roasted bean to steaming mug, coffee and chocolate lead parallel lives in many ways. (Although both require attention, understanding, and judgment from harvest to table, chocolate is the more complex.) Once cocoa beans are roasted and ground, the resulting substance yields two products: One is pure cocoa butter; the other is a mixture of cocoa butter and chocolate liquor. The mixture may either be solidified into unsweetened chocolate; or it may be further dried and ground into cocoa powder; or it may be mixed with pure cocoa butter, plus sugar, to produce chocolate in all its sweetened varieties: from bitter-sweet to semisweet to sweet. Sweetened chocolate plus milk results in milk chocolate. White chocolate contains no chocolate liquor; in its best form it is pure cocoa butter mixed with milk and sugar.

Here we have chocolate in four stages—unsweetened, bittersweet, milk chocolate, and white—captured in a quadruply blessed creation, one of the grandest desserts in this collection.

Cake

8 ounces bittersweet chocolate	5 eggs, separated
2 ounces unsweetened chocolate	1 cup sugar
¼ cup cold coffee	6 tablespoons flour
6 ounces (12 tablespoons) sweet butter	¾ cup finely ground walnuts
	2 ounces milk chocolate, coarsely chopped

Glaze

4 ounces bittersweet chocolate	½ cup heavy cream
2 ounces unsweetened chocolate	2 ounces (4 tablespoons) sweet butter

white chocolate curls (see Note)

To make cake: In top of a double boiler or in a heavy saucepan melt first two chocolates with coffee. Stir in the butter a tablespoon at a time, until mixture is smooth. Remove from heat and let cool slightly. Preheat oven to 350°F and butter and flour a 9-inch cake pan.

Beat yolks in a bowl with sugar until thick and pale. Stir melted chocolate into yolk mixture. Add flour and ground walnuts, and mix together gently.

In a separate bowl beat whites until stiff but not dry. Fold into chocolate mixture in 3 additions. Fold in chopped milk chocolate. Pour batter into the cake pan and bake for 25 minutes or until cake begins to pull away from sides of pan. Let cool about 15 minutes on a cake rack before turning out.

To make glaze: In a double boiler or heavy saucepan melt the chocolates in the cream and add butter a tablespoon at a time, mixing until smooth. Set aside to cool and thicken.

Pour over cooled cake and spread with spatula. When glaze has set, sprinkle outer edge of cake with white chocolate curls.

Serves 10

CHOCOLATE CURL NOTE: To make curls draw a vegetable peeler blade across the flat side of a piece of white chocolate.

White Chocolate Pear Brownies

Brownies are among those sweets—strawberry shortcake and peanut butter cookies are others—that have been used to complete the phrase "There's certainly nothing more American than..." Perhaps because brownies are often a child's first cooking production, they retain and communicate a definite nostalgia. As reminders of home, they tend to revive in popularity during the first move to college or just after getting married, or moving to someplace crazy, like California.

These crumbly squares are brownies of a different color. Made with white chocolate, they are temptingly full of the moistness and subtle fragrance of pears.

3 ounces white chocolate, chopped	½ teaspoon baking soda
½ cup sweet butter	3 eggs
1¾ cups flour	1 cup sugar
¼ teaspoon salt	½ cup ground walnuts
½ teaspoon baking powder	2 pears, peeled, cored, and diced

Preheat oven to 350°F and butter and flour a 9"- × -13" baking pan.

Melt chocolate and butter in a saucepan over low heat or in a double boiler. Let cool.

In a bowl sift together flour, salt, baking powder, and baking soda.

In a separate bowl, beat eggs lightly with sugar. Stir in chocolate mixture, flour mixture, walnuts, and pears. Pour into pan and bake for 35 to 40 minutes, or until tester comes out clean. Let cool and cut into 3-inch squares.

Makes 12 squares

Buried Treasure Truffles

Cocoa beans were used as money among the Mexicans whom Cortez encountered in the early 1500s. The Spaniards were quick to appreciate the value of this newly discovered commodity and they began shipping the beans back to Spain almost immediately. The beans were usually thrown into the sea when they were found by Dutch and English pirates, who clearly underestimated their potential. But eventually everyone caught on, and cocoa beans became valuable for the wealth of pleasure they represented.

Through a long and complicated series of steps, cocoa beans are processed into cocoa powder, the form we need for the final step in this recipe. Cocoa powder is often processed with potash to make it less bitter and more soluble in water, a method called "dutching." Either type will work nicely here.

Whether chocolate or espresso, it is the hidden coffee bean that provides the unexpected treasure in each of these mildly mocha truffles.

½ cup heavy cream
12 ounces bittersweet
   chocolate
¼ cup sweet butter
2 tablespoons coffee liqueur
2 tablespoons brewed
   espresso coffee

about 36 espresso coffee
beans or chocolate-flavored
coffee beans
½ cup unsweetened cocoa
mixed with 2 tablespoons
finely ground espresso
coffee

In a heavy saucepan or in top of a double boiler heat cream with chocolate until melted. Add butter bit by bit and stir until mixture is smooth. Add liqueur and espresso coffee, mix well, cover, and chill until mixture is firm, about 2 hours.

Using a heaping teaspoonful of chocolate mixture, mold chocolate around espresso bean forming an irregularly shaped ball or truffle. Roll truffle in cocoa-espresso mixture and place in paper candy cups. Store airtight in refrigerator or freezer.

Let sit for 20 minutes at room temperature before serving. To further gild the lily, serve with cups of espresso coffee.

Makes about 36 truffles

Ginger-Peachy Roulade

The peach blossom, according to Chinese legend, signifies long life. Toward this end, a Chinese birthday tradition includes the serving of a peach-shaped steamed roll called <u>Shoutao,</u> or "long peach life."

The peach is also important in a birthday celebration of the Shaker religious community, honoring founder Ann Lee. To make the traditional Mother Ann's Birthday Cake, the cook is supposed to cut down some sap-filled peach twigs and beat the batter until it picks up a distinct peach flavor.

This flourless, tortelike roulade embodies the spirit of celebration. It is a bourbon-splashed cake, with a hint of ginger, spread with peach-studded filling. It is then rolled up into a stunning (not to say ginger-peachy) dessert, grand enough for a special birthday, or just about any old day.

Cake

4 eggs, separated
8 tablespoons sugar
1 tablespoon bourbon

1 teaspoon ground ginger
1 cup finely ground pecans

Filling

3 tablespoons bourbon
2 cups heavy cream
3 tablespoons sugar
1 tablespoon finely chopped
candied ginger (optional)

4 peaches, blanched* and
peeled

To make cake: Preheat oven to 350°F, and line an 11"-×-16" jelly-roll pan with parchment* or buttered foil. Beat yolks in a bowl with 5 tablespoons sugar, bourbon, and ginger until light and thick.

In a separate bowl, beat whites to soft-peak stage, adding remaining 3 tablespoons sugar gradually. Beat until stiff and shiny. Into the yolk mixture fold in the whites alternately with the pecans.

Pour batter into jelly-roll pan, tilting pan so that batter covers evenly. Bake for about 20 minutes, or until sides begin to pull away from the pan. Cool for about 5 minutes on a cake rack and turn out on a flat towel. Peel paper off cake gently. Roll cake with towel making an 11-inch roll. Let cake cool completely in towel before filling.

To make filling: Unroll cake and sprinkle with 2 tablespoons bourbon. Beat the cream, sugar, and remaining bourbon in a bowl until soft peaks form. Remove half of cream mixture and combine with chopped ginger in a bowl. Spread over the cake.

Arrange 2 rows of the sliced peaches over the cream and roll cake up tightly. Frost the cake with remaining cream, reserving some for decorative piping. Slice off ends of cake diagonally and place remaining peach slices diagonally down top of cake. With a pastry bag fitted with a star tip, pipe a line of whipped cream on both sides of peaches. Chill for about 1 hour before serving.

Serves 8 to 10

Persimmon Walnut Log

For those who dabble in the art of delayed gratification, the persimmon makes the perfect exercise. When plump, firm, and most visually inviting, persimmons are inedible. A few days later, when they become soft, translucent, and resemble a pallid to-mato well past its prime, they are lusciously sweet, ready.

When the first Europeans found this exotic plumlike fruit growing here, they obviously didn't wait. It can "fur a man's mouth like alum" complained one early persimmon report. Captain John Smith, who obviously practiced the required restraint, wrote that " . . . when it is ripe, it is as delicious as an Apricock."

The Algonquin word for persimmon, pasiminan, means "dried fruit." This tells us how the Indians used it. Persimmons were also fermented for "simmon" beer, and made into breads, puddings, and salads. In Pennsylvania, early settlers made persimmon wine; in Maryland and Virginia, the little orange fruits were distilled into brandy. Persimmon vinegar and molasses were also produced, and tea was made from the leaves and valued as a substitute for sassafras.

Gnaw Bone, Indiana, is the site of the most recent persimmon explorations, those conducted by writer Raymond Sokolov, who was determined to stalk the true American wild persimmon. This he did, asserting in his book Fading Feast that it is terribly fragile but much more succulent than the Japanese type found (if at all) in the supermarket. Since 1855, when Commodore Perry brought it back from Japan, this heartier variety has been grown commercially in the Gulf States, Georgia, and California.

We use only one persimmon in our festive, rolled confection, but its exotic lushness permeates both the creamy filling and the surrounding walnut-rich cake.

Cake

- 4 eggs, separated
- 8 tablespoons sugar
- 1 tablespoon grated orange zest*
- 1 tablespoon orange liqueur
- ½ cup cake flour
- ½ cup finely ground walnuts

Filling

- 1 large persimmon, stem removed
- 2 tablespoons orange juice
- 1 tablespoon orange liqueur
- 1 cup heavy cream
- ⅓ cup powdered sugar
- ½ cup coarsely chopped walnuts

10 walnut halves

To make cake: Preheat oven to 350°F and line an 11″-×-16″ jelly-roll pan with parchment* or buttered foil. Beat the yolks in a bowl with 5 tablespoons sugar, orange zest, and liqueur until light and thick.

In a separate bowl mix flour and walnuts together and set aside.

In another bowl beat whites to soft-peak stage, add remaining 3 tablespoons sugar gradually, and beat until stiff and shiny. Fold flour-nut mixture alternately with whites into the yolk mixture.

Spread batter in the jelly-roll pan and bake for about 20 minutes. Let cool for about 5 minutes and turn cake out onto a flat towel. Roll in towel to form an 11-inch log and let cool.

To make filling: In a food processor puree persimmon, orange juice, and liqueur.

In a separate bowl whip cream with powdered sugar until stiff. Fold persimmon puree into cream. Reserve ½ cup of this cream for piping. Spread remainder on unrolled and cooled cake. Sprinkle with walnuts and roll cake up tightly. Fit a pastry bag with a star tip and pipe rosettes of reserved cream down center of log. Top each rosette with a walnut half. Chill for about 1 hour before serving.

Serves 8 to 10

Apricot-Almond Pound Cake

For many, almond paste recalls the little flat cakes or molded figures served during the Christmas season. Consisting simply of ground almonds, sugar, and either orange, kirsch, or traditional rose water, almond paste is easily made at home and stores very well. It is sometimes confused with marzipan, which starts with almond paste but is fortified with whipped egg whites and confectioners' sugar. This makes it a highly malleable material for forming into intricate shapes, often painted with vegetable coloring.

Of all its uses, none is perhaps more intriguing than the old custom of rubbing almond paste all over the body to make the skin smooth and soft. Admittedly its role is slightly less dramatic in this Cognac-apricot pound cake. Delicious after dinner, topped with a generous scoop of honest vanilla ice cream, it is also welcome the next day with the first hot sips of morning coffee. (To our taste buds, it is even better the third day; and it continues to develop new intrigues on subsequent days, especially if popped into the toaster in the expectant atmosphere of fresh sweet butter.) Tightly wrapped, this and most pound cakes will keep well for about ten days.

¼ cup ground almonds
1 cup coarsely chopped dried apricots soaked in ¼ cup Cognac
1 tablespoon plus 1½ cups flour

1 cup sweet butter, room temperature
½ cup commercial almond paste
1 cup sugar
6 eggs, separated

Preheat oven to 350°F and grease a 9-inch tube pan or loaf pan and dust with ground almonds.

Drain apricots and reserve Cognac. Toss the apricots with 1 tablespoon flour. Set aside.

Cream the butter in a bowl with the almond paste and ½ cup sugar. Add the egg yolks one at a time, beating well after each addition. Add the reserved Cognac and 1½ cups flour and mix just until blended.

In a separate bowl beat whites until soft-peak stage. Gradually beat in remaining ½ cup sugar until stiff and shiny. Fold one quarter of egg white mixture thoroughly into yolk mixture. Gently fold in remaining whites and floured apricots. Fold thoroughly but do not overmix.

Pour batter into prepared pan. Bake for about 50 minutes, or until cake is golden and pulls away slightly from sides of pan.

Serves 12

Mint Julep Pound Cake

We owe this recipe to a Baptist minister named Elijah Craig, who lived in Bourbon County, Kentucky, in 1789. His activities had nothing to do with pound cake but had everything to do with why his particular county is now world famous. Using corn, rye, and the limestone water unique to that area, the Reverend Craig developed the first formula for the sour mash corn whiskey now called "bourbon." Only sour mash whiskeys that meet stringent regulations are today privileged to use the name bourbon. Twenty years ago, the U.S. Congress declared true bourbon "a distinctive product of the United States."

From its tender beginnings, bourbon was but a sip away from the evolution of the Mint Julep. The procedures for creating this drink are usually as intimidating and stringent as the federal bourbon regulations. Fortunately, this cake recipe, which captures the refreshing nature of the Julep, does not entail the nerve-twitching precision demanded for construction of the drink itself. It can, and really should, be made a few days in advance. It is a buttery, caramel-brown cake delicious with, and even without, the mint.

¼ cup ground walnuts	1 tablespoon vanilla
1¾ cups flour	1⅔ cups light brown sugar
¾ teaspoon baking powder	3 eggs
6 ounces sweet butter, room temperature	⅛ cup bourbon
	3 ounces milk
1 teaspoon mace	⅓ cup sugar mixed with ¼
⅛ teaspoon mint flavoring	cup bourbon for glaze

Preheat oven to 350°F and line an 8"- × -4" loaf pan with parchment paper* or buttered foil. Dust with finely ground nuts.

In a bowl sift together flour and baking powder. Cream butter with mace, mint, and vanilla. Add sugar gradually and beat until very light and pale in color. Add eggs one at a time, beating well after each addition.

338

On low speed add dry ingredients alternately with bourbon and milk to the butter mixture in two additions, beating just until smooth.

Pour batter into prepared pan, shaking to level batter. Bake for 1 hour, or just until top springs back when touched.

To make glaze, heat sugar and bourbon until sugar dissolves. Brush the warm glaze over the cake. Let sit for several hours before serving.

Serves 12

California Poppy Seed Coffee Cake

"No tea table, in my opinion, is complete without a good seed-cake. We nursed one all the time . . . . When it was too stale, it was sometimes served toasted and buttered." These were the reminiscences of none other than James Beard, whose mother owned and managed everything in Portland, Oregon's Gladstone Hotel, but most energetically its kitchen. Beard's particular seedcake favorite contained caraway.

Poppy seed cakes and tortes were beloved among the Pennsylvania Dutch and in German settlements everywhere in the country. The Shakers, whose principles of nutrition and religion shared equal importance, raised the little dot-size seeds for cooking and set aside part of the crop for sale. Our triply citrus California cake tastes as fresh as fruit juice when just made. Like any good little seedcake, it makes a glorious comeback even when stale with the help of toaster and butter dish.

1½ cups sweet butter, room
   temperature
1 cup sugar
1 tablespoon each grated
  lemon, lime, and orange
  zest,* plus juice from each
  fruit

½ cup poppy seed
8 eggs, separated
2 cups flour
¼ teaspoon salt
¼ cup superfine sugar*

Preheat oven to 350°F and butter well a 9- or 10-inch bundt pan.

Cream butter and ¾ cup sugar in a bowl. Add grated zests and poppy seed. Beat until mixture is very light and pale in color. Beat in yolks, one at a time, until smooth.

Beat whites in a separate bowl to soft peak stage, and gradually beat in remaining ¼ cup sugar until the whites are stiff.

Mix flour and salt gently into yolk mixture. Stir in a quarter of the whites to lighten mixture, then fold in remaining whites.

Pour batter into bundt pan and bake for 1 hour. Allow cake to cool in pan for 10 minutes before turning out onto a cooling rack.

Mix juices in a bowl with superfine sugar until dissolved. Spoon over cake as it is cooling. (You might want to set rack over wax paper to catch drips.) Allow cake to cool completely before serving.

Serves 12 to 16

New-Fashioned Strawberry Shortcake

We know that his first taste of strawberry bread much impressed the founder of Rhode Island, Roger Williams, because he wrote all about it in his official reports. The recipe was Indian, made from meal mixed with mashed strawberries. Gorgeous New World strawberries from Virginia caused a virtual sensation in England when they were cultivated there in 1629. A benevolent epidemic, referred to as "Strawberry Fever," once raged through this country; its most obvious symptoms were a sudden increase in the number of strawberry-studded dishes. Strawberry Short-cake, possibly the most loved American dessert, remains for many the glory of them all. Regional interpretations vary slightly: A Southern version of the dessert is topped with meringue; New England cooks adorn the same small cakes with their native blueberries and name the piece Blueberry Buckle; San Francisco entrusted its home-town version to Chef Arbogast at the Palace Hotel, who came forth with nothing less than Strawberries Romanoff.

In this recipe, the fresh strawberries are slathered in a puree of raspberries and they marinate awhile together. But otherwise, we have tampered little with the classic compatibility of cake and berry.

Shortcake

2 cups flour
½ teaspoon salt
1 tablespoon baking powder
3 tablespoons sugar
2 teaspoons grated lemon zest*

¼ cup cold sweet butter, plus 2 tablespoons sweet butter, melted
¾ cup heavy cream

Filling

1 10-ounce package frozen raspberries, thawed, or 2 cups fresh raspberries
2 tablespoons sugar
1 tablespoon lemon juice
1 tablespoon framboise or liqueur of your choice

24 ounces fresh strawberries, hulled and halved
1½ cups crème fraiche* for garnish

To make shortcake: Preheat oven to 450°F and grease a cookie sheet.

In a bowl mix flour, salt, baking powder, sugar, and lemon zest. Cut in ¼ cup butter piece by piece until mixture resembles cornmeal. Add cream and mix until dough holds together.

Turn dough out onto a floured surface amd knead a few minutes. Roll dough out to ½-inch thickness and cut 6 rounds with a 3-inch cutter. Place rounds on the cookie sheet and brush with melted butter. Bake for about 12 minutes, or until golden brown. Let cool and split each round in half horizontally.

To make filling: In a processor puree raspberries with sugar, lemon juice, and liqueur. Strain to remove seeds. Pour over strawberries and let marinate for at least 6 hours in the refrigerator.

Place a shortcake half on each plate, cover with strawberries, and top with other shortcake half. Surround with additional strawberries and garnish each with 4 tablespoons crème fraiche.

Serves 6

Sausalito Sophisticated Saucepan Torte

More dishes have evolved from the necessities of the moment than have been artfully created from a universe of possibilities. Some of these are legendary, though like most legends, there may be more than one legend per incident. One explanation for Chess Pie, for example, starts with the versatile pie maker desperately scraping together whatever was around. When someone asked what kind of pie she was making, she answered, "Oh jes' pie," thus bestowing a name that was either misheard, or mispronounced, or both.

Frontier settlements and gold-mining camps were the probable settings for much of our impromptu cookery, like one-pot suppers, fry breads, and steamed puddings, popular when ovens had no temperature controls or where there were no ovens at all.

Dump Cakes and Crazy Cakes need little equipment, since they are mixed and cooked in the same pan. The Miracle Coconut Cake, the Cranberry-Nut Thing, and the Fudge Custard Cake start out in a single bowl and emerge from the oven in several layers, or display some other feature which is, if nothing else, visual.

Our saucepan torte possesses all the beloved qualities of last-minuteness, requires minimal equipment, and allows you to incorporate whatever fruits are at hand. It also tastes complex and time-consuming. You can, of course, get all the specific ingredients and make it deliberately; but you don't have to.

1 cup chopped nuts (walnuts, pecans, almonds, etc.)
¾ cup chopped dried fruit (raisins, apricots, apples, currants, etc.)
1 cup flour
½ cup sweet butter

1 cup plus 1 tablespoon white sugar
4 tablespoons brown sugar
1 cup pureed fruit, cored, seeded, and peeled if necessary (persimmon, apples, bananas, pumpkin, etc.)

1 tablespoon grated lemon zest*	½ teaspoon baking soda
1 teaspoon vanilla	½ teaspoon cinnamon
3 eggs	powdered sugar
¾ teaspoon baking powder	1 cup heavy cream
	2 tablespoons brandy

Preheat oven to 350°F and grease an 8-inch cake pan.

Toss nuts and dried fruit in a bowl with 2 tablespoons flour and set aside.

In a medium saucepan melt butter and add 1 cup white sugar and 4 tablespoons brown sugar. Cook over low heat until sugar starts dissolving. Add pureed fruit, lemon zest, and vanilla. Whisk in eggs one at a time, beating well after each addition.

In a separate bowl combine remaining flour with baking powder, baking soda, and cinnamon, then add to saucepan, stirring just until flour disappears. Mix in fruit-nut mixture.

Pour batter into the cake pan and bake for about 50 minutes. Cool on a rack for about 15 minutes and invert cake onto a serving plate. Allow to cool. Sprinkle with powdered sugar.

In a bowl beat cream with 1 tablespoon white sugar and brandy until soft peaks form. Serve with wedges of torte.

Serves 8

Pear and Cranberry Whole-Wheat Cobbler (Winter Version)

Cranberry sauce, made with maple sugar and honey, was a favorite Native American dish. Because of their high acidity, cranberries can last indefinitely and were used as a preservative in making pemmican, a Native American dried food. By the nineteenth century, cranberries were commonly made into sherbet, jellies, molds, steamed puddings, catsup, and a sauce commonly served with turkey. When they are ripe and firm as they should be, cranberries can be bounced like rubber balls, though most recipes, including ours, eliminate this step.

We cannot recommend too strongly the serving of this tangy cobbler with coffee ice cream, a creamy accent to the two fruits and their buttery, crumbly topping. Coffee ice cream is excellent with many fruit desserts, including the Summer Version of this one.

2 tablespoons sweet butter, plus ½ cup, melted	¾ cup all-purpose flour
	¼ cup whole-wheat flour
2 pounds D'Anjou or Bartlett pears, cored and sliced in ¼-inch-thick wedges	½ cup chopped walnuts
	½ teaspoon salt
	1 teaspoon baking powder
2 cups fresh cranberries, washed	1 egg
	1 teaspoon cinnamon
1½ cups sugar	

Preheat oven to 375°F and butter a 2-quart heat-proof dish.

Heat 2 tablespoons butter in a skillet and sauté pear slices until pears lose some of their juices. Put this mixture in a large bowl, add cranberries, and sprinkle with 5 tablespoons sugar. Mix well and let sit while preparing topping.

In a medium-size bowl mix flours, walnuts, ¾ cup sugar, salt, and baking powder. With a fork, stir in egg and keep stirring until mixture appears crumbly.

Put pear-cranberry mixture into the prepared dish and sprinkle flour mixture over fruit.

Drizzle the ½ cup melted butter over the topping. Mix cinnamon with remaining sugar and sprinkle over butter. Bake for about 20 minutes, or until top is lightly browned. Serve warm with coffee ice cream, if desired.

Serves 8

SUMMER VERSION NOTE: Substitute equal amounts of strawberries and peaches for cranberries and pears.

Apricot Swirl Cheesecake

Startling though the news may be, before there was a Lindy's restaurant in New York, there was cheesecake. In fact, there was cheesecake before there was New York. Without the benefit of graham cracker crust, fresh cheese has long been consumed as "dessert"; it was sometimes sweetened with honey, blended with herbs and spices, or stirred with branches of fig trees to give it sweetness and flavor.

In Pennsylvania, German farm families made their own supplies of a white fresh cheese similar to Philadelphia cream cheese. This now-famous soft, white cheese had nothing to do with Pennsylvania, however. It was created in the small town of South Edmeston, New York, where the dairyman named it for Philadelphia, considered the gourmet capital of the nation, at least in South Edmeston. This country now supplies the world with well over a hundred million pounds of cream cheese every year, by far the most consumed cheese on earth.

Cheese shops and many delicatessens carry fresh cream cheese with no gummy preservatives, a good choice for our very California cheesecake, temptingly streaked with sunny orange swirls of pureed apricots.

½ cup finely ground almonds	1½ pounds cream cheese
3 ounces dried apricots, plus	4 eggs
10 dried apricots soaked in	1 cup sugar
2 tablespoons brandy and	2 tablespoons all-purpose
water to cover	flour
water	½ cup heavy cream
1 tablespoon grated lemon	1 cup apricot preserves
zest*	

Butter an 8-inch springform pan and dust with ground almonds. Set aside in the refrigerator while preparing rest of cake.

In a saucepan cover the 3 ounces of apricots with cold water and cook over a low heat until fruit is tender and almost all water has been absorbed, about 15 minutes. Add the lemon zest and puree apricots until smooth. Set aside. Preheat oven to 350°F.

Beat cream cheese in a bowl until smooth and soft. Add eggs, one at a time, beating well after each addition. Add sugar, flour, and cream and beat again until very smooth.

Remove 1 cup of cream cheese batter and mix with apricot puree. Pour remaining batter into chilled prepared pan, cover with apricot puree batter, and cut through several times with a knife to form a marbleized effect. Bake for 50 minutes. Turn oven off, open door, and let cake rest for 30 minutes. Cool on a rack.

Heat apricot preserves with 2 tablespoons of brandied apricot soaking liquid and strain. Brush glaze over cooled cake, reserving a bit for apricots. Place the 10 soaked apricots decoratively around cake and brush with remaining glaze. Tastes best at room temperature.

Serves 10

Cookies

While no one could claim that the cookie was actually invented in this country, there is strong evidence that the genre has been explored and developed here beyond anyone's wildest dreams. Even the Dutch settlers in New York, who brought with them their rolling pins and baking pans, may have been surprised at the gusto with which their style of koekje (little cake) was adopted.

A cookie recipe in the first American cookbook, Amelia Simmons's 1796 American Cookery, includes sour cream and coriander in a thick buttery dough. Other early recipes also use herbs and spices, as well as seeds, nuts, molasses, maple syrup, and whatever might be rolled, dropped, patted together, or pinched into the small sweet treats. By now the virtue of variety alone might justify American claims to the cookie. The possibilities have still not been exhausted, as evidenced by the following representative jarful.

Oatmeal and Brown Sugar Wafers

These wafer-thin wafers, honest as oatmeal, fit as snugly into the American cookie tradition as they do into the cookie jar. As light as an array of elegant petits fours, these cookies are as satisfying as Brambles, Hermits, Jumbles, or any of our other traditional cookies with their kitchen-cupboard names. Try them as an accompaniment to fruit compotes or to a light dessert, such as the Rhubarb-Strawberry Sherbet.

2 cups quick or regular rolled oats
1 cup brown sugar, tightly packed
1 teaspoon baking powder
¼ pound sweet butter, melted
1 egg, beaten

Preheat oven to 350°F and grease several cookie sheets.

Place oats, brown sugar, and baking powder in a medium-size bowl. Add butter to oat mixture and stir in beaten egg. Mix well.

Drop batter by half teaspoons onto the cookie sheets 3 inches apart. Cookies will spread while baking. Bake for 8 to 10 minutes, then let stand for about 1 minute to firm up cookies before removing from sheets. Wafers crisp as they cool.

Makes about 40 cookies

Black and Whites

The first chocolate-manufacturing plant opened in this country in Dorchester, Massachusetts, in 1765. Its founders, John Hannan and James Baker, in what was certainly to become typical American fashion, took out an ad for the occasion. It said: "Satisfaction or money refunded." Chocolate has seldom needed

347

such guarantees, but we've made the extra effort for universal acceptability by using two kinds in these luscious, double-chocolate cookies.

6 tablespoons sweet butter, room temperature	2 ounces unsweetened chocolate, melted
3 tablespoons sweet margarine, room temperature	1½ cups flour pinch salt
½ cup powdered sugar	3 ounces white chocolate

Cream butter, margarine, and sugar in a bowl until smooth. Add melted chocolate and mix until well blended. Sprinkle in the flour and salt and mix again just until dough holds together. Divide dough in half and roll each half into a cylinder 1 inch in diameter. Wrap each cylinder in waxed paper and refrigerate until firm.

Preheat oven to 350°F and line cookie sheet with parchment.*

Cut each cylinder at 1-inch intervals and place cut side down on cookie sheet. Bake for about 18 minutes, or until firm. Let cool on a rack.

Meanwhile, melt white chocolate over a very low heat. Dip each cooled cookie into the melted chocolate sideways so that one side is coated. Return cookies to rack until chocolate has hardened.

Makes about 36 cookies

Persimmon Peanut Bars

These succulent bars are loosely based on the peanut butter cookie, which American Food author Evan Jones has called perhaps the most "exclusively American" cookie in the New World cookie jar. The chopped nuts make these bars toothsome treats, suffused with the fruity taste of persimmon and just a whisper of orange. They are especially appropriate for those who think they can always guess what things are made of. (Nobody ever can.)

½ cup sweet butter
¼ cup peanut butter
1 cup sugar
2 eggs
1 teaspoon baking soda
2 persimmons, stemmed and pureed
1 teaspoon grated orange zest*

1 cup coarsely chopped unsalted peanuts
2 cups flour
pinch salt
½ teaspoon cinnamon
½ teaspoon ground nutmeg

Preheat oven to 350°F and grease a 9-inch-square pan.

Cream butter, peanut butter, and sugar in a bowl. Add eggs one at a time, beating well after each addition. Stir baking soda into persimmon puree and add to creamed mixture. Blend in orange zest and peanuts.

In a bowl mix flour with salt, cinnamon, and nutmeg and add to creamed mixture until blended.

Pour batter into the baking pan and bake for about 30 minutes. Allow to cool and cut into bars.

Makes 16 bars

Pistachio Meringue-Aroons

Members of the cashew family, pistachios are also called "green almonds." Whatever their name, they have always been a costly luxury. Because they grow well only in temperate climates that are not damp, their areas of cultivation are restricted. Weather conditions in certain parts of California are proving to be ideal, meaning that pistachios are finally becoming available at reasonable prices. Made of ground pistachios and almonds, these light jade green cookies look and taste extravagant.

4 egg whites	1 cup ground pistachios,**
1 cup superfine sugar*	plus 24 whole pistachios
1 cup ground almonds	

Preheat oven to 325°F and line 2 cookie sheets with parchment.*

Beat egg whites in a bowl with sugar until stiff. Add ground nuts and mix until well combined.

Place mixture in a pastry bag fitted with a star tip and pipe out 12 mounds on each cookie sheet. Place a whole pistachio on top of each cookie and bake for about 20 minutes, or until golden brown. Allow cookies to cool before removing.

Makes 24 cookies

Sourdough Bread Pudding

Certainly few dishes can be more sensible in their evolution than puddings. As a medium to incorporate whatever is around, a home-kitchen pudding is usually named after the major leftover it incorporates, such as Potato or Rice or, if it is made fast enough, Hasty. Of them all, bread pudding evokes a universal enthusiasm that is almost primal. Perhaps this appeal comes from its close association with the staff of life or with vivid memories of farm and hearth, real or imagined.

Colonial New Englanders often served a pudding before the main course, possibly to stave off the appetite. This custom gave rise to the phrase "in pudding time" to denote the first part of the meal. Here we use our "native" California sourdough, left-over or just baked, sprinkled with chopped dried fruits whose leisurely bath in applejack is, as you will see, time well spent.

¼ cup golden raisins	¼ cup applejack or brandy
½ cup chopped dried apricots	3 tablespoons sweet butter
¼ cup chopped dried apples	10–15 slices sourdough bread

3 cups milk
6 eggs
⅔ cup sugar
1 teaspoon vanilla

1 cup heavy cream
2 tablespoons powdered
sugar

In a bowl combine dried fruit with applejack and let soak for 1 hour. Butter one side of each slice of bread. Set aside.

In a saucepan bring milk to a boil.

In a bowl mix eggs, sugar, and vanilla until well combined. Add cream to hot milk and stir in egg mixture. Strain through a fine strainer.

Preheat oven to 375°F and butter a 2-quart baking dish.

Layer the fruit and bread in the baking dish starting with the fruit and ending with the bread. Pour egg-milk mixture over all. Place baking dish in bain marie* and bake for about 35 minutes, or until custard is set. Let cool for about 10 minutes and sprinkle with powdered sugar. Serve warm.

Serves 6 to 8

Steamed Apple-Simmon Pudding

"To make a Quakeing Pudding," instructs the three-century-old Martha Washington's Booke of Cookery, you add to your "wheat flowre" about "10 eggs, youlks & whites." You then beat them together for a quarter of an hour at least, after which you would undoubtedly be "quakeing." However, it was the pudding that was supposed to quake, meaning that it should be tender, light, and fluffy, but still hold together like a firm custard. This delicate balance depended on using exactly the right amount of "wheat flowre." In this recipe a mere two tablespoons does nicely. Made from a cinnamon-dusted, persimmon-apple puree, this dessert is easily made and as light as a soufflé.

6 green apples, peeled,
cored, and sliced
½ cup sugar
1 teaspoon cinnamon
3 tablespoons lemon juice
2 persimmons, stemmed and
pureed
2 tablespoons flour

4 tablespoons sweet butter
6 eggs
4 tablespoons ground
almonds
hot water
lightly whipped cream,
barely sweetened, for
garnish

Cook apples in a large saucepan with sugar, cinnamon, and lemon juice until they become very soft. Puree cooked apples and mix with persimmon puree.

Put flour and butter in the saucepan and cook with combined purees over a low heat until thick. Let cool for about 10 minutes. Beat eggs into cooled puree, one at a time.

Butter a 6-cup pudding mold or deep baking dish and dust with ground nuts. Pour puree into the mold and set on a rack in a pot deep enough to hold the mold. Pour about 2 inches of hot water into pot, cover, and simmer over low heat for about 1 hour.

Allow to cool, then unmold pudding. Serve with whipped cream.

Serves 6

Burnt Cream over Huckleberries

When Washington, D.C. was a new city, Burnt Cream was its favorite dessert. Its prominence can be explained by the fact that it was the specialty of Thomas Jefferson's chef, Julien. The recipe has also been traced to a seventeenth-century chef at King's College, Cambridge. Different areas of this country regionalize the dish, also called Grilled Cream, by substituting maple syrup, adding orange, sifting in some ground pecans, or simply using the French name, Crème Brûlée.

This version of the thick and luscious custard is accented on one side by the brittle caramel crown and on the other by plump fresh berries.

2 cups huckleberries or
blueberries, cleaned
2 cups heavy cream
2 tablespoons sugar
pinch salt

8 egg yolks
1 teaspoon vanilla
1 cup sifted brown sugar (or,
if available, use
brownulated sugar)

Put berries in a 10-inch shallow baking dish.

In a saucepan mix cream, sugar, and salt and heat to boiling.

Beat yolks in a double boiler or heavy saucepan over low heat and add the hot cream mixture slowly, whisking continuously. Cook until mixture thickens and heavily coats back of spoon, about 4 to 5 minutes. Strain and stir in vanilla. Pour cream mixture over berries and chill overnight.

Sprinkle brown sugar in an even layer over custard and place under broiler. Do not let sugar burn. As soon as sugar melts, remove from broiler. May be served cold, at room temperature, or straight from the oven.

Serves 6

Pumpkin Custard

On certain October days, from the little California town of Half Moon Bay, you can see on one side of the road the crisp blue waves of the Pacific Ocean and, on the other, the bright and almost endless orange waves of pumpkins. Staring across these bumpy acres of plump golden squash, it is difficult to imagine a more appropriate symbol of a land of plenty. American painter Lewis Miller conveyed this feeling in his pumpkin-filled canvas Thomas McKean Election, After 1811, on which he lettered the words:

"Christian Lehman Big and Large Pumpkin Grown in his Garden, it was as large as A barrel and more in Circumference round, old Dr. John Fisher bought it and Send it to Baltimore to let them See what old York can Raise and Examine it. no man could lift it from the ground."

Our brandied and well-spiced pumpkin dessert is a crustless custard variation on the traditional pie. Full of pumpkin flavor, it can be a welcome light conclusion to any feast, especially the one usually associated with pumpkins.

1 cup milk	½ teaspoon cinnamon
1 cup heavy cream	½ teaspoon freshly ground
2 eggs	nutmeg
3 egg yolks	½ teaspoon allspice
¼ cup honey	½ teaspoon ground cloves
1 teaspoon vanilla	2 tablespoons brandy
1 cup canned pumpkin puree	hot water

Preheat oven to 350°F.

In a saucepan heat milk and cream until almost boiling.

In a bowl beat eggs and yolks with remaining ingredients except hot water. Pour ½ cup of the hot milk mixture into the egg mixture. Mix well, and pour egg mixture back into remaining milk mixture. Stir until well blended.

Pour custard into individual custard cups or ramekins, place in a pan of hot water, and bake for about 1¼ hours, or until cake tester inserted into center of cup comes out clean. May be served hot, cold, or at room temperature.

Serves 6

Tangerine-Coconut Flan

During a stopover in the North African town of Tangier, on its journey to the tables of Europe, the tangerine acquired its name. No one knows what it was doing in Africa, since its origins, like all its orange relations, are probably Chinese. Its relatives include the tangor, mandarin, clementine, and even the ugli, a hybrid of tangerine and grapefruit. The tangerine's distinctiveness is especially pronounced in the spritzy character of its peel, which is dried and used as a flavoring in China and in surprisingly few other places. Our recipe captures the tangerine's elusive taste in custard form, which is the second-best way we know to enjoy the fruit's quiet voluptuousness. The first-best way is reading what, once upon a time, M.F.K. Fisher had to say of it in <u>Serve It Forth:</u>

"In the morning, in the soft sultry chamber, sit in the window peeling tangerines, three or four. Peel them gently; do not bruise them . . . separate each plump little pregnant crescent . . . . You know those white pulpy strings that hold tangerines into their skins? Tear them off. Be careful."

Caramel Syrup

½ cup sugar
⅓ cup water
2 teaspoons grated tangerine zest*

½ cup shredded unsweetened coconut

Flan

2 cups milk
2 tablespoons grated tangerine zest*
½ cup shredded unsweetened coconut
2 eggs

4 egg yolks
8 tablespoons sugar
4 tablespoons frozen tangerine juice concentrate, thawed

To make caramel: Heat sugar and water in a heavy skillet or saucepan, swirling pan occasionally until all the sugar is melted. Continue cooking until syrup is golden in color, about 8 minutes. Add zest and swirl pan again to combine. Pour into a 1½-quart soufflé dish or charlotte mold. Turn dish so that caramel coats most of the inside. Sprinkle with coconut and set aside.

To make flan: Preheat oven to 350°F. Cook milk, zest, and coconut in a heavy saucepan just until boiling. Remove from heat, cover, and let steep for 30 minutes.

In a bowl lightly beat whole eggs, yolks, sugar, and tangerine juice. Pour milk infusion through a strainer and add to eggs while whisking continuously.

Pour flan into the prepared dish. Put into a bain marie* and bake for about 1 hour, or until a knife inserted in the center comes out clean. Cool and refrigerate until cold, about 6 hours.

To unmold, run a knife around the edge of the dish, place a rimmed platter on top, and invert.

Serves 6

Banana Split Soufflé

A hundred years ago, most people in this country had never seen a banana. After the 1876 Philadelphia Centennial Exposition, at which bananas were sold, not many more had seen, but many more had heard about, this "new" exotic fruit. Enterprising shippers finally got them into the major ports, the railroads got them to the Midwest, and cookbooks began to include them, at least under "Vegetables." In their enthusiasm, some people ate them with real determination, skin and all. When nineteenth-century Swedish novelist Fredrika Bremer visited this country, she selected the banana as one of the "greatest refreshments of the mind . . . in the United States."

Probably the oldest of cultivated fruits, the banana is often thought to be the true Forbidden Fruit in the Garden of Eden. Americans consume more bananas than any other fruit, according to some reports. They are an integral part of the Banana Split, a concoction which reinforces the hope that it is still possible to have everything at once: chocolate, nuts, whipped cream, bananas, and shovelings of ice cream.

We've tried to exercise a bit of restraint in our updated Split, a more transcendent interpretation which, you will see, still excites many a childlike grin around the dinner table. It may just be that, no matter what, chocolate conquers all.

Chocolate Sauce

4 ounces semisweet chocolate	1 cup water
2 tablespoons sugar	

Soufflé

3 ripe bananas, quartered	6 egg whites
2 tablespoons lemon juice	½ cup chopped pecans, plus
¾ cup sugar	some for garnish (optional)

To make sauce: In a small saucepan melt chocolate with sugar and water. Boil gently for 2 minutes, stirring continuously. Let cool and refrigerate.

To make soufflé: Preheat oven to 400°F and butter and sugar a 6-cup soufflé dish.

Puree bananas with lemon juice and ¼ cup sugar in a food processor or blender.

In a separate bowl beat egg whites until soft peaks form and then beat in remaining ½ cup sugar, 1 tablespoon at a time, until stiff and shiny. Fold whites and pecans into banana puree.

Pour mixture into prepared dish and bake for about 20 minutes.

To serve, pour some chocolate sauce (about 1½ tablespoons) in each plate and place a serving of hot soufflé on top. Spoon additional sauce over the soufflé and sprinkle with chopped pecans if desired.

Serves 6

SAUCE NOTE: The sauce may be served warm but we think the contrast of hot soufflé and cold sauce is very special. (The soufflé must be served immediately.)

Nectarines in Caramel Cream

If you plant a nectarine, Waverley Root informs us, you may or may not get a nectarine. Once called the "peach-plum," this fruit with the dual personality can go either way. It might even continue to exist as a nectarine. In color, it may be anything from plum red to the exquisitely flavored ivory pink variety. Like peaches, nectarines come in both freestone and clingstone varieties with distinguished-sounding names like Lord Napier, John Rivers, and Dryden, to name a few. Unfortunately, because they are often picked and shipped before being perfectly ready, they are often disappointing; but the best of them are considered more subtle and interesting than either peaches or plums. In fact, few cookbooks contain recipes for nectarines, usually advising they be eaten out of hand for their rich taste and firm flesh. They can be substituted in any peach recipe, they make excellent Bavarian Creams, and they are unsurpassed in this warm dessert, adrift in caramel cream.

6 nectarines, pitted and
   quartered
3 tablespoons sugar

4 tablespoons sweet butter
1 cup heavy cream

Preheat oven to 400°F.

Place nectarines in a shallow baking dish and sprinkle with sugar, adding the butter in small pieces. Place in the oven and bake for about 20 minutes. At this time the sugar should be caramelized and the nectarines tender. Add cream and place back in oven. Bake for another 15 minutes, basting with cream every 5 minutes. The sauce should be thickened and a light golden color. Remove from oven and cool about 15 minutes before serving.

Serves 6

Baked Apples Alaska

A basket of Rome Beauty apples, with their flaming red and yellow streaks, can look like a welcoming bonfire. Because they keep so well, they are known as the "Winter Apples." Firm and mild in flavor, the Beauty has long been regarded as the superlative apple for baked desserts.

"Snowballs" were a nineteenth-century dessert of uncooked apples cored and filled with fruit, smothered in meringue, and baked in individual pastry shells. After baking, each snowball was further "winterized" with snowy frosting and then served warm. In our semisnowball version, we've eliminated the crust completely, kept the golden brown meringue topping on each apple, and even added a little surprise in the centers of each of these baked Beauties.

6 Rome Beauty apples	1 teaspoon lemon juice
3 tablespoons apricot jam	½–1 cup apple cider
3 tablespoons chopped walnuts	4 egg whites
3 tablespoons currants	6 tablespoons sugar
3 tablespoons cream cheese or ricotta cheese	pinch cinnamon

359

Preheat oven to 350°F.

Core apples to make good-size cavity for stuffing. With swivel peeler remove about 1 inch of peel from top of apple and set aside.

In a bowl mix jam, walnuts, currants, cheese, and lemon juice to form a paste. Fill the cavities of each apple with this mixture and place apples in a baking dish just large enough to hold them. Pour apple cider around apples, cover with foil, and bake for about 30 minutes. Remove dish of apples but turn oven up to 450°.

To make meringue: Beat egg whites in a bowl until soft peaks form. Gradually beat in the sugar, 1 tablespoon at a time, until stiff and shiny. Add cinnamon and mix well. Pipe meringue decoratively over each baked apple, return to oven, and bake for about 7 minutes, or just until meringue becomes golden. May be eaten warm or at room temperature.

Serves 6

Fall Fruits Gratin

Because apples and pears belong to the same category of fruits, known as pomes, they are frequently grouped together. Organizations called pomological societies specialize in investigating these two fruits, alone and together. In this country, the fruits have been associated with each other since 1629, when the seeds of both arrived here for possible cultivation. With the first successful harvest, reams of recipes evolved to use and preserve them.

The Shaker religious community, organized in the eighteenth century, was one of the first groups to advocate wholesome eating and the consumption of fresh vegetables and fruits. A mixture of their home-grown pears and apples, topped with farm-fresh cream, was a hallmark Shaker creation.

This pear-apple combination is made in the form of a gratin, a preparation more familiar for vegetables, which gets its golden gratin crust from a sprinkling of crumbs or grated cheese. For the dessert, we use instead a mixture of crushed cookie crumbs and chopped pecans. It is one of those comforting, warm desserts, wonderful for early autumn evenings and well worth some serious pomological attention.

3 large Golden Delicious apples, peeled, cored and cut into sixths	2 tablespoons light rum
	¼ cup currants
	½ cup finely chopped pecans
3 large Bartlett pears, peeled, cored, and cut into sixths	1 cup cake or cookie crumbs
	1 teaspoon cinnamon
½ cup water	2 tablespoons butter
½ cup sugar	1 cup heavy cream
juice and grated zest* of 1 lemon	

Place apples, pears, water, sugar, and lemon juice and zest in a heavy pot. Bring to a boil, cover, and let simmer for about 30 minutes. Uncover, stir, and cook until all liquid has evaporated, about 20 minutes. Remove from heat and stir in rum and currants.

Preheat oven to 375°F and butter a 10-inch shallow baking dish. Fill with apple-pear mixture.

In a bowl mix pecans, crumbs, and cinnamon together and sprinkle on top of fruit. Dot with butter and pour cream over all. Bake for 20 minutes, or until top is golden brown. Delicious served with a dollop of good plain yogurt.

Serves 6

Raspberries with Coffee Sabayon (Zabaglione)

Though highly perishable, the delicate raspberry has made its way into every dinner course from hors d'oeuvre and salad vinaigrette through wild game sauces and the most elegant of desserts. The raspberry is a member of the rose family, which has also expanded its activities beyond the proverbial bouquet to become part of rose vinegars, jams, jellies, and even rose cough drops. Together, raspberries and rose water make one version of the traditional American Raspberry Flummery.

This dessert is a triumph in contrasts: hot with cold; creamy ivory sauce with glinting red berries. Spooned from tall-stemmed glasses, it is lovely to see as well as to eat.

6 egg yolks	¼ cup strong black coffee
1 cup superfine sugar*	2 pints fresh raspberries,
½ cup dry Marsala	cleaned (see Note) and
2 tablespoons coffee liqueur	chilled

In the top of a double boiler, or in a heavy saucepan, beat yolks and sugar until thick and foamy, about 3 minutes. Put over simmering water or low heat and continue beating, while adding the Marsala, liqueur, and coffee. Beat until mixture is very thick and almost tripled in volume. The custard should be very hot to the touch.

Pour about ¼ cup of the sabayon into each individual serving dish (champagne glasses are perfect), add ¾ cup raspberries, and pour remaining sabayon over the fruit. This dessert is at its best if the raspberries are very cold and the sabayon hot.

Serves 6

RASPBERRY NOTE: Raspberries are really too delicate to be washed in running water. Place berries in coarse strainer, sift out loose grit, and examine for creepy crawlies. If this method is too unsterile for you, place berries in a colander and dip in a bowl of cold water for 2 seconds. Shake dry gently.

Babcock Peaches Poached in Champagne with Blueberries

Although great chefs the world over have named some of their most elaborate desserts after the peach, in America the Natchez Indians named one of their thirteen months after it. In colonial Virginia, whatever was not consumed in season was dried and crushed into a paste for use in breads and desserts, or brewed into a much-prized peach beer. Ohio farmers were drinking along the same lines with their favorite, peach brandy. One researcher found over 2,000 peach varieties in New York alone, while another has divided peaches into two simple categories: those that are superb eaten out of hand and those that are superb for preserving.

Babcock peaches, with their pale and ephemeral beauty, are often paired with berries in combinations that have become legendary. To that basic idea, we added a splash of champagne sauce for a dessert that makes the most of the Babcock's all-too-short season.

2 cups water
2 cups champagne
1 cup sugar
   strip of lemon zest*

6 Babock peaches, blanched*
  and peeled
1 pint blueberries, cleaned
  mint leaves for garnish

In a large pot bring water, champagne, sugar, and lemon zest to a boil and continue to cook until sugar is dissolved and mixture becomes syrupy, about 12 minutes. Add peaches and simmer for about 5 minutes. Turn off heat and allow peaches to cool in syrup.

When peaches are cool, slice them in wedges, removing the pits. Arrange peaches on a serving dish, sprinkle with syrup, cover, and allow to chill 6 hours. Scatter with berries and sprinkle with additional syrup. Garnish with mint leaves.

Serves 6

Compote of Dried and Fresh Fruits with Honey-Lime Sauce

The boring nature of canned fruit cocktail is no mere accident. The idea began in 1913 when a California canner realized that there was a new, widespread interest in health and nutrition, and that it was having its effects. Eating fruit was suddenly in vogue. When this enterprising cannery invented and marketed its first fruit cocktail, the product was so well received that other canners soon joined in, each with its own recipe and combination of fruits. The competition became so fierce that the canners decided to eliminate the variables; they developed one single identical formula for the product. Consumers could choose any brand they wished and get exactly the same thing in every can. This uniformity took all the mystery out of canned fruit desserts, removing them from serious consideration as an exciting conclusion to a meal.

This situation was a far cry from the gorgeous "tasting plates" of mixed fruits, cookies, and small cakes once considered the most sumptuous finale for elegant banquets and formal dinners. The fruits were both fresh and dried, some marinated for several hours, others cooked in liqueurs or Cognacs. The times seem right for a revival of "tasting plates" and fruit-full compotes, like this one. You can use any combination of fruits, of course; it's the lime-laced marinade that brings this dessert together.

juice and grated zest* of 1 large lime	1 banana
¼ cup honey	2 pears, peeled and cored
1 tablespoon apricot jam	2 oranges, peeled, pithed, and sectioned
3 tablespoons kirsch	½ cup pitted prunes
1 cup fresh strawberries, washed and hulled	½ cup dried apricots
1 cup grapes	½ cup golden raisins

Combine lime juice and zest, honey, jam, and kirsch in a bowl that is large enough to hold the fruit.

Cut fruit into bite-size pieces and put into bowl. Toss well with marinade, cover, and refrigerate for at least 6 hours, tossing every so often. Most delicious served over our Apricot-Almond Pound Cake, although the compote tastes fine all by itself.

Serves 6 to 8

Fresh Figs and Kiwis in Chardonnay with Crème Fraîche

Like pistachios, the kiwi may be popular in some culinary realms more for its lovely green color than for its taste. Its decorative potential seems less than promising viewed from its potato-brown exterior. But its beauty unfolds when the fruit is sliced in almost any direction. Dots of black seeds swirl between a center of pale, honeydew green and a surrounding rim of deep lime. Kiwis always look cool; they taste like strawberries or melons or some citrus mix. They can even taste like kiwis when you get to know them.

Now an important California crop, kiwis were practically un-known in this country just a few years ago, when Australia's Bay of Plenty was the world's only supplier. Formerly called the "Chinese gooseberry," a name under which it did not sell to the American market, the fruit was renamed to identify it more closely with Australia. The French ignore all three affiliations, calling the fruit souris végétales, or "vegetable mice."

Kiwis look especially magnificent in this presentation and they taste even better. This visually enticing dish is also a showcase for Chardonnay, which we specify for a reason you will know instantly when you taste the finished dessert. Best of all, it uses less than a cup of the wine, leaving the rest to your own devices.

6 fresh figs, quartered
3 kiwis, peeled and sliced in
   thin rounds
¾ cup Chardonnay

2 tablespoons honey
1 cup crème fraiche**
   fresh mint leaves for
   garnish

Place fruits in a bowl. Mix Chardonnay with honey, and pour over fruit. Cover and allow to macerate for at least 12 hours in the refrigerator.

To serve, place several kiwi slices in center of each plate. Surround with fig quarters arranged like petals of a flower. Pour juices over each plate and top with a dollop of crème fraiche and a mint leaf.

Serves 6

Red and Green Grapes in Maple-Walnut Cream

The whistle of the locomotive penetrates my woods summer and winter, sounding like the scream of a hawk sailing over some farmer's yard, informing me that many restless city merchants are arriving within the circle of the town.... Here come your groceries, country.

Henry Thoreau, Walden

Any country originally called Vinland might be expected to develop a few interesting grape recipes along the way. But even Concord Grape Pie had to wait until after 1850, when Ephraim Bull perfected the Concord grape on his vines near Walden Pond. Not far from this idyllic setting, a noisier development, refrigerated railroad cars, soon began to transport produce long distances, making the new Concord grape widely available and initiating a thriving trade in commercial table grapes.

In California, growers eventually specialized in seedless varieties, like the Thompson, which comprises half its present crop of dessert grapes. This jewellike cluster of red and green grapes, anointed with maple crème fraiche, is at its most poetic served in stemmed wineglasses.

1½ cups seedless green grapes,
    washed and stemmed
1½ cups seedless red grapes,
    washed and stemmed
1 cup coarsely chopped
    toasted walnuts* (plus
    some for garnish)

1 cup crème fraiche*
¼ cup maple syrup**

Toss grapes and walnuts together in a bowl.

In a separate bowl lightly whip crème fraiche with maple syrup. Add to grapes and walnuts and stir gently to blend. Cover and store in the refrigerator for about 3 hours.

Serve in wineglasses with additional toasted walnuts sprinkled on top.

Serves 6

Comice Pears Stuffed with Goat Cheese and Rolled in Walnuts

Called the "Queen of Pears," the celebrated Comice was developed by botanists in the year 1849 in the French city of Angers, where a plaque on the site still commemorates the event. Its fragility makes the Comice difficult to transport in the usual, roughhouse manner preferred by most of the carton-throwers who are in charge of getting our produce into our stores. Nevertheless, this buttery, sweet fruit is so prized for its texture, it is often eaten with a spoon, like cream from a bowl. This inviting practice can certainly be applied to our recipe, which adds the musky touch of goat cheese and the crunch of chopped walnuts.

2 ounces mild goat cheese**
2 ounces sweet butter, room
  temperature
6 medium Comice pears

½ cup fresh lemon juice
1 cup finely chopped toasted
  walnuts* mixed with 1
  teaspoon cinnamon

Mix goat cheese and butter in a bowl until smooth.

Peel pears and cut in half lengthwise. Remove cores with a melon baller. Fill cavities with goat cheese mixture and press pear halves together to form whole pears. Roll each pear in lemon juice and then in walnut-cinnamon mixture. Allow to chill for about 1 hour before serving.

Serves 6

Dried Figs Stuffed with Walnuts and Dipped in Chocolate

People fond of strolling through the desert might already be aware of one of its most precious buried treasures. Deep in the hot sand, a wealth of figs may lie, drying in a method as old as antiquity. In Turkey, dried Smyrna figs can be seen in the marketplaces strung into necklaces like the heavy precious jewels they are. Always revered as the most delicious of dried figs, the Turkish Smyrna was planted in fig-productive California in the late 1800s, where, alas, it did not produce a thing. This led to an international hunt for the elusive fig wasp, the necessary go-between for fig trees, which have, as might be suspected, two entirely different genders. The resulting California fruit, named not too mysteriously the Calimyrna, is also at its most succulent when dried. In our recipe, each chocolate-cloaked fig secludes its own buried treasure, an orange-zesty walnut-cheese stuffing.

2 ounces toasted walnuts*
2 ounces ricotta cheese
1 teaspoon grated orange
   zest*

2 teaspoons powdered sugar
1 pound dried figs
4 ounces bittersweet
   chocolate, melted

In a bowl make a paste of the walnuts, cheese, zest, and sugar.

With a sharp knife make a slit in each fig. Place a tablespoon of the walnut paste in the fig and press the cut edges together to seal. Holding the fig by the stem end, dip half into melted chocolate and set on cooling rack to dry. This is an unusual and delightful addition to a petits fours tray.

Serves 8 to 10

White Chocolate–Hazelnut Mousse with Raspberry Sauce

Though it took him until his fourth voyage, Columbus finally did get around to discovering the cocoa bean, which he sent back to Spain to see what, if anything, could be done with it. The rest, as they say, is decadence. In a sense, all chocolate starts out white. When the cocoa tree is in bloom—yes, Virginia, chocolate does grow on trees—its flowers are usually clusters of white petals. Of course, it's the fruit that really commands our attention because eventually it becomes the much-beloved chocolate of cakes, mousses, and midnight snacks. White chocolate does not contain the liquor of dark chocolate, but it does contain the cocoa butter, many of chocolate's delicate properties, and, most intriguing, the element of surprise, as guests savor the first taste of its unexpected chocolatey richness. This dessert also takes full advantage of the heady aroma of toasted hazelnuts and of the brilliant red raspberry-framboise sauce. To top it off, more hazelnuts. It is a sensation.

6 ounces white chocolate, chopped
¼ cup sweet butter
6 egg whites
1 cup heavy cream
4 tablespoons superfine sugar*

3 tablespoons framboise
1 cup finely ground toasted hazelnuts* (see Note)
1 pint fresh raspberries, cleaned, or 1 10-ounce package frozen, thawed

In a heavy saucepan or double boiler melt chocolate with butter over low heat. Alow to cool.

Beat egg whites in a bowl until stiff. In another bowl whip cream with sugar and 2 tablespoons framboise (see Note).

Reserving 2 tablespoons hazelnuts for garnish, fold hazelnuts, whites, and cooled chocolate into cream. Pour into a 6-cup soufflé dish or 6 individual ramekins and refrigerate for at least 2 hours before serving.

Puree raspberries with remaining framboise, sweeten to taste, and drizzle sauce over mousse before serving. Sprinkle with reserved nuts.

Serves 6

CREAM NOTE: Do not whip cream until stiff because it can all too quickly turn to butter. Overwhipped cream will result in a heavy, waxy, cheesy taste instead of the lightness essential to a good mousse.

HAZELNUT NOTE: When grinding hazelnuts, do not stop when they become powdery. They do not release their precious oils until they become pasty.

Rhubarb-Strawberry Sherbet

In cold climates, the first spring growth is often the rhubarb plant. This alone would have assured it a high place in wintery early America, which had, by March, long since run out of the stuff that sweets are made of. Often paired with strawberries, rhubarb was cooked and folded with cream into Fools, baked as Rhubarb Crisps, and stewed into a sauce for ice cream and plain cakes. In Alaska, Eskimos eat the season's first tender rhubarb stalks raw. Most popular with Americans of Dutch, Scandinavian, and German background, rhubarb is really a vegetable, though its most popular use is evident from its nickname, the "pieplant."

In this kirsch-laced sherbet, tart, cooked rhubarb is pureed with fresh strawberries and strawberry-rich jam. It is a remarkably light sherbet with which a generously overfilled tray of Oatmeal and Brown Sugar Wafers makes a nice accompaniment.

1 pound rhubarb, cooked and cooled	1 cup sugar
2 pints strawberries, hulled and washed	2 tablespoons kirsch
2 egg whites	1 tablespoon lemon juice
	4 tablespoons good-quality strawberry jam

Place all ingredients in a food processor fitted with a steel blade. Process until absolutely smooth. Pour into metal ice-cube trays or any shallow metal pans and place in freezer until mixture is crystallized but not solidly frozen. This should take from 1 to 2 hours depending on the temperature of your freezer and depth of pan.

Remove from freezer and spoon into bowl of food processor. Process until thick and light. Pour back into trays and freeze again.

When ready to serve, remove from freezer and place in processor. Puree and serve immediately (or store in airtight freezer container).

Serves 6

Ice Creams

The story of American ice cream is rife with unsung heroes. Certainly the most unsung of all is Nancy Johnson, a Philadelphia woman who invented the hand-cranked ice cream freezer in 1846. Shortly thereafter, a Baltimore milk dealer, Jacob Fussell, began selling ice cream wholesale and soon found himself presiding over the first large-scale business venture of this type. A name completely lost in obscurity is the inventor of the Ice Cream Soda, a creative sort who reportedly introduced the innovation on the spur of the moment after running out of fresh cream. This historic event took place in 1874 at the Semicentennial Exposition of the Franklin Institute in Philadelphia. The 1904 St. Louis Fair provided the setting for the next ice cream advancement, the Ice Cream Cone. This was apparently another happy accident arising from the fact that the ice cream vendor and the waffle vendor, whose booths were side by side, saw a need, as they say, and filled it.

The famous American chant, "I scream, You scream, We all scream..." and so forth, arose from the original name of the Eskimo Pie (I-Scream), invented by an Iowa candy-store manager and schoolteacher, who patented his contribution in 1921. But

Harry Burt of Youngstown, Ohio, must be credited for utilizing the full breadth of American technological state of the art for his still-thriving development: the Good Humor Bar. Selling their ice cream from trucks, neighborhood to neighborhood, Good Humor men and their jangling bells became identified with the welcome delights of summer.

Both versions of our recipe, like the famous Philadelphia ice cream, use only pure cream and no custard base, with resulting flavors that are both rich and delicate. You can use this recipe for any type of ice cream freezer, even an original "Nancy Johnson." Anything is bound to be easier than in Fannie Farmer's day when she counseled, somewhat unconvincingly, in her 1896 cookbook: "With ice cream freezer, burlap bag, wooden mallet or axe, small saucepan, sufficient ice and coarse rock salt, the process neither takes much time nor patience."

Apple Ice Cream à la Mode

2 cups heavy cream	pinch salt
2 cups light cream or half and half	¼ cup frozen apple juice concentrate, thawed
1 cup sugar	¼ teaspoon ground nutmeg
1½ teaspoons vanilla	¾ teaspoon cinnamon

In a bowl stir all ingredients together until sugar dissolves. Pour into the container of an ice cream maker and process according to the manufacturer's directions.

If not serving immediately place in freezer. Let stand at room temperature for 10 minutes after removing from the freezer.

Makes 1 quart

Maple–Pine Nut Ice Cream

2 cups heavy cream
2 cups light cream or half
  and half
½ cup sugar
½ cup maple syrup

pinch salt
1½ teaspoons vanilla
1 teaspoon maple flavoring
1 cup pine nuts

In a bowl stir all ingredients except pine nuts together. When sugar and syrup have been completely incorporated, pour mixture into the container of an ice cream maker. Process according to manufacturer's directions.

After processing, stir in pine nuts, distributing evenly. If not serving immediately, place in freezer.

Makes 1 quart

PANTRY
FANCIES

Until recently, the following foods were available only in specialty stores or from mail order sources. As people discovered and enjoyed these somewhat exotic delicacies, their rising popularity won them a place in regular supermarkets and ordinary grocery stores, although they are still often confined to those unapproachable shelves of "gourmet-type" foods where only intrepid shoppers dare to tread. In most cases, however, little information about these items is readily available and, except for an occasional food magazine article, recipes using them are still rare. (We have tried to remedy that in this book.)

In this section you can obtain information about the background of these foods and some suggestions about how to use and serve them. Although some of these items can be costly, they are particularly valuable for creating an exciting meal or transforming an ordinary dish, especially at the last minute. We always recommend the best of the lot, regardless of whether they are domestic or imported. So long as they help create some fine California/American food, they're worth some space in the pantry.

Flavored Honeys
Chutneys
Flavored Mustards
Hot-Sweet Mustards
Hot Pepper Jellies
Green Peppercorns
Dried Imported Mushrooms
Sun-dried Tomatoes
Tomato Paste in Tubes
Olive Spread
California Olive Oil
Balsamic Vinegar
Raspberry Vinegar
Sherry Vinegar
American Golden Caviar
Smoked Trout
Smoked Salmon
Goat Cheese
Country Ham
Olives
Sweet Onions
Pistachios
Maple Syrup
Semolina Flour
Melon Seed Pasta
Arborio Rice
California Wild Rice
Louisiana Wild Pecan Rice

Flavored Honeys

The flavor of honey depends on what the bee feeds on. Clover was always the bees' everyday fare, but now some beekeepers are controlling their bees' food sources so they can produce honeys flavored with acacia, lavender, and even mesquite. One of our favorites is a raspberry honey that perfumes the air with the aroma of the fruit the moment the jar is opened. Use these unusual honeys as you would your favorite old one: in fruit salad dressings, meat glazes, or toppings for hot home-made biscuits.

Chutneys

The old standby mango chutney is now no longer the only jar on the shelf. Unusual concoctions, such as nectarine-almond or sour cherry–walnut, can enhance a fish or poultry salad or give a new dimension to old favorite curries.

Flavored Mustards

In this world of many flavored mustards, our favorites are those with fresh-tasting herbs and spices. Speckled with dill, shallot, garlic, tarragon, and herbs de Provence, flavored mustards invigorate otherwise ordinary salad dressings, sauces, and marinades.

Hot-Sweet Mustards

This special type of flavored mustard tastes mild and sweet initially but heats up substantially once on the tongue. Although there are several now available, many are a bit too cloying for our taste. Those with the right balance are wonderful for glazing meats and poultry or enlivening the tastes of salad dressings, soups, and sauces.

Hot Pepper Jellies

Made from hot or sweet peppers, these jellies can range in taste from sweet/hot to hot/sweet. They make an intriguing glaze for poultry or pork; one spoonful transforms a plain vegetable sauté into an imaginative dish.

Green Peppercorns

Green peppercorns are actually common, everyday black peppercorns that have not quite matured. Their flavor is strong but accommodating: They complement other flavors and can be added to sauces and herb butters. Available in small cans or bottles, they are generally packaged in brine or vinegar, which must be rinsed off. Before using, mash them with the back of a spoon.

Dried Imported Mushrooms

Porcini, shitakes, cepes, and chanterelles are now available in dried form. The flavor of these exotic and sometimes wild mushrooms is often much more intense than in fresh form. Therefore, although they are expensive, a small amount easily works its wonders. Dried mushrooms must be soaked in hot water for about thirty minutes before adding them to sauces or omelettes or mixing them with fresh mushrooms for pastas or vegetable dishes. The soaking liquid must be filtered to remove sand and may be refrigerated for later use in soups, stews, or sauces.

Sun-dried Tomatoes

These Italian plum tomatoes are picked at their absolute peak, halved, and dried in indirect sunlight. They then may be sold as they are, or packed in olive oil with herbs and spices, left to ferment a month or more, drained and repacked in extra-virgin olive oil. Because of their highly concentrated flavor, a little of these expensive imports goes a long way. California is also bottling its own sun-dried tomatoes, which have an entirely different flavor, just as canned domestic tomatoes differ from canned Italian plum tomatoes. Any of them may be chopped into a cream sauce or slivered onto a salad with their oil incorporated into the dressings. Strips of sun-dried tomatoes make a lovely topping for pizza and pasta.

Tomato Paste in Tubes

No more foil-topped, half-used cans of tomato paste lurking in the back of the refrigerator shelves. Used in Europe for years, these imported, ingeniously packaged tubes contain highly concentrated tomato paste derived from rich sweet Italian tomatoes. They are available in specialty shops and have now begun to surface in general supermarkets. After squeezing out the desired amount, you simply recap the tube and store in the refrigerator for future use.

Olive Spread

Imported from Italy, this mixture of Tuscan olives, herbs, spices, and anchovies gives a surprising Mediterranean touch to a Sunday morning bagel and cream cheese. Used in sauces and salad dressings, it can also be mixed with soft cheese to make a handsome, caviar-colored spread for raw vegetables or crisp wafers. All-olive pastes—no anchovies or other flavorings—also are available.

California Olive Oil

For some reason, olive oil is a relatively young enterprise in this country's only olive-producing state. Recently, however, some very fine fruity oils, with good acidic balance, have become available from a few California producers. Like limited bottlings of good wines, they tend to be in short supply. But they are worth searching for and the price compares favorably with the imports.

Balsamic Vinegar

A relative newcomer to this country, this rich, red Italian vinegar is aged in oak barrels for at least ten years. It has a smooth, mellow taste that adds distinction to marinades and augments the flavors of ripe strawberries and other sliced fruits. Mixed into some good olive oil, it is superlative with fresh greens.

Raspberry Vinegar

In the past few years, this flavored vinegar has maintained its status as the darling of the French-inspired nouvelle cuisine. Today we think the best raspberry vinegar on the market is produced in California from a white wine vinegar and crushed fresh raspberries. It is not syrupy sweet, like many of the imported brands. Its true raspberry richness permeates marinades for poultry and dressings for fruit or cooked vegetables.

Sherry Vinegar

The best sherry vinegars come from Spain and are aged in wood barrels for as long as twenty years. Their nutty flavor marries well with olive oil and with all nut oils. We love to use this flavorful vinegar in a freshly made mayonnaise destined to top a fish or seafood salad.

American Golden Caviar

This amber, jewellike caviar is the roe from lake-bred whitefish. Aside from the caviar's aesthetic effects, its taste is buoyant and delicate, not as strong and salty as sturgeon roe. Toss a bit of it in a seafood pasta or treat it as you would your favorite Beluga caviar. Its fine flavor will never betray its low cost, about $36 a pound. Surprisingly, it freezes well.

Smoked Trout

The fresh fish is hot-smoked slowly over flavored wood chips with tiny amounts of salt and brown sugar. After being vacuum packed, it may be refrigerated or frozen for quite a while before using. Consult your grocers for storage information on their brands. Creamed with some butter and herbs, smoked trout makes an incomparable pâté. It can also be cut into strips and secluded among an array of new greens for a truly regal salad.

Smoked Salmon

The price of smoked salmon is a good indication of its place of origin, which may be anywhere from Norway to Washington. We like the Pacific Northwest variety that gets its mildly sweet flavor and moist texture from being cold-smoked with alder chips. Serve it in very thin slices on some buttered black bread, dice it into omelettes, or add it to cream sauce for pastas or risottos.

Goat Cheese

This specialty cheese, sometimes know as chèvre, comes from California and France. Available in cylinders, pyramids, and a variety of shapes, its flavor depends on age, the young cheese being the mildest. Four major California producers offer chèvres in styles from plain bulk and spiced rounds to small discs wrapped in black pepper or herbs. Crumbled into a green salad or stirred into a creamy sauce, chèvre brings a definitive character to any dish. Spread on some thickly sliced, crusty baguettes, chèvres make welcome and easily organized snacks and appetizers.

Country Ham

Slow-cured country hams come from North Carolina, Georgia, Missouri, and Pennsylvania. The famous peanut-fed Smithfields result from a 300-year-old curing method done only in Virginia. The hams from Kentucky come coated with brown sugar and ground cloves. Oregon's are pepper-coated and Vermont's are corncob-smoked. More of them than ever before are being sold in specialty shops as well as by mail order. Even in small amounts they add earthiness to salads, mousses, rice, and pasta dishes.

Olives

Cured in oil, brine, water, or even in the sun, olives can be flavored with fennel, orange peel, rosemary, garlic, and any number of spices. Ranging in color from purple to green and black, they can be stuffed with pimentos, anchovies, nuts, or onions. Spain, France, Greece, and Italy provide most of the imports, California all of the domestics. In our opinion, the olive is one of the wonders of the world just as it is; but you can also make green olive sauce, garlic cream soup, and black olive muffins.

Sweet Onions

Vidalia, Georgia; Walla Walla, Washington; and Maui, Hawaii, have at least one thing in common. They know their onions. Each of these areas produces onions so sweet they may be eaten raw without flinching. All three originate from the same Granex seed, but the soil nourishes them into their honeyed flavor. Because they are more perishable than the common variety of yellow onion, they are usually more costly. When cooked, they become sweet enough to use as a vegetable marmalade. Raw slices add a sweet crispness to salads. Another of their unsung features is that you can look at them squarely while cutting: no more tears.

Pistachios

California pistachios are now in full production after the usual fifteen to twenty years of patient tending. Actually, pistachio trees thrive in less than ideal circumstances, like rocky hills and dry, hot weather. Once gathered, they are dried for several days, during which time they open naturally, requiring none of the usual strenuous cracking ceremonies of other nuts. Also produced in Texas and Arizona, pistachios have traditionally been associated with North Africa and the Middle East and the foods of those areas. Pistachios add color and crunch to pâtés, stuffings, and rice dishes. Desserts like ice cream, tortes, cakes, and cookies containing any significant number of pistachios radiate the tell-tale pistachio green color and distinctive taste.

Maple Syrup

The high price of maple syrup derives from the labor-intensive aspects of its production and also from the fact that it takes twenty to eighty gallons of sap to make one gallon of syrup. "Sugaring off" is the seasonal ritual of collection in those few areas in the Northeast, in Pennsylvania, and west to Wisconsin, favored with the precise temperatures (twenty-eight degrees to minus forty degrees) necessary for sap flow. Maple syrup is graded: Fancy—light and delicately flavored; Grade A—more maply in taste; and Grade B—stronger in flavor with dark color, usually used for cooking. It makes a great glaze for meats as well as for vegetables such as parsnips, carrots, and squashes. Bake it into breads, use it to sweeten fruit compotes, whip it into cream as a dessert topping. Or use it in the dessert itself: mousses, ice creams, pies.

Semolina Flour

Semolina is milled from hard durum wheat and produces a tender, golden pasta with a definite bite. Because semolina is rich in gluten, it produces a dough that is difficult to handle if used alone. We recommend a 1:1 ratio of finely ground semolina to all-purpose flour. Semolina also makes great bread.

Melon Seed Pasta

Sometimes known as orzo or *semi di melone,* this tiny, barley-shaped pasta is most frequently found among the imported brands. It is a nice change from rice and lends itself well to creamy sauces. A cold pesto pasta salad made with this unique macaroni delights guests and keeps them guessing.

Arborio Rice

A short-grained rice from Piedmont, Italy, this grain lends itself to long, slow cooking. Carefully simmered in stock and/or wine, it has a nutlike flavor with an unbelievably creamy consistency. With bits of seafood, asparagus, or chicken livers, it makes a mouth-watering main course or "Littlemeal."

California Wild Rice

Usually defined as the grain of an aquatic grass, wild rice is found in its natural habitat around the freshwater lakes of northern Minnesota. About ten years ago California growers succeeded in adapting wild rice to the climate and conditions of the rice-producing regions in the Sacramento area. Now available internationally, California wild rice has a nutlike and chewy texture that combines well with game and poultry.

Louisiana Wild Pecan Rice

There are no nut pieces in this unusual long-grain rice, but because it grows near pecan orchards, its nutty aroma and flavor are strongly reminiscent of pecans. It makes a delicious pilaf with raisins for serving with poultry and game, or it can be substituted in favorite rice salads.

SUGGESTED
MENUS AND
WINES

SUMMER DINNER I

Strawberry Melon Soup
Grilled Squab with Lavender Honey and Black Pepper
Red Pepper and Onion Marmalade with Celery
Grilled Baby Corn and Chive Butter
Wild Blueberry and Cheese Open-Pie
Wines: White Zinfandel, Gamay Beaujolais

SUMMER DINNER II

Seafood Gazpacho
Green Bean, Corn, and Red Pepper Salad
Grilled Leg of Lamb with Hot-Sweet Mustard and Sherry Vinegar
Tortellini and Artichokes in Fresh Tomato and
Sun-Dried Tomato Vinaigrette
Blackberry Sour Cream Pie
Wine: Cabernet Sauvignon

SUMMER DINNER III

Cool Cucumber and Hot Mustard Soup
Carrot and Zucchini Sticks in Raspberry Vinegar
Grilled Salmon with Four Butters
Artichoke, Mushroom, and Potato Stew
Santa Rosa Plum Tart
Wine: Sauvignon Blanc

SUMMER BRUNCH

Babcock Peaches Poached in Champagne with Blueberries
Smoked Salmon and Sweet Onion Pie
Tomato, Onion, and Cucumber Salad Ribboned with
Ricotta Pesto Cream
Apricot-Almond Pound Cake
Breads from "The Bread Basket"
Wine: Blanc de Blancs

‖ S U G G E S T E D   M E N U S   A N D   W I N E S ‖

AUTUMN DINNER I

Mixed Mushrooms with Vermont Cheddar
Breast of Chicken Poached on Shredded Baby Carrots and Leeks
Potatoes with Lemon, Garlic, and Parsley
Fall Fruits Gratin
Wine: Fumé Blanc

AUTUMN DINNER II

Coriandered Carrot Soup
Marinated Mexicali Eggplant Salad
Grilled Red Snapper with Tomato Salsa Cruda
Fresh Corn Flapjacks with Basil
Apple Ice Cream à la Mode
Wine: California Gewürztraminer

AUTUMN DINNER III

Crookneck Squash and Tomato Soup
Pan-fried Sand Dabs with Ginger-Lemon Butter
Gratin of Celery Root and Basil
Tangerine-Coconut Flan
Wine: Chenin Blanc

WINTER DINNER

Mussels in Mustard
Zinfandel Beef Stew with Celery Root and Parsnips
Buttered Egg Pasta
Red and Green Grapes in Maple-Walnut Cream
Wine: Zinfandel

385

WINTER HOLIDAY DINNER

Corn and Oyster Bisque
Black Bean, Cranberry, and Roasted Pepper Salad
Roast Duck Glazed with Green Peppercorn Mustard and
Nectarine Chutney
Walnut Brussels Sprouts
Sweet Potato Fritters
Chile-Cornmeal Biscuits
Steamed Apple-Simmon Pudding
Pumpkin Custard
Wines: Sauvignon Blanc, Merlot, Muscat Blanc

WINTER BRUNCH

Fresh Cherry Tomato Soup with Grated Jack and
Sourdough Croutons
Golden Caviar–Mascarpone Roulade
Compote of Dried and Fresh Fruits with Honey-Lime Sauce
Peaches and Cream Scones
Wine: Napa Gamay

SPRING DINNER I

Very Democratic Double-Mushroom Soup with
Pernod and Tarragon
Veal Scallops Sauced with Asparagus Puree
Tomato Pasta
Burnt Cream over Huckleberries
Wine: Grey Riesling

SPRING DINNER II

Asparagus with Orange-Sherry Vinaigrette
Basil Pasta with Two Salmons
Pan-fried Cherry Tomatoes in Garlic Butter
New-Fashioned Strawberry Shortcake
Wine: Oregon Pinot Gris

‖ SUGGESTED MENUS AND WINES ‖

ANYTIME DINNER I

Broccoli-Jicama Salad
Berkeley Bouillabaisse
Basil Baguettes
Sausalito Sophisticated Saucepan Torte
Wine: Zinfandel

ANYTIME DINNER II

Good Green Soup
Leeks and Goat Cheese in a Flaky Drum
Balsamic Broccoli with Golden Raisins and Toasted Walnuts
Mint Julep Pound Cake
Wine: Fumé Blanc

ANYTIME DINNER III

Red Pepper and Eggplant Soup
Poussin Pot Pie
Broccoli Spears with Walnuts and Raspberry Vinegar
Baked Apples Alaska
Wine: Semillon

SUNDAY NIGHT SUPPER

Zucchini and Peppery Watercress Soup
Hot Cajun Sausage Calzone
Banana Split Soufflé
Wine: Merlot

A COCKTAIL PARTY

Mushroom-Hazelnut Pâté
Seviche of Scallops and Snapper
Tomato-Coriander Tartlets
Triangle Crepes Filled with Boursin and Smoked Salmon
California Caponata
Wine: Blanc de Blancs (sparkling)

A SALAD SOIRÉE

Sushi Salad
Potato Pesto Chicken with Red Pepper Strips
Curried Tuna and Mango Chutney on Garden Lettuces
Coriandered Carrot Coins
Smoked Trout, Red and White Radish, and Watercress
Salad Scheherazade
Green Bean, Corn, and Red Pepper Salad
Herbed Olive Muffins
Whole-Wheat Garlic French Bread
Wine: Pinot Blanc, Blanc de Noirs

TAILGATE PICNIC

Goat Cheese Tarts with Sun-dried Tomatoes
Smoked Trout Mousse with Horseradish and Golden Caviar
Basil Baguettes
Spiced Walnuts
Marinated Lamb, Corn, and Baby Bean Salad with
Cherry Tomatoes
Red Pepper and Onion Marmalade with Celery
White Chocolate Pear Brownies
Wines: Chenin Blanc, California Barbera

FIRESIDE — V.C.R. — PICNIC

Palace Chile
Parsnip-Carrot Salad in Raspberry Vinaigrette with
Walnuts and Currants
Chile-Cornmeal Biscuits
Pear and Cranberry Whole-Wheat Cobbler
Wines: California Burgundy, Johannisberg Riesling

PANTRY FANCY DINNER

Lentil, Parsley, and Goat Cheese Salad
Shrimp with Vermouth and Sun-dried Tomatoes
Green Risotto
Pistachio Meringue-Aroons
Maple—Pine Nut Ice Cream
Wine: California Gewürztraminer

VALENTINE'S DAY DINNER FOR TWO

Red Pepper Pasta with Tapenade
Sautéed Baby Lamb Chops with Shallot Puree
Carrot Cream in Artichoke Bottoms
Blush Bread
White Chocolate—Hazelnut Mousse with Raspberry Sauce
Wine: Oregon Pinot Noir

A CELEBRATION DINNER

Spinach-Parsnip Soup
Comice Pear Wedges and Endives Julienne on Watercress
Veal Ragout with Artichokes, Brandied Raisins, and Crème Fraiche
Melon Seed Pasta with Butter and Parsley
Zucchini in Lime and Thyme
Mocha Mousse Mud Pie
Wines: California Champagne, Chardonnay

GATHERED CRUMBS:
Kitchen Techniques and Terms

Chicken Stock
Fish Stock
Beef or Veal Stock
Duck Stock
Pâte Brisée
Pesto
Mayonnaise
Crème Fraiche
Bouquet Garni

Bain Marie or Water Bath
Blanching
Chiffonade
Cooking Fresh Artichoke Hearts
Deglazing a Pan
Handling Jalapeño Peppers
Julienne
Parchment Paper
Peeling Tomatoes
Proofing Yeast
Reduce
Roasting Peppers
Superfine Sugar
Toasting Nuts
Trussing
Zest

Chicken Stock

1 leek, white part, with
about 1 inch of green
2 carrots
2 celery stalks
1 whole chicken or a 5-
pound mixture of necks,
backs, and wings

1 onion, halved and stuck
with 6 cloves
6 peppercorns
½ teaspoon thyme
1 bay leaf
4 quarts water

Cut leek, carrots, and celery into 1-inch pieces. Place into a large stockpot with remaining ingredients and bring to a boil. Skim foam as it accumulates. Reduce to a simmer and cook for about 2 hours, uncovered or partially covered. Add more water if more than 1 cup evaporates during cooking time.

Strain into a bowl or storage container and refrigerate or freeze.

Makes about 4 quarts

STOCK NOTES: You may easily remove all fat from these stocks by refrigerating until a solid layer of fat forms on surface. The fat can be removed practically in one piece.

Stock may be refrigerated for 3 to 4 days. After that time, if you wish to refrigerate it longer, bring it to a boil and store again for 3 days, or freeze. Stock may be frozen for up to 6 months in an airtight container. Always let your nose be your guide to its freshness. Rancid stock will smell inedible.

Fish Stock

2 pounds fish bones from
  nonoily fish (not salmon)
1 carrot, sliced
1 leek, white part only,
  sliced
1 celery stalk, sliced
½ teaspoon thyme

1 bay leaf
1 sprig parsley
3 peppercorns
  pinch salt
1 slice of lemon
2 cups dry white wine
2 cups water

Place all ingredients in a large pot and bring to a boil. Reduce to a simmer and cook for 25 minutes. Strain and store in refrigerator or freezer.

Makes about 1 quart

ALTERNATE METHOD: In some areas fish bones are difficult to obtain. A suitable substitute can be made using 2 cups bottled or canned clam juice, 1 cup dry white wine, 1 cup water, and above herbs and spices simmered for 5 minutes.

Beef or Veal Stock

8 pounds beef and/or veal
  bones, cut into 3-inch
  pieces by butcher
2 onions, sliced
2 carrots, sliced

2 celery stalks, sliced
2 tomatoes, quartered
1 bouquet garni*
4 quarts water, plus 1 cup

Arrange beef and onions in a large roasting pan and place in preheated 450°F oven. Brown on all sides, turning as necessary.

  Transfer bones and onions to a large stockpot with remaining ingredients except cup of water. Discard fat from roasting pan and deglaze* with 1 cup water, scraping up all particles sticking to bottom of pan. (This will give your stock flavor and color.) Add to stockpot and bring entire contents to a boil. Reduce to a simmer and skim foam as it accumulates on surface. Let simmer for at least 4 hours, adding more water if more than 1 cup evaporates during cooking time.

Strain into a bowl or storage container and refrigerate or freeze.

Makes about 3½ quarts

Duck Stock

Use same procedure as for beef stock substituting duck bones, cooked or uncooked, for beef bones.

Pâte Brisée

1½ cups all-purpose flour
    pinch salt
8 tablespoons cold sweet
    butter

2 tablespoons cold vegetable
    shortening
about 5 tablespoons ice
    water

In a bowl or food processor mix flour and salt. Cut in butter and shortening piece by piece until mixture is crumbly. Add half the water and mix or process just until dough holds together. If it seems too dry, add remaining water.

Form into a disc, wrap, and refrigerate for at least 1 hour before using.

Makes enough pastry for one 9- or 10-inch tart

Pesto

2 cups fresh basil leaves
4 cloves garlic
¼ cup toasted pine nuts*
½ cup grated Parmesan cheese

1 teaspoon oregano
salt and pepper
½–¾ cup olive oil

Puree all ingredients in a food processor or blender.

If storing for future use, cover surface with a layer of oil to prevent discoloration. May be refrigerated up to a week and frozen up to 4 months.

Makes about 1½ cups

Mayonnaise

2 egg yolks
1 teaspoon good-quality
    mustard

2 teaspoons fresh lemon juice
salt and pepper
1–1½ cups olive or vegetable oil

Blender or processor method: Combine all ingredients except oil in a bowl of a food processor or blender. While machine is still running, pour in oil in a slow steady stream. For a light mayonnaise, use 1 cup oil. For a stiffer, thicker mayonnaise, use 1½ cups oil.

By hand: In a bowl whisk together all ingredients except oil. Whisking constantly, add the oil drop by drop at first. When sauce starts to thicken, pour in remaining oil in a thin, steady stream, still whisking constantly.

Makes 1–1½ cups

Crème Fraîche

Authentic crème fraiche is a naturally fermented cream that can now be found in the dairy cases of some specialty food shops. The price is very high, from $3 to $4 a pint. It has a wonderfully nutty flavor and reacts very favorably in sauces that are exposed to long and high heat because it does not curdle. The following is a most satisfactory and less costly substitute:

1 cup heavy cream (preferably not ultra-pasteurized)	½ cup sour cream, or 2 tablespoons cultured buttermilk

In a saucepan heat cream to approximately 80°F. Pour into a clean jar and add sour cream or buttermilk. Stir gently and cover loosely.

Allow to sit at room temperature until thickened, which may take anywhere from 8 to 24 hours. Cover tightly and store in the refrigerator for up to 1 week. It will continue to thicken after refrigerated.

Makes 1¼ to 1½ cups

Bouquet Garni

a few celery leaves	6 peppercorns
3 sprigs parsley	1 bay leaf
½ teaspoon thyme	

Make a bundle of the above ingredients by tying in a piece of cheesecloth, or enclosing them between 2 pieces of celery stalk and tying with kitchen twine.

Always remove the bouquet garni before serving.

Bain Marie or Water Bath: Most frequently used for delicate custard-based dishes, a bain marie is simply a large pan filled with hot water in which the custard molds are placed to be cooked or kept warm.

Blanching: Place vegetables or fruits briefly in lots of boiling water (not more than a few minutes) to remove raw taste, set color, or facilitate the peeling of fruits and tomatoes.

Chiffonade: To cut greens in a chiffonade, stack the leaves of sorrel, basil, spinach, chard, etc.; roll them up like a cigarette and cut into shreds crosswise with a sharp knife.

Cooking Fresh Artichoke Hearts: Remove stem. Pull out outer leaves until you reach the tender, inner leaves, which are a pale green color. Spread open with fingers to expose purple-tinged choke. Remove choke by scraping with a spoon. To cook artichoke hearts, place in pot with boiling water and 1 tablespoon lemon juice. Simmer, uncovered, about 8 minutes. Drain well.

Deglazing a Pan: To capture precious pan juices and browned particles after the sautéing or roasting process, first pour off fat. Add liquid (stock, wine, water, or cream) and cook over medium heat while scraping and stirring.

Handling Jalapeño Peppers: Due to the volatile oils in these peppers, they require careful handling. Kitchen gloves should be worn when cutting them, especially if there are cuts or wounds on hands. If working without gloves, wash hands well after handling peppers because any remaining oils can cause painful and sometimes dangerous irritations, particularly to the eyes.

Julienne: Cut food into matchstick-size pieces.

Parchment Paper: Packaged in rolls like wax paper, this silicone-treated paper is excellent as a nonstick lining in baking pans. Wiped clean, the paper may be reused. Food may be wrapped and baked in parchment for an effect very much like steaming. This is because the paper is nonporous and the food cooks in its own juices and vapors. This paper can usually be found in specialty cookware shops.

Peeling Tomatoes: Place tomatoes in boiling water for 30 seconds. Remove, allow to cool, and peel with a small paring knife.

Proofing Yeast: To be activated, yeast must be dissolved in warm liquid, about 105° to 115°F. Stir yeast into warm liquid and allow to stand for 5 to 10 minutes. If yeast is active and alive, a foam will form on the surface. If yeast is no longer active, it will sink to the bottom. If inactive, discard mixture and begin again with a fresh package of yeast.

Reduce: This technique is used to evaporate and thicken a liquid, such as stock, soup, or sauce. Boil liquid rapidly in order to concentrate its flavor and reduce its volume.

Roasting Peppers: Place peppers over a gas burner, under a broiler, or on a barbecue grill. Roast until skin blisters and blackens, turning peppers often. Place in a plastic bag until cool enough to handle and scrape skin away with a small paring knife.

Superfine Sugar: Place desired amount of regular sugar in a food processor bowl fitted with a steel blade and process until very fine.

Toasting Nuts: Spread desired amount of nuts on a cookie sheet and place in a preheated 350°F oven for about 10 minutes, shaking pan once during that time. Nuts should be no darker than a light golden brown.

Trussing: Using kitchen twine, tie a chicken or any bird into a compact shape before cooking.

Zest: The outer colored part of the rind of citrus fruits (lemon, orange, lime) contains the flavorful oils. It is removed with a tool called a zester, grater, or peeler and added to various dishes.

SELECTED BIBLIOGRAPHY

Beard, James. *Delights and Prejudices*. New York, 1964.
———. *James Beard's American Cookery*. Boston, 1972.
———. *The New James Beard*. New York, 1981.
———. *Theory and Practice of Good Cooking*. New York, 1977
Betty Crocker's Cooking American Style. New York, 1975.
Botkin, B. A., ed. *A Treasury of Western Folklore*. New York, 1975.
Brown, Helen Evans. *West Coast Cook Book*. Boston, 1952.
Callahan, Genevieve. *California Cook Book*. New York, 1946.
———. *Sunset All Western Foods*. Menlo Park, California, 1947.
Cannon, Poppy. *The New Can-Opener Cookbook*. New York, 1959.
Coyle, J. Patrick, Jr. *The World Encyclopedia of Food*. New York, 1982.
Cummings, R. O. *The American and His Food: A History of the Food Habits in the United States*. Chicago, 1940.
Damon, Berthe. *A Sense of Humus*. New York, 1943.
David, Elizabeth. *French Provincial Cooking,* rev. ed. New York, 1967.
———. *Spices, Salt and Aromatics in the English Kitchen*. New York, 1970.
Donovan, Mary, et al. *The Thirteen Colonies Cookbook*. New York, 1975.
Dorson, Richard M., ed. *Folklore and Folklife: An Introduction*. Chicago, 1972.
Estragon, Vladimir. *Waiting for Dessert*. New York, 1982.
Farb, Peter, and George Armelagos. *Consuming Passions: The Anthropology of Eating*. Boston, 1980.
Farmer, Fannie Merritt. *The Boston Cooking-School Cook Book*. Boston, 1909.

Fisher, M.F.K. *The Art of Eating*. New York, 1954.

———. *Among Friends*. New York, 1971.

———. *As They Were*. New York, 1982.

Furnas, C. C. and S. M. Furnas, *Man, Bread and Destiny: the Story of Man's Food*. New York, 1937.

Grigson, Jane. *Jane Grigson's Fruit Book*. New York, 1982.

———. *Jane Grigson's Vegetable Book*. New York, 1979.

———. *The Mushroom Feast*. New York, 1975.

Hazelton, Nika. *American Home Cooking*. New York, 1980.

Heatter, Maida. *Maida Heatter's Book of Great Chocolate Desserts*. New York, 1980.

Herter, George Leonard, and Berthe E. Herter. *Bull Cook and Authentic Historical Recipes and Practices*. Waseca, Minnesota, 1969.

Hess, Karen, ed. *Martha Washington's Booke of Cookery*. New York, 1981.

Hooker, Richard J. *A History of Food and Drink in America*. New York, 1981.

Jones, Evan. *American Food: The Gastronomic Story*. New York, 1981.

Leonard, Jonathan Norton. *American Cooking: The Great West*. New York, 1971.

Lewis, Oscar. *This Was San Francisco*. New York, 1962.

McPhee, John. *Oranges*. New York, 1966.

Marcus, Adrianne. *The Chocolate Bible*. New York, 1979.

Mariani, John F. *The Dictionary of American Food and Drink*. New York, 1983.

Miller, Amy Bess, and Persis Fuller. *The Best of Shaker Cooking*. New York, 1970.

Montagne, Prosper. *The New Larousse Gastronomique*. New York, 1978.

Paddleford, Clementine. *How America Eats*. New York, 1960.

Perle, Lila. *Red-Flannel Hash and Shoo-Fly Pie: American Regional Foods and Festivals*. New York, 1965.

Pullar, Phillipa. *Consuming Passions*. Boston, 1970.

Roberson, John and Marie. *The Famous American Recipes Cookbook*. Englewood Cliffs, New Jersey, 1957.

Root, Waverley. *Food*. New York, 1980.

———. *The Food of Italy*. New York, 1971.

———. *The Food of France*. New York, 1958.

Root, Waverley, and Richard de Rochemont. *Eating in America: A History*. New York, 1976.

Rorer, Sarah T. *Mrs. Rorer's Cookbook.* Philadelphia, n.d.

Simon, Andre L. *A Concise Encyclopedia of Gastronomy.* 7 vols. London, 1939–1945.

Smith, Page, and Charles Daniel. *The Chicken Book.* San Francisco, 1982.

Sokolov, Raymond. *Fading Feast.* New York, 1981.

Soyer, Alexis. *The Pantropheon.* London, 1977.

Starr, Kevin. *Americans and the California Dream, 1850–1915.* New York, 1973.

Stern, Jane and Michael. *Goodfood.* New York, 1983.

Stobart, Tom. *The Cook's Encyclopedia.* New York, 1980.

Tannahill, Reay. *Food in History.* New York, 1973.

Thorne, John. *Down East Chowder.* Boston, 1982.

Trager, James. *The Foodbook.* New York, 1970.

Villas, James. *American Taste: A Celebration of Gastronomy Coast to Coast.* New York, 1982.

Walden, Howard T., II. *Native Inheritance: The Story of Corn in America.* New York, 1966.

INDEX

Jeannette Ferrary

Jeannette Ferrary was born in Brooklyn, New York, and graduated from Southern Connecticut State College. She has published articles, book reviews, and fiction in the *San Francisco Chronicle,* the *San Francisco Examiner, Harvard Magazine, San Francisco Bay Guardian, Food & Wine* magazine, the *Journal of Gastronomy,* and *Focus Magazine.* She lives near San Francisco with Peter Carroll and their daughter, Natasha.

Louise Fiszer

Louise Fiszer serves as Director of Louise's Pantry Cooking School, which she founded in 1978. She and the school have been featured in the *New York Times* and other publications for their innovative contributions to California cookery and regional cooking. A former Special Education teacher in New York City, Louise moved to California in 1974, where she presently resides with her husband, Max (and two sons when they get hungry enough for Mother's cooking to come home from college). She is owner of Louise's Pantry Cookware Shop.